PLANNING EFFECTIVE PROGRESS

Planning and implementing the
curriculum for
children with learning difficulties

Edited by

Mike Hinson and Martin Hughes

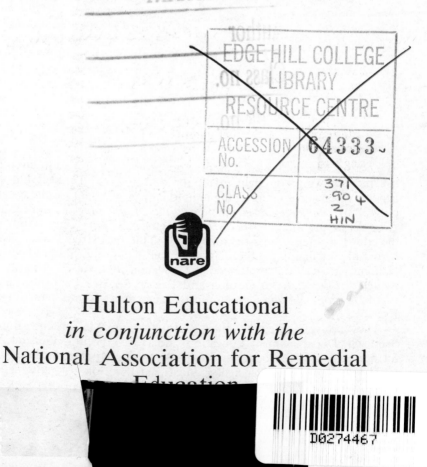

Hulton Educational
in conjunction with the
National Association for Remedial
Education

D0274467

First published in Great Britain 1982
by Hulton Educational Publications Ltd
Raans Road, Amersham, Bucks HP6 6JJ

ISBN 0 7175 1007 7

Printed in Great Britain by
Richard Clay (The Chaucer Press) Ltd, Bungay, Suffolk

Acknowledgements

The editors and publishers gratefully acknowledge permission given to pub-
lish the following copyright material: to Holmes McDougall Ltd and the
Schools Council for figure 1, the individual scoring sheet for the checklist on
page 38 of *Language Development and the Disadvantaged Child*; to Edward
Arnold Ltd and the authors of *Helping Language Development* for figure 2,
the criterion-referenced assessment grid; to the Industrial Training Research
Unit Ltd, for figure 18, the diagram from the A – Z Study (1979); to the
National Association for Remedial Education for extracts from its journal
Remedial Education; to Gordon and Breach Science Publishers and *Early
Child Development and Care* to reproduce extracts from a paper by Dr Roy
Evans.

   They also wish to express their gratitude to the Metropolitan Borough of
Sandwell, Department of Education and J. R. Griffiths, General Adviser,
for permission to reproduce two extracts from a discussion document, also
to Thomas A. Kelly, Principal Educational Psychologist, and his staff for
their assistance ʒ   of this book.

Contents

Notes on contributors

Terence Bailey is the Adviser for Special Education in the London Borough of Enfield. Previously, he has worked as a teacher, an educational psychologist and as an adviser for remedial education.

Michael Cahill is Deputy Headteacher at the Frank Harrison Comprehensive School, Walsall. He was formerly National Co-ordinator of the Schools Council *Skills for Employment Project.*

Wendy Dewhirst is a Senior Lecturer in Curriculum Studies at Wolverhampton Polytechnic, Faculty of Education, Dudley. She is an author of the *Bronto Books* for the Nuffield *5–11 Mathematics Project.*

Roy Evans is Head of the Education Department at Roehampton Institute and is based at Southlands College, London. He is editor of the international journal *Early Child Development and Care* and a former Assistant Director of the National Children's Bureau.

Roy Hallam is a Principal Lecturer in the Department of Professional Studies at the College of Ripon and York St John and Area Adviser for the Historical Association in North Yorkshire.

Mike Hinson is Head of the Remedial Education and Advisory Department of the Sandwell Child Psychology Service. He is a Past President of NARE.

Paula Hodson trained as an educational psychologist. She has worked in a tutorial unit in Dorset for pupils with severe reading difficulties.

Martin Hughes is a Principal Lecturer at Hull College of Higher Education, where he is currently responsible for the one-year, full-time in-service course in the education of handicapped children.

Peter Jones is a fifth-year tutor and Head of Department at Aston Manor School, Birmingham.

Avril Lofthouse is a Lecturer at the Colchester Institute where she acts as a tutor to the Manpower Services Commission, Youth Opportunities Programme courses.

Colin McCall is a Lecturer in the School of Education, University of Exeter. He has previously worked as a teacher, as an educational psychologist and a curriculum development officer.

Jim McNicholas is a Senior Lecturer at Edge Hill College of Higher Education, Ormskirk, where he is concerned with in-service education in the area of special educational needs.

Gordon Pidgeon is the Warden of Charlemont Teachers' Centre, Sandwell. He is Chairman of the Educational Drama Association and tutor to its course in drama for the handicapped.

Barry Pinfield is Curriculum Development Leader for Mathematics with the Manchester Education Authority. He is also Publications Secretary of the Northern Mathematics Council (NORMAC).

Carol Stevens is a Specialist Teacher involved in the Sandwell Parental Involvement Project. Previously, she was deputy headmistress of an infant school.

Michael Williams is a Senior Lecturer in the Department of Education at the University of Manchester. He is also Joint Honorary Secretary (Education) of the Geographical Association.

Introduction

After Tyndale

The Rt Hon. James Callaghan, in his historic speech at Ruskin College, Oxford, on 18 October 1976, defined the goals of education as to equip children, to the best of their ability, for a lively, constructive place in society, also to fit them to do a job of work — 'Not one or the other, but both'.

During the years that have elapsed since his inauguration of education's Great Debate, there has been intense discussion of existing school curricula and their effectiveness in a rapidly changing world. The planning and implementation of curricula suited to the needs of children with learning difficulties has received greater emphasis than ever before. This was chosen as the topical theme of the NARE Easter Course in 1981, held at Wolverhampton Polytechnic, Faculty of Education. Its success underlines the need for practical guidance in this hitherto neglected area. The Course provided the inspiration for this book, and a number of chapters are based upon papers given at Wolverhampton (though extensively revised for publication within the framework of the book). To these have been added a chapter by Dr Roy Evans, based on his challenging introduction to the NARE Annual Conference (held at the University of Essex during the same year), guest contributions dealing with certain specialized areas, and relevant articles from *Remedial Education*.

As a starting point, contributors have accepted the definition of curriculum to be found in the HMI Discussion Paper *A View of the Curriculum* (1980):

> 'The curriculum in its full sense comprises all the opportunities for learning provided by the school. It includes the formal programme of lessons in the timetable: the so-called "extra-curricular" and "out-of-school" activities deliberately promoted or supported by the school; and the climate of relationships, attitudes, styles of behaviour and the general quality of life established in the school community as a whole.'

We have also accepted the assertions of the Warnock Report (1978) that the purpose and goals of education are the same for all children. However, the help that individuals need in attaining these goals, particularly those pupils who have learning difficulties, will be different. It is the nature of this help that contributors discuss, also offering some guidelines for curriculum planning and implementation.

In his opening chapter, Colin McCall sets the scene by considering the curricular needs of children with learning difficulties and the relevance to such needs of some national reports and surveys:

DES, *Primary Education in England*, HMSO, 1978.
DES, *Special Educational Needs*, HMSO, 1978.
Brennan, W.K., *Curricular Needs of Slow Learners*, Schools Council Working Pager 63, Evans/Methuen, 1979.
DES, *Aspects of Secondary Education in England*, 1979.
DES, *A View of the Curriculum*, HMSO, 1980.
DES/Welsh Office, *A Framework for the School Curriculum*, HMSO, 1980.
DES, *The School Curriculum*, HMSO, 1981.

The remainder of the book has been divided into three broad inter-related sections in order to consider more closely curricular needs throughout the school years. The first section deals with pre-school and primary education, stressing preventive measures and the fostering of early skills in language and mathematics. In the second section, authors consider three major subjects areas in which both primary and secondary-school children can experience difficulties. The third section deals with the basic curriculum for children in the 11–16+ age-range. Following chapters concerned with language and mathematics, there are four studies dealing with life skills and education for employment.

The Practical Curriculum (Schools Council Working Paper 70, 1980) argues that we need to develop a visible structure for the curriculum and that a useful starting point is to consider each pupil's right of access to different areas of human knowledge and experience. The paper emphasizes that *'for the children themselves the effective curriculum is what each child takes away'*. We feel that effectiveness must be central to curriculum planning for children with learning difficulties. It emphasizes the whole focus of the book, hence our title *Planning Effective Progress*.

The School Curriculum outlines the ministerially recommended approach to a broad and largely common curriculum for all pupils. It can be regarded as a statement of what central government requires for educational continuity from 5–16. Local education authorities are charged with the responsibility to 'formulate curricular policies which meet national procedures and objectives, command local assent and can be applied by each school to its own local circumstances' (para.9). Schools must be prepared to produce reasoned written statements about the curricula which they offer. Teachers need to be able to produce rationales for the subjects they teach, to defend them and see them in the context of the school curriculum as a whole.

Here, then, is our best opportunity, so far, to secure a curriculum which gives equal consideration to the special needs of those children who have received scant attention in the past. Of course, this will not be easy to achieve. Remedial teachers will find their idealism strained to the utmost in persuading some colleagues.

This book does not set out to provide 'cook-book' answers. It has been written by a group of concerned educationists with a wide spectrum of experience, who have considered the major questions more deeply and who wish to share with readers their enthusiasm for resolving them. *Planning Effective Progress* is intended as a stimulus to discussion, reading, enquiry and planned action. Understandably, in such a composite effort, gaps and omissions may occur, for which we apologize in advance. From whatever sector of education readers are drawn, we hope that they will read the entire book. We all need to see the broad picture of education if our curriculum planning is to be effective.

Mike Hinson and Martin Hughes
April 1982

1

Some recent national reports and surveys: implications for the remedial specialist

COLIN McCALL

Introduction

Planning and implementing the curriculum for children with learning difficulties is neither a straightforward task nor a simple set of practical procedures. It involves, at the very least, careful, detailed thought, with full consideration being given to the intense discussion surrounding general school curricula and their effectiveness in a rapidly changing world.

This latter discussion generated a number of important national surveys and reports. If one also adds important publications pertaining directly to children with learning difficulties, there is now a substantial amount of literature related to their curricular needs. This literature requires detailed investigation by all who desire to plan and assist in the development of better school programmes for children exhibiting learning difficulties.

Towards this end, this chapter attempts a brief review of the major strands of thought to be found in publications (up until 1982) which are of direct relevance to the work of remedial specialists. The strategy employed is to relate much of the content of these publications to an actual child and to seek from an examination of this relationship the primary questions and implications of relevance to the work of remedial teachers.

A while ago, 'M' was described by the portmanteau expression 'slow learner'. He is currently described by a second portmanteau label as a child with mild or moderate learning difficulties (Warnock, 1978). I note 'M' demonstrates many of the general characteristics offered in much of the educational literature as 'typical' of this kind of child (Haigh, 1977, Younie, 1974) *if* we can believe such criteria. I stress *if* we can believe such criteria because, in reality, we do not know much about children with learning difficulties. Information about them is quite inadequate. The fact that we know little about such children, especially in describing their educational needs in terms of curricular provision or adaptation, is emphasized by Brennan (1979), the Warnock Report and hinted at within a number of the other sources. It is also a fact which has been known for a long time. For example, Featherstone (reported by Younie) wrote in 1941:

'Comparatively little is known, in a scientific way, about the growth patterns of individual slow learners but there is evidence to suggest that they have the same quality of uniqueness that one finds in studying the growth pattern of other children.'

Whilst Younie *(op. cit.)*, commenting on Featherstone's statements, suggested that:

> 'In the ensuing forty years we have seen the development of jet propulsion, interplanetary visits, atomic energy, micro-processors, transistors, replacement hearts and many other scientific and social advances, yet little has occurred to date Featherstone's comment.'

As a consequence of this lack of hard information, most of the 'needs' of these children as we envisage them arise from:

(a) a few small group studies of variously defined children with learning difficulties;
(b) a great number of general statements made by teachers and other professionals who work with such children.

Thus, what we have, in 1982, in respect of the curricular needs of any child with a learning difficulty is a tentative picture that must suffice until more precise information is available.

Brennan's *(op. cit.)* classification system, in which he relates pupil characteristics to suggested types of curriculum, has been helpful in focusing thought on the likely curricular implications of learning difficulties and in reminding us that the curriculum for all children should be more concerned with *objectives* than *content*. However, there is an enormous job to be done to develop his blueprint, and its successful development will only take place if remedial specialists show that they are more prepared to understand children with difficulties in terms of their total curricular requirements rather than in terms of what they lack.

It has never been more urgent for remedial specialists, as a professional association and as individuals, to study their charges more intensively and systematically in respect of their full curricular requirements. For what all the sources reflect is that various definitions are coupled with recurring worries and uncertainties about curricular needs and planning implications. This state of affairs, together with new ideas, new legislation and new economic restrictions, indicates that the only certainty about curriculum planning for children with learning difficulties is that many uncertainties exist.

Indeed, in talking specifically about definition and curricular description for those children served by remedial specialists, it is not unrealistic to suggest the latter are currently in the position of the unhappy centipede:

> A centipede was happy quite
> Until a frog in fun,
> Said, 'Pray, which leg comes after which?'
> This raised her mind to such a pitch
> She lay distracted in the ditch,
> Considering how to run.

How, perhaps, remedial specialists ought to run in the next decade is hinted at most strongly in the sources under consideration and can be best made explicitly by reference again to 'M'.

Accepting that identification of his curricular needs is still more tentative than absolute, we can seek guidance for further thinking from these reports and surveys by asking four fundamental questions about 'M' and seeing what the sources offer in reply.

1. What is an appropriate curriculum for 'M'?
2. What exactly is his curriculum experience directed towards?
3. How will his curriculum experience be offered so as to match his needs but not limit his horizons?
4. How will his progress and the efficacy of his planned programme be monitored so as to meet his needs but not limit his horizons?

An appropriate curriculum

What is an appropriate curriculum for 'M'? There are no certainties here. The question immediately raises two other questions, neither of which is without controversy or uncertainty: *What experiences ought remedial specialists to promote on 'M' 's behalf? Are there curricular activities he ought to be removed from?* The Warnock Report (*op. cit.*) outlines the necessary factors to examine before attempting to answer these questions.

Firstly, any chosen activities and experiences for particular children in a school are necessarily a selection from a wider range of possibilities and such selection is not a decision to be taken lightly.

Secondly, the manner by which such a selection is made is influenced by the rationale that comprises the backcloth for selection. The report suggests we need to consider:

(a) the detailed specification of each child's personal qualities and needs, and
(b) to seek clear experience and knowledge of the problems faced by children with learning difficulties at home, in the neighbourhood and as young adults seeking independence.

Thirdly, that when we make our selection we should ensure that, as far as is practicable, the chosen programme intentions *are as near in scope and quality to those of other children of the same age.*

Finally, providing an appropriate curriculum for some children is not just a question of selection, but may involve modification. However, the report strongly emphasizes the important point that there are at least two senses in which modifications may be necessary (or which have arisen in practice whether they are necessary or not):

(a) Some children may be able to follow an ordinary curriculum provided that special materials are prepared in advance. This requires that lessons are carefully planned and prepared and that materials are selected in good time. (The emphasis is on having the same objectives, but using different materials and methods to achieve them.)
(b) For some children, modification of teaching objectives as well as materials may be needed. (The emphasis is on an alternative curriculum for all or part of the time.)

This seems a simple, practical division, yet it raises very important considerations which, if Brennan (*op. cit.*) is right, remedial specialists have not debated rigorously enough. He reminds us of a central problem if we choose (b):

'If the curriculum is to be differentiated in order to meet the special needs of slow learners, then at what point does that very differentiation become a separatist device, in that it "cuts off" the slow learner from the common aspects of curriculum which contribute to cultural and social cohesion in our society?

Put another way, if the transmission of some degree of common culture through a common curriculum is one purpose of education, at what point does the differentiated curriculum for the slow learner depart from that purpose? If so, should it? By what right is any child denied access to any area of human knowledge? The specific literature on the slow learner shows little awareness of these important questions.'

(For 'slow learner' substitute any other portmanteau expression describing a type of special need — the argument still holds.)

There is a real dilemma here and one worthy of detailed, long-term debate at school, regional and national level. Several written sources are of value in informing such debate (e.g., Wilson, 1980). However, what one can say at this point about this 'curriculum divide' is that there are indications in many parts of all the aforementioned reports and surveys that remedial specialists have been guilty of opting too quickly and certainly for (b), rather than using their skills within the general curriculum to promote (a) as the reality for most children with learning difficulties. Brennan (*op. cit.*) suggests that before the formidable obstacles to such support are simply rehearsed and the idea of more curriculum modification of type (a) is resisted, all remedial specialists should take cognizance of Hirst's (1965) words that 'there are no adequate grounds for saying this is impossible when we have, in fact, spent so little of our effort trying to achieve this'.

How might remedial specialists achieve this goal of supporting more children within mainstream curricular activity? Here are three suggestions:

Suggestion 1

They can join vigorously with mainstream colleagues in defining carefully what is being taught — that is, by encouraging the definition of learning by objectives rather than by lists of content. Such endeavour permits the promotion of 'learning-to-learn' objectives as primarily more important than the learning of specific information. Additionally, where teaching intentions are explicitly stated, there is an increase in opportunity for curriculum-based assessment, that is, the progress of individual children monitored against specific criteria of development. A representative example of this endeavour is likely to embrace the following stages:

Example

Third-year history syllabus (chosen extract — The English Overseas: in India). Syllabus as presented reads:

Topic outline — in India
The European traders — Portugal, France and England in India
Formation of the British East India Company
Rivalry between France and England
India at the time of Clive

13

Story of Clive of India
Black Hole of Calcutta
Battle of Plassey
Reference to India today in relationship with the U.K.

Stage A — clarification of specific teaching intentions.
What is required here is to define more explicitly the nature of the content in terms of observable final results in pupils (see Ainscow and Tweddle, 1979, and Holt, 1980) and also to make very clear which learning skills the content aims to teach. This latter step is particularly important, since it has to be accepted that, given the best teacher working in optimal conditions, even the most able child is likely, in the long term, to retain little specific information from this particular unit of work. Thus, if the central goal is not that of using the content to enhance learning-to-learn skills, all pupils, the most and least academically able, are likely to be very restricted in furthering their own knowledge and development.

Stage B — statement of learning outcomes.
The following can be the behavioural objectives (a sample drawn from a larger sequence) for a pupil doing this unit of work:

Topic outline — the English Overseas: in India

Learning-to-learn objectives	*Content objectives*
Identifies differences between pictures, charts, graphs, maps, etc., and distinguishes appropriate use.	Identifies two influences on modern life from this historical period.
Understands written comprehension questions and responds with appropriate reading strategy.	Can name three major personalities and relate basic facts associated with them.
Given a selection of major reference sources, identifies three appropriate to a given assignment and orders them in terms of priority.	Can think of etc. modern counterparts of these three historical figures. Draws a simple sketch of India and locates key places.
Uses contents table and index when locating information.	Draws and reads a simple relief map of India.
Demonstrates competence in the use of a variety of writing and drawing implements.	Can name main differences between major religions practised in India and other world religions.
Uses following equipment effectively: compass, simple camera, tape-recorder, atlas, film-strip.	Spells correctly and knows appropriate meaning for the following key vocabulary: India, ruled, power, century, British, French, trade, rivalry, conquered, princes, Bengal, Plassey.
Demonstrates appropriate use of the school library classification system.	

14

Compiles short statements summarizing a text.

Demonstrates elementary competence at note-taking.

Demonstrates elementary skill in critical evaluation.

Demonstrates elementary skill in critical evaluation.

Demonstrates a rough notion of chronology using: ladder, pie-chart indicator, sequence of important events.

Knows Sanskrit equivalent for five common English words.

Appreciates some of the trials and tribulations faced by: ordinary people, and the leading personalities during this period.

Stage C — discussion of appropriate decision regarding children with learning difficulties and this unit of work.

A clear statement of teaching intentions helps when deciding to include or exclude children from a particular course. Even if a department refused the support of a remedial specialist or the timetable did not allow such a specialist to give direct support, the obligation to explicitly state teaching and learning intentions is still worthwhile. By such a procedure a department (and ultimately a school) clarifies the demands it is placing upon a child's linguistic and cognitive development. Clarification of these demands often serves as a first step in curriculum change.

In respect of the unit of work under discussion here, the behavioural objectives seem to focus attention on four possible courses of action:

Decision

1. No change in objectives. Use of adapted materials, plus support within general curriculum timetable by subject and remedial specialist working together, are considered suitable for meeting the needs of the children with learning difficulties.
2. A 'crash course' on enabling objectives (i.e., pre-requisite skills for entry to the outlined programme) is provided by remedial specialist or department representative with special responsibility for children with learning difficulties — e.g., the department's 'link figure' (see McCall, 1980).
3. The programme is considered unsuitable and an alternative is offered by the remedial team.
4. The programme is considered unsuitable for a large number of children and the remedial team insist on, and participate in, modifying the whole programme.

Each decision would need appropriate changes to be made in the learning-to-learn and the content objectives.

Setting clear objectives is not the all of programme planning, especially where children with learning difficulties are concerned. Careful choice of

15

teaching methods, materials and classroom exercises is necessary to ensure the focus of the unit of work is learning experience, rather than mere academic content. A number of sources now exist offering embryonic thinking regarding these important areas (see, for example, Griffin (1978), Haigh (*op.cit.*), Hinson (1978) and McCall and Salmon (in preparation)).

Suggestion 2

Remedial specialists can try to list clear principles for adapting teaching methods and materials to more readily suit children experiencing learning difficulties. Such principles must be related to the general curriculum so that more subject-based courses offer greater variety of learning experience, group arrangements, and style of task set for children to work on. So far, little direct effort has been made to chart clear principles for the adaptation of conventional classroom approaches and materials, but considerable interest and energy is developing and some exploratory ideas are emerging. For example, McCall and Salmon (in preparation) suggest the following principles for the adaptation of conventional materials:

1. Reducing the content of the material in volume and complexity.
2. Altering emphasis of material to match immediate interests.
3. Replacing abstract illustrations or text with more concrete examples supported by easier reading matter.
4. Expanding background material so that the pupil has a greater basis for understanding.
5. Presenting the material in ways that involve more than one sensory pathway to learning.
6. Enlivening the normal presentation through novel methods of introducing materials or subject matter.

Suggestion 3

Remedial specialists can give their support and energies to the resurgent wave of interest in a broad-based common curriculum for all children (DES, 1980).

Over the last ten or fifteen years, consideration has been given to distinguishing the *essential areas of experience* to which every pupil has the right of access during his years of compulsory education. Indeed, HM Inspectorate have recently documented their views on this matter (DES, 1979, 1980) and used eight areas of experience as a set of reference points for their surveys of the curriculum in primary and secondary schools.

As a basis for curriculum planning, these areas of experience have had a mixed reception within the teaching profession. They are important, however, for the child with learning difficulties, and remedial specialists ought to seek a full understanding of what these areas mean. For, if adopted, this approach is likely to encourage a reconsideration of the curriculum as a whole, since there is no one-to-one correspondence between the areas of experience and subjects on the timetable.

Indeed, this formulation of curricular needs not as subjects but as areas of experience demonstrates how important it is for all teachers to see the school curriculum as a whole, something that remedial specialists have often argued is to the benefit of the particular children they serve.

Below is a summary of possible answers to this first question, 'What is an appropriate curriculum for 'M'?'

1. It must give him access, in some shape or form, to all eight areas of experience listed in the HMI surveys of primary and secondary education.
2. Ideally, any modification of a programme should primarily aim to change teaching methods and resources within the general programme, or alter the general programme objectives, rather than adopting different objectives for children with learning difficulties taught in a separate context.
3. Whether the support work is offered within the main programme or outside it, the objectives of 'M' 's curriculum ought to be expressed as skills and knowledge he will acquire and attitudes and work habits we hope he will adopt, rather than lists of content or activities to which he will be exposed.
4. In writing objectives there is a need to indicate clearly the level of achievement in skills development and the acquisition of knowledge which is being aimed at. When specifying skills, it is helpful to distinguish between mastery and familiarity. Similarly, for knowledge, it is useful to distinguish between understanding and awareness (Brennan, *op. cit.*).

If these points are accepted, an appropriate curriculum for 'M' can be devised more easily if remedial specialists can be encouraged to extend their province from assessment and reading help, to that of curriculum planning and development.

Directing curriculum experience

What exactly is his curriculum experience directed towards? The long-term aims of educational programmes are well discussed in all the considered sources. Utilitarian goals and employment still receive considerable emphasis, and remedial specialists are urged to make sure that each pupil's curriculum and the intensity of study are compatible with post-school requirements. Only then, in some of the sources, is attention directed to remind the same professionals to ensure young people acquire the self-confidence to manage their personal life.

No-one wants to get any of these vital developments out of balance, and it is perfectly correct for the reports and surveys to make strong representation to teachers of children with learning difficulties to bear the realities of the post-school world clearly in mind when selecting and motivating educational activities. However, how do the sources compare if we scrutinize their content with the following question in mind? *What exactly are the skills, knowledge, attitudes and values required by a child who will serve his or her schooling period and early adult life in the closing years of the twentieth century with its technological revolution?* Hardly any of the sources explore this vital question in detail.

The way the question is phrased deliberately does not differentiate between children, because it seems plausible that the skills and qualities required in the later part of this century, attributes which support happiness and personal richness, are very much the same for the child with learning difficulties as for all children, in making the transition from school to the outside world. In fact, a number of studies referred to by Brennan (*op. cit.*) and Warnock (*op. cit.*) suggest that post-school failure both in personal and vocational development relate far more to instability and social immaturity than to the level of tested intelligence or academic attainment.

Given these findings, it seems reasonable to suggest that the objectives listed for broad-based courses such as *Man: A Course of Study* (Bruner, 1969) and *Social Education* (1974) are far more significant as long-term curriculum targets for the child with learning difficulties than are those narrow objectives of rather sterile basic skills and social competence courses featured in some remedial department syllabuses. This point again raises the vital need to remediate or compensate within existing good programmes, rather than develop separate programmes. Often the latter seem to turn out as pale reflections of the former, and over-emphasize mere acquisition of skills. Indeed, if the DES (1979) interpretation is accurate, it implies that many of the alternative courses turn out to be time-filling activities.

On the overall curriculum front, in order to ensure that curricular activity is directed towards considered criteria of development, all sources agree there is a need for more systematic planning. They continually re-iterate that:

(a) some clear model of curriculum planning is needed;
(b) programme intentions should be stated far more specifically, particularly by using behavioural objectives where these are appropriate;
(c) monitoring needs to be linked with curriculum objectives to offer record-keeping procedures which are curriculum-based;
(d) a definite attempt should be made to register clearly what constitutes a minimum level of competence in a particular basic skill or subject area.

These criteria represent a substantial demand. To provide this quality of programme planning and evaluation requires that all teachers come to terms with what each of these points means in practice. In respect of teachers who are primarily concerned with children with learning difficulties, Wilson's (*op. cit.*) paper for the Schools Council offers some valuable advice to help meet these demands.

Curriculum experience: needs and horizons

How will his curriculum experience be offered so as to match his needs but not limit his horizons? The third question is not easy to answer and all the sources contain little material that begins to provide a reply.

The Warnock Committee suggested (particularly of the child with moderate learning difficulties — the old ESN(M) category) that more research is needed into the development of curricula, including methods and materials, to determine what will be of most benefit to such children. Additionally, the committee strongly hints that much good material (particularly Schools Council projects) exists, but it has not influenced the special education or remedial education scene adequately. It registers its concern that little effort has been made to modify these materials to give more children access to rich curricular experience. Towards this end Warnock strongly recommends (para. 11:68) that resources be made available to the Schools Council and local teachers' centres so that national curriculum projects can be translated into forms useful to special units, special classes and special schools. In respect of the Schools Council, such work is already under way (Schools Council Programme 4, 1980) and within its brief, a number of activities are directed specifically at fulfilling the requirement of Warnock 11:68.

The teachers' task

However, all sources do agree, with relevance to this third question, that the pace and pattern of improvements in the curriculum for children with learning difficulties will depend above all else on the energy, imagination and professional skill of the teachers. If we analyse this statement in respect of the work of many remedial specialists, it implies a change in attitudes, broader skills and wider areas of professional endeavour.

Energy and effort

There has never been any shortage of energy in most remedial specialists, quite the reverse. The majority are most impressive in the amount of drive they possess and the amount of work they do. Yet, many of the sources seem to question if that energy is always channelled in the best direction. Some hint at the fact that remedial teachers work hard on new methods, new materials and new arrangements for teaching basic skills, but do not direct their energies towards long-term goals which would bring about innovation and curriculum change. Without this, it is argued, children with learning difficulties can only profit in very limited terms from the energy the teacher has left.

This theme has been argued strongly of late. For example, Golby and Gulliver (1979) accuse remedial specialists of acting as 'ambulance-men to an accident-prone curriculum' rather than serving as agents of curricular and institutional change. A number of sections in the various considered sources indicate they also believe this is the case.

The challenge seems to be for more remedial specialists to direct the bulk of their energy to being more active in the planning of broader-based curriculum courses.

Imaginative thinking

Ellis (1981) comments on a widespread feeling amongst remedial teachers that 'remedial education is largely concerned with basic skills and that development of imaginative thinking is beyond their brief'. He argues powerfully for the inclusion of such thinking regularly in the curricular experience offered to children with learning difficulties. Surely Ellis is right to do so? A more forcible attempt to break away from the simplistic notion that skills come first, using them and using them imaginatively comes second, is long overdue. Many authors (for example, Weber (1974)) have suggested the two areas of development are integral and their joint promotion essential if a balanced curriculum is to be offered.

Several sections in the considered reports and surveys echo this appeal for more imaginative curricular activity. They describe:

(a) over-concern by remedial teachers with the teaching of basic skills in isolation;
(b) the lack of attempts by such specialists to engage children in developing basic skills through more creative, aesthetic, problem-solving activities;
(c) the virtual non-existence of remedial specialists working alongside a subject specialist in obvious imaginative areas of the curriculum, i.e., literature and drama (DES, 1979, 1980).

Professional skills

The range and direction of the professional skills required of the remedial specialist, to ensure that the pupils' curricular experiences match their needs but do not limit their horizons, have been well documented by the National Association for Remedial Education. It offers the following ambitious brief for the remedial specialist (NARE, 1979).

'THE DEVELOPING ROLE OF THE REMEDIAL TEACHER
Ideally, the specialist remedial teacher should fulfil several functions.
(a) An assessment role
   (i) The supervision and correct administration of standardized tests as part of a comprehensive screening procedure.
   (ii) The follow-up and diagnosis of specific learning difficulties in children who are identified as being 'at risk'.
(b) A prescriptive role
   (i) The preparation and implementation of individualized programmes for children with particular learning difficulties.
   (ii) The preparation and implementation of school strategies in the basic subject areas.
   (iii) Costing such exercises and requisitioning accordingly.
(c) A teaching/therapeutic role
   (i) Teaching individuals and groups where the nature of the problem makes it impossible for it to be contained within the normal classroom situation.
   (ii) Treating children with associated behavioural difficulties.
   (iii) Where appropriate, co-operating with other colleagues on a team-teaching basis.
(d) A supportive role
   Advising colleagues on:
   (i) appropriate group/setting procedures;
   (ii) ideas and techniques for the whole range of children with special educational needs;
   (iii) the range of materials and apparatus available;
   (iv) remedial work 'across the curriculum'.
(e) A liaison role
   Where appropriate, liaising with:
   (i) support services, in particular the school psychological, school health, educational welfare and career guidance services;
   (ii) parents;
   (iii) the community at large.

In presenting this discussion model of the remedial teacher's role, we are aware that many colleagues are already operating effectively in more than one of these areas. It is still all too rare, however, to find many examples where they have been allowed to operate effectively in all five.

There is obviously a need for the specialist remedial teacher to become more closely involved in decision-making processes at the highest level within schools.

In the past, remedial teachers have often been accorded a low status within schools, having had to struggle for parity with other colleagues. In their eagerness to gain esteem, they have tended to establish the same vertical structure of organization as that employed by departments dealing with particular subject areas of the curriculum.

Remedial education is both a horizontal and vertical concept. Children carry their problems across the curriculum and long-term benefits can only be achieved within the context of genuine team effort and co-operation.'

In the light of the comments so far highlighted in the sources under consideration, the NARE criteria seem realistic if remedial specialists are to be seen to be effective, determined, developing professionals. The role registered within section (d) above is the main area for future growth.

Monitoring progress and programmes

How will his progress and the efficacy of his planned programme be monitored so as to meet his needs but not limit his horizons? A short answer to this question is to say, as Brennan (*op. cit.*) does, that what is required is technical expertise in making use of normative and criterion-referenced assessment measures together with teaching information from the classroom. Certainly, the importance of classroom information ought to be increased as teachers come to realize that the teaching and learning situations represent the richest possible source of diagnostic information leading to more realistic insights concerning the curricular needs of children with learning difficulties. Such information must, however, be authoritative, and both normative and criterion assessment procedures must be appropriately applied.

In connection with the appropriate application of such procedures, the Warnock Report (*op. cit.*) and several of the DES papers (1979, 1980) emphasize that effective assessment aims to discover how a child learns and responds over a period of time and not merely how he or she performs on a single occasion. Thus, there is general acknowledgement of the validity of criterion-based assessment of pupil competence from teachers who know the children well, and a statement of desirability for broader assessment focus. This means, at the very least, that remedial specialists must fully understand assessment procedures overall (as opposed to possessing knowledge of certain tests) and to realize the relationship between assessment and curriculum objectives (for a clear statement of this relationship, see Mackintosh, 1976).

In addition to the points made above, comments occurring throughout most of these documents indicate further issues of relevance to this final question. Briefly, these are:

(a) evaluation of programmes is as important as the monitoring of pupil progress within them;
(b) assessment of personal development and achievement is of equal importance to the assessment of development in basic skills and academic knowledge (Burgess and Adams, 1980);
(c) monitoring performance by pupils themselves is an important ingredient in assessment routines.

Conclusion

Taken overall, many of the comments from these various reports and surveys are similar in emphasis and direction. They express challenges and concerns well recognized by remedial specialists themselves (Gains and McNicholas, 1979). Thus, in the early 1980s, much enthusiasm and energy is forthcoming from such specialists towards extending horizons for children such as 'M' and finding tentative answers to the four questions raised about the nature of his curricular needs and experiences.

Undoubtedly, there are many uncertainties (such as shown by the reference to the 'unhappy centipede' earlier), especially since calling into question the curriculum for children with learning difficulties inevitably means calling into question the total school curriculum. However, there is much determined local and national collective effort, and certain guidelines for future effort can be stated. Indeed, by taking the word 'we' to represent this collective effort and summarizing the essential messages from the considered sources, nine strands can be offered for further thought and action.

Implications for the role of remedial specialists

1. We must study the child with learning difficulties more systematically and scientifically.
2. We need to supplement our 'tests' with broad-based knowledge of assessment procedures and understand their relationship with curriculum design and planning.
3. We must become well-acquainted with curriculum design, development and evaluation.
4. We must give vigorous support to the current moves for a broad-based, common-content 11–16 curriculum and seek its level one primary equivalent.
5. The bulk of our support work must be within the general curriculum and not away from it. Towards this end, we must urgently seek to catalogue clear principles for adapting traditional teaching methods- and learning resources.
6. If we elect to offer a 'differentiated curriculum', we must:
   (a) offer definite evidence for doing so;
   (b) ensure that the 'alternative package' is better than an adapted existing one.
7. We must lift the expectations of some remedial specialists.
8. We must present our professional energies and skills in a more forward-reaching, exploratory and determined fashion — especially working alongside a subject teacher.

9. We must seek a new description to convey the full essence of our future role and expertise.

References

Ainscow, M. and Tweddle, D., *Preventing Classroom Failure: An Objectives Approach*, Wiley, 1979.

Brennan, W. K., *Curricular Needs of Slow Learners*, Schools Council Working Paper 63, Evans/Methuen, 1979.

Bruner, J. S., *Man: A Course of Study*, Guide to the Course, Cambridge, USA, 1969.

Burgess, T. and Adams, E., *Outcomes of Education*, Macmillan, 1980.

DES, *Aspects of Secondary Education in England*, HMSO, 1979.

DES/Welsh Office, *A Framework for the School Curriculum*, HMSO, 1980.

DES, *Primary Education in England*, HMSO, 1978.

DES, *A View of the Curriculum*, HMI Series: Matters for Discussion 11, HMSO, 1980.

Ellis, J. (1981), 'Imaginative thinking for the less-able adolescent' in *Remedial Education*, Vol. 16, No. 1.

Gains, C. and McNicholas, J., (eds) *Remedial Education; Guidelines for the Future*, Longman, 1979.

Golby, M. and Gulliver, J. (1979), 'Whose remedies, whose ills? A critical review of remedial education', in the *Journal of Curriculum Studies*, Vol.11.

Griffin, D., *Slow Learners: A Break in the Circle*, Woburn Press, 1978.

Haigh, G., *Teaching Slow Learners*, Temple Smith, 1978.

Hinson, M. (ed.), *Encouraging Results: Helping Children with Learning Difficulties in the Secondary School*, Macdonald Educational, 1978.

Hirst, P. J. (1965), 'The logic of the new curriculum', in the *Journal of Curriculum Studies*, Vol.1.

Holt, M. C., *Schools and Curriculum Change*, McGraw-Hill, 1980.

Mackintosh, H. G., *Assessing Attainment in the Classroom*, Hodder and Stoughton, 1976.

McCall, C. (1978) 'Ways of providing for the low achiever in the secondary school' in Raybould, E., *Helping the Low Achiever in the Secondary School*, Educational Review, 1978.

McCall, C. and Salmon, J., Preparation materials for intended new publication on 'Remedial Education Across the Curriculum' (1982).

National Association for Remedial Education, *The Role of Remedial Teachers, Guidelines* No. 2, 1979.

Schools Council, *Social Education: an Experiment in Four Secondary Schools*, Evans/Methuen, 1974.

Warnock, M. (Chairman), *Special Educational Needs*, HMSO, 1978.

Weber, K. J., *Yes, They Can!*, Open University Press, 1974.

Wilson, M. D., *The Curriculum in Special Schools*, Schools Council, 1981.

Younie, W. J., *Instructional Approaches to Slow Learning*, Teachers College Press, 1974.

Section 1
Pre-school and primary education

In his comprehensive chapter, Roy Evans suggests that the 1975 Children's Act represents the spirit of the decade: a respect for the individuality of the child and a concern for his or her needs and aspirations. The 1970s have also been described as the decade in which the family was rediscovered. Evans regards parents as 'managers of change' whose needs must be recognized and met if their children's development is to proceed in a socially valued sense. This view is amply supported by Carol Stevens' study of a project centred around the involvement of parents in the education of their pre-school children. Her account underlines the necessity for developing a true understanding of parents and their needs. She describes one approach representing the many adopted by similar projects in other parts of the country. Her own colleagues, working in different ways in multi-racial areas, have developed equally close relationships with families from ethnic minority groups.

Early identification of learning and behavioural difficulties is of prime importance, and early school-based intervention is vital if educational action, appropriate to children's needs, is to be effective. NARE has not been neglectful in this field. *Identification of Learning Difficulties: A Model for Intervention* by Sheila Wolfendale and Trevor Bryans was published in 1980. The authors use the principles and processes of child development as a framework for a psycho-educational approach to intervention into early-appearing learning and behavioural problems in school. They outline and illustrate methods of observing children, intervention programmes and methods of evaluation. This helpful book is of significance in the planning and implementation of a curriculum geared to the needs of the young child with learning difficulties.

Wendy Dewhirst describes recent studies of language development which provide a positive basis for planning programmes which will extend children's language. Despite exposure to differing teaching strategies, a small number of children do not appear to improve their reading skills. Paula Hodson describes an objectives approach to this problem, developed during her work in a tutorial unit. Finally, Barry Pinfield adopts an empirical approach to the balanced mathematics curriculum in the primary school. He discusses twelve reasons for children's early mathematical difficulties and outlines ways in which these may be overcome.

Primary Education in England (1978) found that, during the years when the public at large had seemed to be critical of schools, the relations between teachers and individual parents had become closer and more friendly, while the curriculum had broadened to include much that is of value. Whilst this may be true for the majority, other strong evidence shows that many other children are still failing at school for non-educational reasons. This section concentrates on the preventive aspects of education for children with learning difficulties at the expense of a more conventional 'ambulance-service' approach. Each chapter deserves a book in its own right — nevertheless, we hope that this overview of the more salient problems will act as a stimulus to the implementation of more effective strategies.

2

The early years of education: practice and precept

ROY EVANS

Introduction

During the late 1970s and early 1980s, the entire framework of public education has been the subject of more intense scrutiny and national debate than at any other period in the century or so since the extension of elementary education to all. Against a background of economic difficulties arising through shifts in the balance of world trade and the global recession of recent years, over-laid with more 'local' demographic, social and cultural trends, the resources available to education have progressively declined, whilst the process of education itself has been increasingly urged in the direction of greater accountability, efficiency and social utility.

However, the re-evaluation of means and ends, of policy and practice, is an inevitable and necessary pre-condition to the evolution of an institutional framework which is sensitive to the changing needs of individuals and groups, in response to general cultural and social change. Principles need to be affirmed and articulated which will serve to guide policy and permit priorities to be established. Good practice (as it affects children) must be identified and described, and patterns of organization developed which will allow new knowledge to transform the physical and psycho-social environments of the child.

In the context of the wider national community which constitutes British society in the 1980s, there are notable features which, although not unique to this country, nevertheless affect children's life-chances and influence the extent to which they adjust to and benefit from schooling. The progressive industrialization of society, developing urbanization, high-density living and the unprecedented rate of cultural change create social stress and may lead to individual crises of identity, feelings of political impotence and sub-cultural alienation. The increasing incidence of family breakdown, of psycho-social illnesses of various sorts, of child abuse, violence and disaffection are facts of modern-day living with which the Western countries in particular are all too familiar.

Efforts to ameliorate social pathology, prevent it where possible, and to provide programmes of individual or family support which are rehabilitative or compensatory in character are generally perceived as multi-disciplinary and representing a challenge to co-ordinated policy and practice in fields which include the distribution of incomes, housing, community and race relations, environmental planning, health care, as well as education and social welfare services of all forms. Presented with a diversity of claims against finite (and, in the 1980s, curtailed) resources at national and local level, priorities are established through a process of informed advocacy, influenced by the prevailing political philosophy. Furthermore, it is through such processes that the management framework is defined, the agents of change identified and their roles and responsibilities clarified. As society evolves, so also must the management structure and the roles of all involved within it. Within the context of education *per se*, the agreed priorities for distributable resources are, by the same token, the tangible outcome of the advocacy process.

The purpose of the present chapter is two-fold: (a) to review briefly the major shifts in priorities and developments in practice as they have occurred in this country over the last decade or so, and particularly as they affect the development of young children; and (b) to consider developments in policy and practice related directly to identifying and meeting children's special needs, set against practice elsewhere — notably the USA.

Priorities for children: needs and rights

Any overview of the many issues relevant to childhood that are taken up in the course of a decade suffers the potential handicap of professional bias. One's own membership of a particular professional group has a determining effect on the importance that one attaches to issues and even the extent to which one is capable of achieving a balanced perspective on the significance of proposed changes to policy and practice in disciplines and services outside of education. Nevertheless, if the recent past has revealed anything of the nature of the forces which shape children's lives, it has above all emphasized their multi-disciplinarity and the hazards which can accrue to children and families from action which is professionally isolated. There is particular relevance in this for children of all ages who are in any sense 'different' and for those who show signs of learning difficulty, educational handicap or maladaptive development.

With this in mind, it may be suggested that the formulation of policy throughout the seventies has been guided by two major principles: (a) the paramountcy of the child, and (b) the primacy of the family. These are evidently inter-related in a complex manner. The former indicates the pivotal significance of the child and his or her needs, to decisions taken on his or her behalf. Whilst child-oriented education has claimed this principle for many decades, it has not always operated within the legal framework of broadly-conceived social policy. The second principle re-affirms society's belief in the central importance of the child's family, and in addition carries implications for the *manner* in which decisions are taken and practice implemented on behalf of the child. These two principles may appear self-evident, but their relevance for statutory law, for professional practice in the health and welfare services, in education and in social work is profound.

The paramountcy of the child

This principle recognizes the individuality of each child and that his or her needs should be systematically met and his or her wishes taken account of, if his or her *rights as a citizen* are to be protected. For instance, the 1975 Children's Act was constructed around the concept of the 'child's welfare'.

It laid a duty on courts to base any decision regarding the adoption of a child on the 'need to safeguard and promote the child's welfare throughout his childhood' (Section 3) and to give due consideration to the child's wishes. At all stages in adoption proceedings since January 1976, 'the child's views must be ascertained and his feelings must be considered'. The Act also extended the welfare principle to cover decisions taken by local authorities in relation to children in their care. Further provisions of the Act relate to making the child a *party* to court proceedings in cases of local authority resolutions on parental rights and obligations (Section 58).

The effects of Plowden and Warnock

The 1975 Act represented the spirit of the decade: a respect for the individuality of the child and a concern for his or her needs and aspirations. It is possible to find evidence of this concern in the reports of every major committee of enquiry sponsored by government from the Plowden enquiry in 1967, up to and including the Warnock Report in 1978. The latter report said forcibly that society was 'now committed not merely to tending and caring for its handicapped members, as a matter of charity, but to educating them as a matter of right'. The Warnock Committee dealt substantially with the issue of children's needs, and saw their development, education and social integration as dependent on the extent to which these personal needs could be systematically identified and met.

A similar point had been made by the Plowden Committee eleven years earlier, when it was argued that 'the early and accurate identification of children who are deprived or disadvantaged' was the essential first step in meeting their needs and preventing educational failure. This enquiry, concerned as it was with the effects of social disadvantage on the course of children's life chances, pricked the national conscience over the plight of hundreds of thousands of British families. It legitimized intervention on behalf of children living under conditions of poverty by demonstrating the crass immorality of doing nothing. British society has subsequently recognized that the socializing and educational forces which operate in deprived and disadvantaged sections of the community are divisive and alienating, and contribute to the inter-generational transmission of deprivation. Equality of educational opportunity is incompatible with vast inequalities of life experience, and social policy must necessarily determine its priorities with a view to alleviating society's worst excesses.

Children's survival needs

Even at a very basic level, it is evident that at this point in time we are unable to ensure the survival needs of *all* of our children: twice as many children of unskilled workers die in the first year of life as children of professional workers; children still die today for nineteenth-century reasons. Within the last five years, official estimates place the number of households living in accommodation that is considered to be unfit for human habitation or lacking in basic amenities at around the 1·5 million mark; more than half a million children live in families where the total income is below the official poverty line. From evidence provided by the National Child Development Study, it is evident that within the last decade one in 16 of all British children were in large families, receiving low incomes and who were also poorly housed. The demonstrably poorer health, social adjustment and educational development of this group of children continue to give great cause for concern.

How do we effect *change* to the benefit of such children? An educational policy alone is not sufficient to meet their needs. Their concept of social reality is constructed within the poverty of their own homes and neighbourhood. School constitutes a cultural discontinuity, a clash of attitudes and values which many of these children reject. The social reality of classrooms is one in which many children from disadvantaged backgrounds feel alienated and of little worth; negative self-evaluations are reinforced and poor self-concepts *learned*. Whole communities are at risk and minority groups feel disadvantaged and discriminated against.

The past decade too has witnessed growing concern over child abuse by parents. The Court Report (1976) commenting on the 'disturbing phenomena of non-accidental injury to children' suggests that this is 'but *a* manifestation of a range of child abuse'. Of deaths in the 0 to 5-year-old age-group, violence in the family is presently the fourth most common cause. Court (*op. cit.*) gives evidence to indicate the gravity of the problem. Of the children who survive violence, 11 per cent have brain damage, 5 per cent some degree of visual impairment.

Children's basic rights

Beyond the survival needs, the child's need for security, for love, respect and recognition by significant adults as well as his or her need to feel a sense of 'belonging' (*c.f.* Kellmer Pringle, 1975) are basic human needs. They are also *fundamental human rights*. Psychologists have accepted for many years, although they may not always agree on the mechanisms involved, that the roots of human motivation are associated in a complex manner with the satisfaction of basic needs (*c.f.* Maslow, 1954, Adler, 1964, Barker, 1960, Elkind, 1969, Erikson, 1972, Fischbein, 1980, Frankenstein, 1966, Freud, 1953, Kohen-Raz, 1977, Rey, 1935, Sullivan, 1953, and so on). Where these needs are not met, the child is at risk of maladaptive development, social deviance and psycho-social stress. Where opportunities for new experiences have been limited, where the environment has restricted exploratory behaviour and language experience, then the development of higher cognitive abilities may be curtailed.

Jarman (1980) examines this thesis in the context of recent studies of adult-child interaction. He suggests that current evidence points to the ability of the very young baby — a few days after birth — to take part in complex interactive sequences with the principal caring adult (usually the mother), 'moreover, the baby displays *initiative* in interaction and by this means sets about learning about his world, especially the meaning of his social world'. Jarman continues to suggest that because this interactive process is dependent on complex signalling and the synchronization of behaviour sequences, it may be easily disrupted and result in the child losing 'initiative and hence the power to direct the interaction process in his quest to make sense of his world'. Citing the unresponsive or depressed mother as a possible source of such disruption, Jarman asks whether it is on this level that a child's cognitive potential is reduced. 'Perhaps the child's loss of initiative is a connecting factor between educational handicap and the socio-cultural correlates variously identified within an extensive literature'.

Tamburrini (1982) examines the interaction hypothesis from a somewhat different perspective and focuses particularly on teachers' intervention in children's play at nursery school. Arguing that adult interaction may facilitate and enhance the imaginative quality of representational play, Tamburrini distinguishes between the redirecting and extending style of interaction, and suggests that the one which is educationally profitable is the extending style which also has the virtue of valuing children's play in its own right whilst synchronizing with the child's intentions.

The role of attitudes and values

Being sensitive, then, to children's intentions, responsive to their initiatives and valuing their exploratory and representational behaviours are all aspects of attempts by caring adults and teachers to meet young children's needs. These are all necessary, but Tamburrini suggests that they are not inevitably sufficient. The educator must understand the relationship between the activity and its cognitive outcome, i.e., the principle of extension in socially-valued directions is basic to the educational enterprise. It evokes questions relating to the teacher's role and directs attention to the *means* employed within the educational environment at all levels. Differences in attitudes and values influence the course of human transactions, and misunderstandings are frequently rooted in different conceptions of social reality. Allport (1968) observed that 'No problem is more challenging than the degree and manner to which the structure of a person's thought reflects his own personal life history'.

Schools and other social institutions may inadvertently reinforce the negative self-evaluations of some children and, moreover, provide an intrinsic mechanism for the perpetuation of social and cultural stereotypes to the further disadvantage of some children and young people. Over the last ten years particularly, developments in social psychology have allowed a much clearer recognition that the child's 'self-concept' or 'self-picture' is itself an educational *outcome*, which is both influenced by the conditions of learning, as well as forming an element of them. (See, for example, Staines, 1971). Milner (1975) has provided a sensitive account of the way in which prejudiced attitudes and racial stereotypes influence the behaviour of minority-group children and intervene in their development through the process of response to expectations that 'significant others' hold of them. Again, the works of Birns (1976), Serbin (1978), and Loban (1974), are good accounts of how gender identification is 'hidden' in the unofficial curriculum of schools and pre-schools. Equally, the message conveyed by the results of the study by Rutter *et al.* (1979) on attainment within a group of London comprehensive schools is broadly to the effect that social and organizational parameters of an institution can have a substantial influence on the response and progress of pupils.

Every social situation with its implicit attitudes and values provides opportunities for incidental learning which contribute to children's developing 'world view'.

Trends and their influence

Some trends in educational practice which emerged in the past decade should perhaps be viewed with caution — although these developments, largely interventionist in character and compensatory by intent, can be placed within the general context of efforts to identify and meet children's needs. The caution is inclined less to the intent than to the balance of emphasis:

Firstly, the curriculum development trend emphasizes cognitive processes. Chazan (1978) in an overview of international research in this field notes that 'efforts have been made to define objectives in terms of observable behaviour and the acquisition of measurable skills with an emphasis on linguistic and cognitive development'.

Secondly, individualization is increasingly being sought through a technological approach to learning which is rooted in behavioural psychology. It focuses on the tasks to be taught rather than on the processes in the child which need to be studied. Whilst not irrelevant to the practice of education at any level, and even of particular value in some circumstances and to specified ends, its place within the curriculum of early childhood education requires careful consideration.

Thirdly, the pressure on the school system to attend to the problems of illiteracy, innumeracy and lack of scientific understanding, whilst of themselves the proper objects of formal education, i.e. schooling, has been accompanied by overt attempts at quality control through product monitoring. The inauguration of the Assessment of Performance Unit by the DES indicates clearly an intention to measure what can be measured in terms of school learning and to provide a comparative base to track performance nationally. There is an inherent danger in that 'what can be measured' will influence the balance of objectives pursued.

Fourthly, there has been relatively little research into the effects of institutional arrangements, or curricular activity on children's social or emotional development, behaviour or adjustment. The review of Headstart research since 1969 conducted by Mann et al. (1977) cited only 16 studies — of the many hundreds conducted — which examined Headstart impact on children's social development. Stukat's (1976) review of trends in European pre-school research reveals that few studies actively embrace evaluation of any merit in the area of social development, even though social behaviour objectives were contained within the various curriculum models.

The above reservations notwithstanding, the broad lines of policy during the years recently past have re-affirmed society's commitment to supporting and promoting the individuality of the child in all its varied aspects, and of his or her rights as a citizen. To these ends, the broad framework of policy has re-iterated the central significance of *the family*.

The primacy of the family

The 1970s have been variously referred to as the decade in which 'the family' was re-discovered. Its value as a social institution has been re-affirmed both in its own right and as a principal agency of socialization and early education of children. Parents are 'managers of change' whose own needs must be recognized and met if their children's development is to proceed in a socially

32

valued sense. The strength of the family lies in its 'naturalness', its intimacy, and in the security it may afford the child. Conversely, its pathology can be the generative base for childhood difficulties of many kinds. The broad base of policy formulation has increasingly recognized that the needs of children can not be seen in isolation from the needs of the family. Disadvantaged families, one-parent families, and families of exceptional children have had their special problems examined and their rights and responsibilities underlined.

The Court Committee on Child Health Services (1976) observed:

> 'If our services are to be based on working with and through the family, then the professionals concerned must unders and has respond appropriately to the new conditions. If families can now no longer do everything that they were formerly supposed to do, and services have to provide instead, they must do so in a way that supports rather than denigrates the family.'

And again: 'We want to see a service which is child-centred . . . that is, geared to ensuring that parents are well informed and increasingly involved in their children's development and health.'

Parental involvement

These recommendations effectively reinforced the position taken by Plowden nine years earlier, the latter being itself a turning-point in British education as far as the barriers to parental involvement were concerned, providing the impetus to the EPA projects directed by Halsey (see, e.g., Halsey, 1972) and representing the corner-stone of the substantial developments in home-school liaison which have evolved subsequently. The more recent report of the Taylor Committee (1977) extended the parental involvement debate to the arena of school management and raised important — if difficult — questions related to the accountability of schools to the communities they serve and notably to parents. In the area of special educational needs, the Warnock Committee (1978) provided a framework for parents' participation at all relevant stages in their child's education, and in so doing synthesized the various strands of a debate that had been actively canvassed more than a decade earlier (see, e.g., the Report of the Carnegie UK Trust, *Handicapped Children and Their Families*, 1964, and also the National Children's Bureau Report, *Living with Handicap*, 1970).

The shift of emphasis in policy and practice to greater parental involvement is in recognition:

(a) of their *rights* as parents;
(b) of the specialized and intimate knowledge they possess (see, e.g., Brimblecombe, 1976), and their potential for contributing positively to the therapeutic (e.g., Jeffrey and McConkey, 1974) and early educational process (e.g., Levenstein, 1970);
(c) of the reciprocal value to them of being involved.

Whilst there is an inevitable gap between precept and practice (e.g., Booth, 1981), between the formulation of policy and its implementation, it is equally the case that a growing literature of evaluated practice and innovative action within the spectrum of concern over 'parenting' has furthered the identification of significant features of a co-ordinated approach to supporting parents and providing education appropriate to their needs and stage of development (Honig, 1980, Wolfendale, 1981). Pugh (1981) provides an excellent overview of the current status of parent-education programmes in the UK and points to the disparate aims, objectives and methodologies which they exhibit. She suggests that parents should be offered a range of services which 'build upon their own parenting skills, rather than undermining their self-confidence with "professional expertise" '. The latter point relates to communication between parents and professionals which, as Evans (1980) has noted, 'may produce a different set of outcomes to those sought: help for their children may be rejected by parents because of the *manner* in which it is offered'.

The significance of involving parents actively in the sense of (b) above is amply demonstrated by intervention programmes such as the Heber (1973, 1975) project at Milwaukee, and through Headstart evaluations by Bronfenbrenner (1972), Lazar (1977), and Mann *et al.* (1977).

The relevance of such evidence to the development of an effective technology of intervention with young children 'at risk' of educational handicap has been described by Evans (1979). The central feature of the whole thrust of practice in this context is broadly similar in intent to the range of programmes described in Wolfendale (1981): simply put, parents have a determining influence on the course of children's development from the moment of conception (see, e.g., Wedge and Prosser, 1973, Davie, Butler and Goldstein, 1972) through the quality of care they provide, the opportunities they create for exploratory and imaginative play, through the nature of the interactions within the total dynamic of the family situation, the attitudes expressed and the values held, through the families' knowledge of support services when these are necessary.

Professional action which can support or extend parents' competencies in rearing their children, which is offered in a manner that parents can accept, offers possibilities for positive change to the totality of early childhood experience — and on an enduring basis. It may, moreover, lay the foundation for effective co-operation between sets of significant adults in a child's life, facilitate mutual understanding of problems, objectives and attitudes and establish a basis of respect for the potential that each 'partner' can contribute to the full development of the child. The notion of 'reciprocal value' is rooted in the benefits which can accrue from active partnership — information essential to decision-making is unlocked, and at the same time opportunities exist for creating learning situations for parents.

Parental self-development

From another viewpoint, involvement may be overtly concerned with parental self-development. The work of SCOPE, for instance, (Poulton and Poulton, 1979) 'is concerned with elevating the self-esteem of mothers and fathers, enhancing their consciousness not only about their role as educators of their children, but also their functioning as members of a larger community'. In the UK, the Pre-school Playgroups Association sees involvement as centrally connected with personal development in the realization that this will ultimately benefit the whole family.

Today, such concern is very necessary. In Britain, as in many industrialized countries, the nature of family life has undergone a rapid change. Urbanization and occupational mobility have resulted in the demise of the extended family (see, e.g., Cooper, 1974) programmes of urban renewal and high-rise dwellings have exacerbated the isolation of nuclear families (Fairbairns and Wintour, 1977) and perpetuated social problems (Latournerie, 1982). This has been particularly marked for families with young children: depression in young mothers has increased its incidence throughout the decade (e.g., Brown, 1975). In this country, too, the divorce rate has doubled since the passage of the Divorce Reform Act in 1969, and the number of children in one-parent families is also increasing. The traditional conceptions of parental roles are changing in response to pressure from radical female pressure groups and legislation on sex discrimination.

These changes in family life carry great significance for the education and socialization of young children and make increasing demands on the welfare services to provide flexible day-care arrangements for the under-fives. Successive UK governments over the past decade have been under pressure to expand provision and develop a range of day-care institutions so as to provide a better 'fit' with society's changing needs. In the degree to which such provision, in all its variety, is sensitive to the changing needs of children and parents, it can contribute positively to the achievement of socially valued goals. However as Dorothy Day (1982) has observed, whilst there is general agreement on these needs, 'published opinion on how these needs should be fulfilled continues to be partisan and in some cases extremely polarised'.

Surprisingly, the actual number of children being catered for in all forms of pre-school provision rose throughout the decade despite the general cutback in resourcing (Osborn, 1979, 1981). The pattern of provision nevertheless remains patchy, with marked regional variation in the predominance of one or other of playgroup or nursery class (van der Eyken, 1979). In a very real sense, the continuing lack of coherent, comprehensive and flexible arrangements for the care and early education of *all* children between birth and school entry with the opportunities this holds for health-care surveillance and routine developmental checks (*c.f.* provision in France: *The Social Institutions of France*, Documentation Française, 1980), limits opportunities for preventive work which should begin as early as possible.

Identifying and meeting special educational needs

The Warnock Report (1978)

Few public documents in recent years can have been awaited with the eagerness that was evident in the case of the Warnock Report, *Special Educational Needs*. Whilst little enough of the committee's principal body of recommendations has found its way into the statutory and regulatory framework, there is little doubt that its pervading philosophy of 'difference' rather than 'handicap', of 'provision' on the evidence of 'need', will influence practice in the years ahead.

Extending the concept of special need to one in five of the school-age population, the Report emphasizes the importance of preventative practice and views early identification of children 'in need' or 'at risk' of educational failure as the essential first step in the helping process. A multi-stage model for identification is proposed which begins with the teacher in the classroom and culminates, for a small minority of children, with comprehensive and specialist functional evaluation.

Acknowledging the complex and multifaceted character of a whole range of problems which children may display at school, the Warnock Committttee elaborate the concept of multi-professional co-operation and parental involvement, and recommend an operational procedure for its implementation and co-ordination. Whilst the 1981 Education Bill provides some statutory powers to local authorities in the area of 'co-ordination', the effectiveness of such practice, if evaluated in terms of ultimate benefit to the child rather than as an administrative exercise, will be controlled by factors such as individual competencies of the professionals concerned, their attitude towards co-operation, the level of resourcing for specialist or consultative purposes in a particular area or region, the range of institutions available for special placement in a given authority or to which that authority has access.

Establishing the need for case-finding procedures

Because of the clear importance of 'case-finding' to all subsequent educational decision-making on behalf of the child, it is worth examining the directions of development in this area during the 1970s, as a reflection of policy and as a precursor to educational planning.

In the late 1960s, in the aftermath of Plowden (1967) and the flood of compensatory education activity in the USA, the Schools Council funded a research and development project based at University College Swansea, part of whose purpose was to develop a screening procedure to identify children who were 'at risk' of educational handicap. The conceptual basis for the instrument was the *prediction* of future school failure or under-functioning on the basis of child-orientated evaluations made at school entry. The identification was thus to be made on a pre-symptomatic basis, the hypothesis being that within the general population of children from all social backgrounds, it would be possible to discover combinations of personal/developmental, socio-cultural, medical and familial factors which provided an efficient indication of 'need for' compensatory educational provision. To put this rather differently, the purpose was to discover where possible, risk factors which, taken either singly or in combination, efficiently identified young school-entrants who, in the absence of special help, were likely to under-achieve before entry to junior school. The results of the study have been variously reported (Evans, 1973, 1976, Evans *et al.*, 1976), and the screening instrument made available through NFER.

There are two reasons for referring to that research here. Firstly, the experience of the research team between 1968 and 1970 is relevant in that the normal review process which aimed at compiling a battery of psychological tests for use with the sample of school entrants was largely found to be fruitless. At that time, and for some years after, there existed a clear deficit in the availability of reliable, valid and efficient screening techniques and prediction scales. In 1974, Evans and Ferguson noted that 'it is in relation to the availability and adequacy of normative data for devices currently available that the major criticisms may be made . . . too few have really acceptable psychometric properties or report their normative samples in ways that allow objective assessment of their worth'. At that time too, a few local authorities had developed imaginative systematic screening programmes and even fewer employed these at the stage of school entry.

Secondly, since the late 1960s, the whole concept of pre-symptomatic identification has undergone substantial re-evaluation, largely as a result of a re-orientation of policy in medicine based on evaluated practice and the move towards population surveillance with the aim of identifying (with young children) the early symptoms of a delay or disorder of development (see, e.g. Rogers, 1971). During the 1970s, most area health authorities abandoned the practice of risk-screening in favour of frequent routine health and development checks for all infants prior to school — all, that is, who attend appointments at well-baby clinics (see Wedge and Prosser, 1973). The responsibility for early symptomatic evaluation thus rests with the pediatrician and his or her competency in the area of developmental delay.

At this point in time, there are indications that 'practice' in education is moving in a direction similar to that taken in preventive medicine, although it may be argued that even here the concept of risk-screening was too hastily abandoned (see Alberman and Goldstein, 1971 and Goldstein, 1975). A review of current practice in the field of education and educational psychology is presented by Wolfendale and Bryans (1980) in their book *Identification of Learning Difficulties*. A striking feature is the number of experimental procedures for early identification being developed and evaluated by educational psychologists in different parts of the country. Equally striking is the greatly increasing number of assessment devices for use with pre-school-age children and school entrants. Moreover, many of these devices are checklists and developmental schedules, and give evidence of a sustained trend towards criterion-referenced assessment which, as Ward (1970) noted, requires a change of emphasis 'from the assessment of individual differences to the identification of learning criteria and individual performance relative to these'.

Ward further suggested that this form of assessment would be particularly relevant to the construction of tests for diagnostic remediation programmes in special education. It should be recalled that the monitoring of individual children's performance within the ordinary classroom as advocated by the Bullock Committee in 1975, and later by Warnock, represents both the means by which teachers may more effectively match the child with learning experiences appropriate to his or her needs, and the means by which the first stage of multi-level screening is effected. This strategy puts considerable stress on the teacher's knowledge of developmental processes in children and challenges his or her diagnostic and pedagogical abilities. In this sense, the teacher is working within a framework of clearly perceived objectives for each child, where the child himself or herself has effectively mediated in the specification of those goals. The value of developmental checklists in this context is discussed by Sparrow (1975).

It must be noted, however, that the practice of symptomatic identification is heavily reliant on the practical situation enabling an early realization of the onset of delay — if practice is to be in any sense preventative; failure to draw attention to the problem usually leaves the way open for the problem to draw attention to itself! One cannot fail to note, either, that the level of support that teachers can expect from the local authority in creating and sustaining the conditions for good practice to flourish is variable.

After more than a decade of agitation for effective preventive educational policy, and two decades of active preventative policy in fields allied to education — notably health care — the attitude of LEAs towards children with special needs *appears* ambivalent. From one perspective, the continuing discovery at successive follow-ups by the National Child Development Study of handicaps not noted in earlier follow-ups add support to the view that, despite the obligation laid upon LEAs in 1944 to discover cases of childhood handicap from the age of two years, there is still a substantial need for coherent and systematic case-finding procedures. Again, the most recent evidence indicates that not all authorities have instituted screening procedures at *primary* school. On the basis of replies to Circular 14/77, made available through HMSO in November 1979, it appears that:

(a) Two in three local authorities employ some form of screening during primary school, mostly in the area of reading. Of those who employ diagnostic screening, in half the authorities this operates with children older than seven years.
(b) Fewer than one in ten authorities report screening in number.
(c) Almost all authorities reported that they maintained services to provide guidance and support for slow learners.
(d) One in five did not refer to the work of a remedial advisory service.
(e) Seven in ten did not mention assistance to schools needing resource material for remedial teaching.
(f) A few responses from LEAs included comments on the importance of involving parents in the education of young children who showed signs of making slow progress in basic skills.

The above observations which have been paraphrased from the published report are not a complete summary of the responses to circular 14/77. What the list does do, however, is to indicate that, whilst systematic progress has been recorded over a decade, such progress is largely consistent with a policy of remediation and is not, on the whole, operative until the third or even fourth year at school. Allowing that care has to be taken in interpreting the results from a circular enquiry, the evidence presented suggests that in one in three authorities either no screening programme existed, or it was not mentioned. Nevertheless, if the spirit of Warnock is to be effected, it argues for more systematic resourcing, applied earlier.

A comparison with the USA

How does current practice compare with efforts in favour of children with special needs in the USA?

On 29 November 1975, the United States Congress approved legislation which has since become regarded as a landmark. Commonly known as the Education for All Handicapped Children Act, Public Law 94–142 has had a profound effect on the entire field of early childhood education, notably in the effort to serve the needs of the pre-school handicapped population. Effectively for the first time in US history, the different states are mandated to provide a public education for children below the age of five. Zweifel and Varney (1980) describe the major provisions of the Act as giving:

(a) assurance that all handicapped children aged three to 18 must have available free public education and all other guaranteed rights (by 1 September 1978). This requirement must be extended to handicapped children aged 18 to 21 by 1 September 1980;
(b) assurance of the maintenance of an Individualized Education Program (IEP) for all handicapped children;
(c) a guarantee of complete due process procedures;
(d) the assurance of special education being provided to all handicapped children in the 'least restrictive' environment;
(e) assurance of non-discriminatory testing and evaluation;
(f) a guarantee of policies and procedures to protect the confidentiality of data and information.

The public school system has responded to the mandate of PL 94–142 in what Slavenas (1982) has called 'a veritable beehive of activity . . . already in a state of crisis due to declining enrolments, shortage of funds and a variety of other socio-economic problems'. Fascinating developments have taken place on several fronts. Two are particularly worthy of note in the light of the foregoing.

Child Find

PL 94–142 established Child Find procedures to locate all handicapped children in a defined geographical area. The legislative mandate emphasizes the importance of public awareness of the services available. Child Find includes locating, identifying and screening children within the 3–5-year age-group. Professionals from a variety of disciplines are responsible for referring children to the 'least restrictive' setting.

The Edna Smith Child Development Centre in Aurora, Illinois, serves mildly to moderately handicapped children aged between 3 and 5. Zweifel and Varney (1980) describe its Child Find procedure:

'A routine community screening is conducted at least twice a year. Parents are invited through local media and by flyers distributed to school-age children, to bring their pre-schoolers for evaluation at a neighbourhood school. Each ten to fifteen-minute gross screening is performed by a professional staff member of either Edna Smith or the local school. A child's developmental level is compared to established norms, and vision and hearing are also tested. Those individuals suspected of development delay are recommended for a six-week diagnostic summer school program at the Center which provides in-depth evaluation. Approximately 60 to 70 per cent of those attending this diagnostic program are recommended for placement at Edna Smith for the following school year.'

Donna Read (1982) describing a Child Find programme in Broward County, Florida, writes:

'The program consists of multi-disciplinary screenings for children aged two through five. An eight-step screening procedure is initiated on Saturdays, approximately seven through ten times per year. Between 100 and 200 children are serviced during each screening: a total of about 1200 children are seen during an entire calendar year. All children identified as possibly having conditions bearing upon their learning abilities are given complete physical and psychological evaluations. Those found to require intervention are either referred to appropriate community organisations for health or social services or referred to a public school classroom for remedial services.'

The evidence from two states, widely different from geographic, demographic and socio-economic perspectives, is of a vigorous effort to operate within the spirit and the text of the legislative mandate. It would be a mistake to believe that in all states, and indeed in all school districts, the same degree of vigour applied — and for not dissimilar reasons to those erected in this country to explain variations in practice and provision: lack of financial and manpower resources, rurality of the area and thus poor cost-effectiveness of some services, inner urban problems and associated difficulties of 'reaching' certain sectors of the population, and so on. However, the positive thrust into the community which is the essence of both approaches described above would certainly be in the spirit of prevailing concepts of good practice in the UK, and make preventative action on behalf of children with special needs eminently more possible than it is at present.

The Individualized Education Program (IEP)

PL 94–142 emphasizes individual programming for children to meet their unique needs. The requirement is established by Law:

'Individualized means that the IEP must be addressed to the educational needs of a single child rather than a class or group of children. A written statement for each handicapped child shall include:

(a) a statement of the present levels of educational performance of such child;
(b) a statement of the annual goals, including shorter term instructional objectives;
(c) a statement of the special educational services to be provided to such child and the extent to which such child will be able to participate in regular educational programmes;
(d) the projected date for initiation and anticipated duration of such services;
(e) appropriate objective criteria and evaluation procedures and schedules for determining, on at least an annual basis, whether instructional objectives are being achieved'.

This programme requirement has the familiar ring of the competency-based curriculum which Cardarelli (1974) argued would be 'based on explicit demonstrable objectives. Each broad goal must ultimately generate specific objectives. It is not enough to say that the child must have a variety of language experiences; the curriculum must specify what these language experiences will aid the child in attaining'.

An interesting paradox exists in British early childhood education, for whilst few teachers would disagree with the merits of what is proposed in the context of such a plan, there is nevertheless a grave suspicion that the approach is altogether too mechanistic to fit easily within the framework of current practice. The error here, of course, is that such a procedure should *constitute* the framework of practice, methodologies being selected to match the learning styles of the child and the broader concepts of the educational experience held by the teacher. Structure is not a word that falls easily off the tongue of some of our educators — being associated with rigid programming with little room for intelligent manipulation of the material or the learning environment. It can certainly have that complexion, but it is not inevitable; for some children the use of closely-programmed material is frequently necessary, and many classroom teachers today are adept at this process. Those antagonistic to the notion should perhaps reflect that daily their children are exposed to *their* structuring of the learning environment — and however 'open' that environment may appear to be, what the children gain is a function of the clarity with which the teacher himself or herself perceives the richness of opportunity it holds. The curriculum plan of the Edna Smith Centre, when seen in operation, is not too different from good practice as one might witness it in a British nursery class.

'A thorough grasp of the developmental stages of early childhood, finely tuned observational skills, understanding of the emotional needs of young children and the ability to use one's own person to establish a therapeutic relationship, are the abstract tools which enable the teacher to create and to implement the IEP. Continued assessment of progress and evolving needs makes the curriculum a fluid process. The environment, the daily schedule, the directiveness of the teacher and the aide, the goals and objectives — all change in relation to changing growth needs.' (Zweifel and Varney, 1980.)

What must not be lost sight of, however, is the mandatory nature of the IEP. It is produced as a result of a multi-disciplinary team-meeting, parents have the right of consultation and appeal — the due process requirement — and access to information and decision-making in respect of their child. IEP specification is also a lengthy and involved process. The regional information and dissemination centre based at the University of Northern Illinois, which facilitates public information and awareness of PL 94–142, has provided a handbook for teachers on writing an IEP. The handbook lays out 18 sequential steps in making and recording *decisions* on the written Programme by the multi-disciplinary case conference. The implementation of the mandated goals and instructional objectives is then a matter for the teacher and his or her aide(s).

Conclusion

Taking a broad view — for it is always tempting to see other people's grass as greener — and leaving aside the possible differences in the technical aspects of screening or prevailing pedagogy, the one trend within the context of American practice that is worthy of note and emulation in this country is the sense of *purpose* that is being brought to bear in locating and identifying

41

pre-school-age children who show evidence of development delay, handicap or learning disability. The efforts to inform and assure the community of their rights in this regard are laudatory.

In the UK, too much is too often left to chance. As the early part of this chapter has attempted to show, the trend of the 1970s has been towards child-oriented and family-based policies, better co-ordination of services, increased access to a broader range of pre-school facilities and a greater understanding of the ecology of childhood. However, at the same time children are still failing at school for non-educational reasons and the trend of cultural change has been towards increasing psycho-social stress and social disintegration.

The continuation of social trauma such as is produced by high unemployment argues for extended and imaginative policies of social welfare and community support; with the future generations particularly in mind, it is regrettable that virtually all agencies have operated in a reverse climate. Much of value in the preventative sense can nevertheless still be accomplished through re-allocating existing resources or applying them earlier. Even adminstrative mechanisms such as making maternity and child welfare allowances contingent upon compulsory health checks — as in France — provide an opportunity to assure the health and developmental progress of the child, throughout gestation and subsequently.

At the end of the day, however, additional resourcing is necessary if teachers are to be enabled to employ their clinical and pedagogical skills fully and apply them appropriately.

References and further reading

Adler, A., *Problems of Neurosis*, Harper and Row, New York, 1964.

Alberman, E. D. and Goldstein, H. (1970) 'The "at risk" register: a statistical evaluation' in the *British Journal of Preventive and Social Medicine*, Vol. 24.

Barker, R. G. (1960), 'Ecology and motivation' in the *Nebraska Symposium on Motivations*, Vol. 8.

Birns, B. (1976), 'The emergence and socialization of sex difference in the earliest years' in the *Merrill-Palmer Quarterly of Behaviour and Development*, Vol. 22, No. 3.

Booth, T. (1981), 'Educating children with Down's Syndrome in an ordinary school' in *Early Child Development and Care*, Vol. 7, Nos. 2/3.

Brimblecombe, F. S. W., 'Pediatricians and parents as partners' in Oppe and Woodford (eds), *Early Management of Handicapping Disorders*, ASP, Amsterdam, 1976.

Bronfenbrenner, U. (1972), 'Is early intervention effective?' Cornell University (mimeo).

Brown, G. W. (1975), 'Social class and psychiatric disturbance among women in an urban population' in *Sociology*, Vol. 9.

Bullock, Lord (Chairman), *A Language for Life*, HMSO, 1975.

Cardarelli, S. (1974), 'How to evolve an individualized pre-school curriculum' in *Educational Technology*, Vol. 14, No. 11.

Chazan, M., *International Research in Early Childhood Education*, NFER, 1978.

Cooper, J. D., 'Dimensions of parenthood' in *The Family in Society*, HMSO, 1974.

Court, Prof. S. D. M. (Chairman), *Child Health Services*, HMSO, 1976.

Davie, R., Butler, N. and Goldstein, H., *From Birth to Seven*, Longman, 1972.

Day, D. (1982), 'Focusing on under-fives' in *Early Child Development and Care*, Vol. 8, No. 3.

DES, *Local Authority Arrangements for the School Curriculum*, HMSO, 1979.

Elkind, D., 'Egocentrism in adolescence' in Grinder R. E. (ed.), *Studies in Adolescence*, Macmillan, New York, 1969.

Erikson, E. H., *Childhood and Society*, Penguin, 1972.

Evans, R. (1973), 'The development and evaluation of some techniques used to predict educational handicap in the primary school' (unpublished PhD thesis, University of Swansea).

Evans, R. (1976), 'The prediction of educational handicap' in *Educational Research*, Vol. 19, No. 1.

Evans, R. *et al.*, *The Swansea Evaluation Profile: School Entrants*, NFER, 1976.

Evans, R., 'Identification and intervention' in Gains and McNicholas (eds), *Remedial Education — Guidelines for the Future*, Longman, 1979.

Evans R. (1980), 'The social integration of the young child' (paper to 16th World Assembly, OMEP, Quebec).

Fairbairns, Z. and Wintour, J., *No Place to Grow Up*, Shelter, 1977.

Ferri, E., *Growing Up in a One-parent Family*, NFER, 1976.

Fischbein, S. (1980), 'Heredity-environment influences on growth and development during adolescence' (paper presented to Third International Congress on Twin-studies, Jerusalem).

Frankenstein, C., *The Roots of the Ego*, Williams and Wilkins, Baltimore, 1966.

Freud, A., *The Ego and Mechanisms of Defence*, International University Press, New York, 1953.

Goldstein, H. (1975), 'A mathematical model for population disease screening' in the *Bulletin of the Institute of Mathematics and its Applications*, Vol. 11.

Halsey, A. H. (ed.), *Educational Priority*, Vol. 1, *EPA, Problems and Policies*, HMSO, 1972.

Heber, R. *et al.*, (1973) 'Rehabilitation of families at risk for mental retardation' (progress report, University of Wisconsin).

Honig, A. S. (1980), 'Parent involvement and the development of children with special needs' in *Early Child Development and Care*, Vol. 6, Nos. 3/4.

Jarman, D. (1980), 'Some implications for the child's educational potential of recent investigations into early childhood interaction' in *Early Child Development and Care*, Vol. 6, Nos. 3/4.

Jeffrey, D. M. and McConkey, R. (1974), Parental Involvement Project, Development Charts, Hester Adrian Research Centre, University of Manchester.

Kellmer Pringle, M., *The Needs of Children*, Hutchinson, 1974.

Kohen-Raz, R. (1977), 'Special education needs at adolescence' in Feinstein, S. C. (ed.), *Adolescent Psychiatry*, Vol. V.

Latournerie, M-A., 'The planning of urban and rural development, housing and urban transport' in Evans, R. (ed.), *The Social Institutions of France*, Gordon and Breach, Paris, 1982.

Lazar, I. *et al.*, *The Persistence of Pre-school Effects*, US Government Printing Office, Washington, 1977.

Levenstein, P. (1970), 'Cognitive growth in pre-schoolers through verbal inter-actions with mothers' in the *American Journal of Orthopsychiatry*, Vol. 40, No. 426.

Loban, G. (1974), 'Presentation of sex roles in British reading schemes' in *New Trends in Education*, Vol. 16, Spring.

Mann, *et al.* (1977), *A Review of Headstart Research Since 1969*, OHEW, Pub(OHDS), 78–31102.

Maslow, A. H., *Motivation and Personality*, Harper, New York, 1954.

Milner, D., *Children and Race*, Penguin, 1975.

Osborn, A. (1979), 'Sources of variation in uptake of pre-school provision', Department of Child Health, Bristol.

Osborn, A. (1981), 'Under-fives in school in England and Wales, 1971–1979', in *Educational Research*, Vol. 23, No. 2.

Poulton, L. and Poulton, G. (1979), 'Neighbourhood support for young families' in *Early Child Development and Care*, Vol. 6, Nos. 1/2.

Plowden, Lady (Chairman), *Children and Their Primary schools*, HMSO, 1967.

Pugh, G. (1981), 'Parenthood: towards a framework for education and support' in *Early Child Development and Care*, Vol. 7, Nos. 2/3.

Read, D. J. (1982), 'Project Child Find: an intervention program that works' in *Early Child Development and Care*, Vol. 8, No. 1.

Rey, A., *L'intelligence pratique chez l'enfant (observations et expériences)*, Alcan, Paris, 1935.

Rogers, M. G. H. (1971), 'The early recognition of handicapping disorders in childhood' in *Developmental Medicine and Child Neurology*, Vol. 13, No. 88.

Rutter, M. *et al.*, *Fifteen Thousand Hours*, Open Books, 1979.

Serbin, L.A., 'Teachers, peers and play preferences; an environmental approach to sex-typing in the pre-school' in Sprung (ed.), *Perspectives on Non-sexist Early Childhood Education*, Teachers College Press, New York, 1978.

Slavenas, R. D. (1982), guest editorial comment in *Early Child Development and Care*, Vol. 8, No. 1.

Sparrow, M., *Charting Child Development, Concern 15*, National Children's Bureau, 1975.

Staines, J. W., 'Self-picture as a factor in the classroom' in Cashdan *et al.* (eds.), *Personality Growth and Learning*, Longman, 1971.

Stukat, K., *Current Trends in European Pre-school Research*, NFER, 1976.

Sullivan, H. S., *Interpersonal Theory of Psychiatry*, Norton, New York, 1953.

Tamburrini, J. (1982), 'Play and the role of the teacher' in *Early Child Development and Care*, Vol. 8, No. 3.

Taylor, T. (Chairman), *A New Partnership for our Schools*, HMSO, 1977.

van der Eyken, W. *et al.*, (1979), *Pre-schooling in England, Scotland and Wales*, Department of Child Health Research Unit, University of Bristol.

Ward, J. (1970), 'On the concept of criterion–referenced measurement' in the *British Journal of Educational Psychology*, Vol. 40, No. 3.

Warnock, M. (Chairman), *Special Educational Needs*, HMSO, 1978.

Wedge, P. and Prosser, H., *Born to Fail?*, Arrow Books, 1973.

Wolfendale, S. (ed.) (1981), 'Parent involvement' in *Early Child Development and Care*, Special Issue, Vol. 7, Nos. 2/3.

Wolfendale, S. and Bryans, T., *Identification of Learning Difficulties*, NARE, 1980.

Zweifel, J. J. and Varney, J.H. (1980), 'Servicing the pre-school non-categorically handicapped: the Edna Smith Child Development Centre' in *Early Child Development and Care*, Vol. 6, Nos. 3/4.

3

Parental involvement

CAROL STEVENS

Introduction

There is a rapid period of growth in a child's measurable intelligence during the first five years of life. This finding emerged from a number of painstaking analyses of data from several longitudinal studies, carried out by Professor Benjamin Bloom at the University of Chicago (quoted by Hutt and Hutt, 1974). Bloom found that of intelligence measured at 17 years, 20 per cent had developed by the age of one year, 50 per cent by the age of four years, 80 per cent by eight years and 92 per cent by thirteen. He concluded that any procedures carried out during the pre-school period are likely to be far more effective than comparable procedures later on. He estimated, for example, that extreme environments (good or bad) in each of the first four years of life could affect the development of intelligence by 2·5 IQ points per year, whereas similarly extreme environments during 8–17 years may have an average effect of only 0·4 IQ points per year. He then went on to say that since 1968 five independent studies have demonstrated the significance of the mother's role in the child's development.

In January 1974, the Parental Involvement Project was set up in the North of Sandwell by the Child Psychology Service. It was regarded as a very necessary extension of the services already offered to parents, children and schools, becoming integrated with the network of the Remedial Education and Advisory Service by extending its provision to the 0–5 range.

Background to the project

Initially, four teachers with the necessary training, experience and motivation were appointed and started their work, each in a specific area of Sandwell where many families were experiencing problems such as poor housing conditions, high-rise flats, financial difficulties, high incidence of physical illness and handicap.

Many of the families involved in the Project would by definition already have been in contact with the Service in respect of an older child. Perhaps it was too late for that older child to be helped. Nevertheless, it was envisaged that by consistent visiting of the younger pre-school siblings on a weekly basis, there would develop relationships of mutual trust and understanding between the Specialist Teacher from the Parental Involvement Project (hereafter known as the PIP) and parent that would help to change attitudes to education in particular, and to life in general. Then the vicious circle of deprivation with all its manifestations could be broken.

46

Prejudice in some families is so great that, from cradle onwards, the baby is aware of parental attitudes towards the school experiences of her older brothers and sisters. If he is born into a family who put formal education at the very bottom of their list of priorities, the following process evolves: they condone truancy and poor attendance for domestic reasons; they only communicate with the school in an aggressive manner, and much verbal comment, or lack of verbal comment, will convey the antagonism they feel. The pre-school child will absorb all of these signals often subconsciously and feel enormous guilt when at five, or before, he encounters the 'establishment' for the first time. His instinct, even while coping just adequately with the classroom situation, will be to keep any success to a minimum, subdue natural responses of pleasure and eagerness and withdraw into himself, under achieving almost deliberately because of loyalty to his mum and dad. If they don't like the place or the people, he has an uneasy feeling that he shouldn't either. Thus, at the start of his formal education his potential for achievement, class participation, language development and eventual reading skills is limited by his conscience.

A new direction was to offer an opportunity for personal awareness, a chance to re-evaluate (without loss of face) all of those ideas about children, school and teacher which have been inherited from previous generations. The aim of the Project was to provide a chance for many young mums and dads to have a fresh start in feeling themselves capable of giving to their small children the comfort of knowing that school is to be approved of, and that their eventual achievement there will not merely be condoned but praised. With this in mind we began, armed not only with the tools of our trade, in the form of educational equipment, but also with the optimism, tolerance and stamina which were to prove so necessary to the success of the scheme.

Assessment procedure

The *English Picture Vocabulary Test* 1 (Brimer and Dunn, 1962) was used throughout the Project. Children in the first year of infant schooling with a chronological age of less than 5 years 7 months were tested in order to ascertain those who were failing to realize their potential. Those who failed to achieve a score of 90 were regarded as experiencing difficulties based on language deprivation. Families with pre-school children were selected from this group for inclusion in the project.

Strategies

1. Parents were approached with a view to arranging a weekly educational visit to either mother or father and their pre-school child or children. The visit would last approximately 30–60 minutes, depending upon the age and ability of the child.

   Stimulation of language development was the essential part of the visit in order that parents might understand the importance of talking to their children during the normal course of a day.

2. This was reinforced by equipment suited to the age and ability of the children. It was designed to provide play experience with children who

had previously lacked the opportunity for exploration and gross motor development.

Toys were left in the home for use by other members of the family (parent, grandparent, etc.) in order to reinforce skills and to provide an area of common pleasure and learning for both adult and child.

3. The PIP continued to visit these selected families until the last sibling entered formal education.

4. Each new intake to the infant school continued to be tested, thereby providing statistical evidence of any improvement in test scores after intervention when they were compared with the results of the first contact child in the family.

5. Where necessary PIPs liaised with other agencies in order that distress and difficulty could be alleviated as much as possible.

Review of the Project over a seven-year period

The importance of a one-to-one relationship in the home

It is a mammoth task to attempt to summarize the events of the past seven years. In my own particular area, the cumulative effect on the community has been beyond our wildest expectations. Education is such a boundless concept, defying specific definition and in no way limited to those participating in the formal system. It is this 're-education' of so many of these families as a whole that has shown such positive results.

The consistent nature of visiting has enabled the parent, usually the mother, to establish an on-going relationship with the PIP which has often lasted for the entire seven years and still goes on as new babies appear. It is inevitable that friendships and connections of this duration do much to produce new thinking and awareness in both partners, often leading to a new direction for the family. This 'relationship' is of paramount importance and is the key to any real and permanent change in the attitudes and behaviour of the family. In the long term, it is foreseen that where this relationship exists, self-help and personal motivation will continue long after regular visiting has ceased.

The Project demonstrated that families who have previously been totally destroyed by their difficulties can, with the support and friendship of someone who really cares, discover new resources within themselves. They can maintain improvement and finally will cope alone, confident in their newly discovered ability to do so. In the majority of cases, all the children who have been involved in the scheme have produced a higher test result that the contact child on entry to school, many of them at a lower chronological age.

In addition to this, there is an obvious improvement in the performance in school by other members of the same family, even when actual personal contact between themselves and the PIP has been limited, i.e., to lunchtime visits and during school holidays. As the children become less inhibited, so their performance in school improves and they are able to participate, feeling that now a teacher visits their own home their parents will view their school activities with teachers more favourably. These are all direct offshoots of mum's growing awareness of her newly discovered abilities. She is feeling very much a part of the family's general improvement.

At this stage, dad is also likely to become part of the process too. With both parents willingly involved with a 'teacher' in their own kitchen, the confidence of the child is restored, a freedom is gained and he feels released from the constant pressure of juggling school attitude with home attitudes. Of course, we must be realistic. These two attitudes can both be poles apart concerning specific values, but there is the chance now of a basic tolerance on both sides and a genuine wish to understand the other's point of view. This is an advantage when, for example, there is a probability that parental co-operation may be required on the selection of special schooling for a less-able child with special educational needs and where the total co-operation and support of the family is desirable. This situation has been achieved only because of the relationships between the PIP and the family, and made easier by close liaison with the remedial and advisory teacher, educational psychologist and school. That the transfer should be a 'comfortable' one for the child is of paramount importance, but reassurance for the parents does much to reduce stress and fear of the unknown. A relationship of long standing with parents and a pattern of consistent welcome into their home proves invaluable when 'bad news' or difficult decisions need to be discussed and acted upon.

Deprivation in the urban area

Short (1974) states that linguistic deprivation is the commonest and intellectually most damaging of all. He goes on to say that, whatever educational provision we make, mother is the young child's principal teacher. Very often, she is untrained and ill-equipped for such tasks as teaching her child his or her native language.

While stimulation of language development is the essential part of the weekly visit, it has to be encouraged not in isolation, but in the context of the child's environment. My experiences over the past seven years point to the consequences for the child of the many forms of deprivation that can and have reduced many (young) parents to the very depths of despair and eventually real (clinical) depression.

Depression is likely to be the 'disease of the decade'. Valium and Librium have become household words. Pills are swallowed hopefully by so many mums when I first meet them, distributed by overworked GPs who know that they should listen, but the surgery is so full and the stories are all the same.

Redundancy and unemployment are no longer social stigmas since they have become so common. It is quite unusual for any of my families to include a 'working male', although one or two mums still hold on to office cleaning jobs on the twilight shift. Electricity and other fuel bills are enormously high, and so unrealistic that to switch the heating off for a few hours seems totally irrelevant to the sum on the piece of paper which drops through the letter box each quarter (usually over £100).

Many of the mothers have few personal resources to cope with the ordinary difficulties and health problems caused by frequent pregnancies, lack of correct nourishment and constant and debilitating tiredness. The specific problems of the 1980s are an almost impossible additional burden.

I offer a situation which is typical of my area because of the nature of the housing.

A mother is having extreme difficulty in coping with her son in a high-rise flat. She is tense, isolated, worried about discipline, aware that she must have some structure, but torn by the need to over-compensate to the child for all she imagines he lacks. She is defeated before she starts by the pessimism of other mothers and her exposure to the media which continue to brainwash her into thinking that 'high-rise' living is totally impossible, negative, even permanently damaging.

With all the adverse publicity, she longs only for a house, with a back door and a garden — a life, in fact, anywhere else but here. Her one desire is to 'get out'. This desperation turns into a positive resentment of her lifestyle, or envy of others she considers to be more fortunate than herself. Her daily actions and words are destructive rather than constructive, negative rather than positive, and counter-productive to herself and the child. She sees herself as a prisoner, totally isolated, although this might not be the case at all. The husband in his role as provider comes home, if he is at work, to an anxious weeping wife and a child who demands attention and reassurance. He feels guilt and self-recrimination for failing in his role, and escapes as soon as possible to the local pub, where he finds other husbands feeling exactly the same. With both parents unable to communicate adequately or reasonably with each other about their different pressures and expectations, the marital situation deteriorates and the children become increasingly disturbed.

It is all a question of attitude. Of course, the lifts will still break down and mum, caught with the pram and two pre-school toddlers at the bottom of the block, will still have to walk around for hours, cold and wet and furiously waiting for someone to help her to carry both pram and children up eight flights of dark stairways. There will be days when mum is marooned inside her flat and doesn't see a soul. There will still be nights when the lifts which are working will be occupied by bored and rowdy teenagers and left indescribably filthy. These are facts of high-rise living and cannot be easily altered. It is a way of life to which children adjust early. They do not have the comparison of 'better days' experienced by their parents.

It is seven years since I first encountered my high-rise families. Many of them are still there, but no longer do they regard their lives as a treadmill of constant difficulty. Of course, they still put up with the disadvantages, but rarely notice them. The tensions have gone, there is an ability to see the bright side, even the funny side to their daily problems. They seek to help others who are new to the 'horror of the block'. Their doors are open all day, they say 'Welcome, come in. We are part of the system. We have beaten the system. We have a good life which, on the whole, we enjoy. We think positively about our lives, our children and our expectations. We are not using our energy constantly striving to get out, but to accept what we have, make it work for us and for our families.' *There* is the difference that the support of the PIP has made to them, producing very little effective change in their physical situation, but a complete turn-about in their outlook on life.

From home to another place

We have seen in the previous paragraphs that the one-to-one relationship must come first, and that the natural and right place for its development is in the home. The mother who is experiencing difficulties will find it hard to mix in group situations, either because of her depression, or because she feels unable to present an acceptable public image in a group setting. This is particularly true of statutory playgroups or PTA groups attached to schools. As the self-confidence grows through the support and 'companionship' of the PIP the mother will gradually allow herself to be drawn into a group of other people experiencing similar problems and fears.

During the past two years, it has become increasingly obvious that there was a need for a common meeting ground available to all school catchment areas, yet completely independent of the school system, where mothers and children could meet for various reasons. Such a building presented itself in the form of a youth centre, available and empty during the day.

By opening on Wednesday, the building has become a mid-week focus for surrounding families, a centre with which they identify. They attend sessions upon which the remainder of their week can be structured.

Weekly jumble sales and auctions are held, providing good clothing, bed-linen, even furniture at extremely low prices. Those who gather there contribute to the turnover of goods by bringing to the sale all their own outgrown clothing. There is also a thriving mother and toddler club. Many pregnant mothers have only a week away from the club and return with their new baby for the next session and thereafter.

Home visiting continues during the rest of the week, but Wednesday has become increasingly special as people have developed confidence and undertaken jobs of responsibility within the Centre. Counselling, advice, practical help, friendship, company and education are all available and offered willingly by a voluntary staff of mothers who were ready for such a development. Canteen facilities mean that hot meals are provided throughout the day, all organized and funded through the efforts of the community who use the premises.

Personal achievement in the group setting has been rapid. As new people come needing help and support, so those already integrated become the supporters and input team. They now feel able to offer to others the commodity they have received from me during the long weeks and months of undivided home visiting, even though few if asked could put into words exactly what motivates them to respond in such a warm and direct way to the needs of other mothers.

The resulting sense of fellowship and belonging produces an atmosphere which would have been impossible to establish had the initiation of the scheme involved a purpose-built site, staffed by professionals.

We now have a Probation Office extension into Thursday, involving a great many unemployed youths and 'fathers' who use the facilities for clubs, fishing, woodwork, football teams, and as a less official reporting centre if they are on probation. Because the 'staff' who provide the canteen facilities are Wednesday families, the two days now run very much in harness, offering a supportive and happy, lively environment for a large number of families.

During the summer holiday period when all the schools are closed, our sessions continue. They change in character by offering a large range of creative activities, handicrafts and leisure pursuits for everyone, young and old alike. The attendance in the summer holiday is, on average, 80–100 per week (Wednesday session only). As all children must be accompanied by an adult, there is an opportunity for all the family to enjoy their leisure together, finding that the six-week period passes quickly and pleasantly.

Our 'other place' provides the second stage in a self-help process. Born leaders emerge, mums and dads are able to offer special skills confidently without fear of rejection or failure. The new, shy, wary people who are just at the start of the process know that no one in this other place will ridicule them if they try tentatively to offer help. Expectations are low, there is tolerance and genuine understanding in abundance.

Our early mums and dads look back and marvel at the process that brought them to this place, the process that has kept them at this place and the automatic way in which they go out of this place back into homes in a one-to-one situation with someone who needs support, and start at the beginning as I did with them.

Home-visiting by the people from the Centre

This is the third stage. This constructive and planned 'befriending' can involve 'listening visits', comforting visits or even 'Let's roll up our sleeves and tackle the mess together' type visits. The therapy offered instructively by non-professional neighbours, based upon their own experiences, is often exactly right for the situation because, unlike me, they have often themselves experienced so many of the problems endemic in the area. In addition to my once-weekly teaching visit, this may be providing a spread of support which may be necessary for a short time only.

The men involved at the Centre will also offer extensive help within the community. Men with transport will take wives on prison visits which they otherwise could not manage with young children. They move furniture and help in 'house moves' with one-parent families. The outcome of the Day Centre is, in fact, an ever-growing web of willingly offered voluntary help from the community for the community, geared mainly to provide support for those who need it most.

Implications for the future

Mia Kellmer Pringle (1975) said:

> 'Just as the foundations in a house are much more important to put right than if something is wrong with the roof, so the foundations for later behaviour, for relations with other people and for how we get on with ourselves, are laid down during the earlier months and years. These months are vital for later life.'

It was with this in mind that we set out to encourage all the parents involved to see their role in the early years more clearly, and to assist directly in the realization of this goal. Undoubtedly, goodwill exists, hidden under numerous layers of other less desirable attitudes, but is there to be drawn upon. The process which has evolved in the course of the Project does not take their children out of parents' hands but gives them the confidence to mould and develop their child in a full and worthwhile preparation for formal learning and all that follows.

This parental 'osmosis' involves three stages, each one taking a varying amount of time and effort, depending on the degree of apathy or antagonism encountered: thesis, antithesis and finally synthesis. The thesis is that I am a teacher. Because of pre-conceived attitudes towards teachers, the parents are not prepared to like or trust me, but accept me with reservations because it is part of a free educational service. The antithesis occurs when they learn to trust me, then to like me and rely upon me to accompany them through this personal crisis of their own development. In this role, they cannot possibly think of me as a teacher because, on the whole, teachers by the very nature of their criteria and working conditions are unable, however willing, to be all things to all people.

The synthesis finally occurs when the two roles blend and become one. The teacher who can convey her educational skills to them and their children, is also the friend, confidante and trusted extension of the family, able to ease their part in negotiations between themselves and other agencies, including the school. This continues until they have become competent in doing so themselves. That they do eventually acquire the right sequence of acceptable communication skills is indisputable, but the learning and teaching of these patterns of behaviour has only occurred by example, encouragement and varying degrees of support.

The implications for the school are clear. Teachers and heads should be aware that while their role in education of the child is of paramount importance, enough consideration must always be given to the pressures and influences which are at work in the home. Such judgements should also be under constant review in order that changing behaviour and response patterns within the family can be accommodated and provided for in any dialogue concerning the child. As a teacher, working for many years right across the age-range, I had always assumed that I did enough and fully understood why certain children were experiencing emotional difficulties which affected their school performance. I now realize how impossibly impoverished I had been in this area of knowledge and perception. Like my families, I have learned so much which indicates a need for this constant reviewing of tolerance levels and assumptions, even in the most caring school.

I am not suggesting that it is necessary for staff to be aware of all the most intimate and personal details of family life in order better to understand the child. I am asking only that parents should not be labelled so readily as difficult and unco-operative and that teachers should be more willing to share some of their professional mystique to encourage parents who, although capable of great personal resources and initiative, find it difficult to display such abilities in an acceptable way.

References

Hutt, C. and S. J., 'Egg-head starters' in the *Guardian*, 22 January 1974.
Kellmer Pringle, M. L., 'Young children need full-time mothers' in the *Listener*, 10 October 1975.
Short, E., *Birth to Five*, Pitman, 1974.

4

Language

WENDY DEWHIRST

Introduction

The focus in this chapter will be on how the researches into the process of language development and its relationship to language curriculum can inform the primary-school teacher.

Fundamental issues such as the attitude of the teacher to the learning process will be discussed and how examples of spoken-language projects reflect broad patterns of aims, objectives and assessment principles in the language curriculum.

Resources and materials to promote spoken language skills will be briefly referred to, whilst research into the organization and management of the group context will be reviewed, and related to the promotion of writing and reading skills.

In the previous chapter it has been demonstrated that the potential for a child's learning extends far beyond the school gate. Therefore, it is of crucial importance to be aware of the young child within the context of the home as well as school.

Research projects specifically concerned with language have shown how, in a variety of contexts, parents can and do influence their children's ability to learn. (Clark and Jerrams, 1976 and 1979), Tizard (1981), Hewison and Tizard (1980), Beveridge (1981).

Teacher attitude to the learning process

For a teacher to make decisions about the curriculum, she needs to recognize the major influences and variables contingent on a child's learning, of which parental influence is a major factor.

Alongside and equal to this understanding of the learner is the need for the teacher to have a fundamental knowledge of the learning process itself, so that she can recognize at what developmental stage the learner is, and make professionally informed decisions as to his immediate and future needs. These decisions in turn will be influenced by the view or views that the teacher has of the learning process. A behaviourist view of learning, of which *Distar* (Bereiter and Englemann, 1966) and the *Peabody Kit* are examples, suggest a teacher uses carefully programmed learning objectives. Progress is then dependent on the mastery of early skills before more complex ones are undertaken. Language competence within this framework is measured by an observable change of behaviour.

This approach demands a clarity of teaching aims and objectives. Many of the language projects for children with specific learning difficulties have adopted this rationale.

Criticisms of this view of language learning is that it can lead to inflexibility on the part of the learner. Specific objectives can be learned but not always applied to new situations.

A cognitive development approach, on the other hand, evolved from Piagetian theory, is essentially child-centred. The child is viewed as an active agent in her own learning through interaction with the environment and people around her. This approach provides learning opportunities and outcomes, which are not so readily assessed in terms of measures, but more in the recognition of the stages of learning. Tough's Schools Council Communication Projects (1973, 1977) are examples of such an approach.

These two approaches are just examples of the many views of the learning process.

Language projects

The curriculum language studies available to the primary teacher present a multi-faceted view of the learning process. They arrive by various routes at a general consensus as to the main aims for language development.

The three projects chosen are representative only of such projects and curriculum materials available. They do, however, reflect some of the general aims and principles of language development that can be applied across classrooms, cultures, age-groups and individuals.

Schools Council Project in Compensatory Education

Although the focus of the Project (1967–1972) was mainly on the compensatory aspects of language development, the principles of practice that emerged from the curriculum publication (1978) can be applied to any primary or nursery classroom. Downes (1978) wrote in the introduction to the curriculum handbook: 'Little is to be gained by either the teacher or the child in pursuing literacy, numeracy or other areas of education if the development of oral language is not adequate.'

The research project considered that there were seven identifiable main aims in the development of young children's language skills. They stressed that language is more than the accumulation of separate skills, but a separation of the skills helps the teacher in promoting activities and materials to develop them:

1. Listening
2. Naming
3. Categorizing
4. Describing
5. Denoting position
6. Sequencing
7. Reasoning

These broad aims are translated into specific and developmental objectives within the context of the curriculum.

There is a checklist (figure 1) linked directly to the objectives by which

55

the teacher can identify individual strengths and weaknesses. He can, as a result, plan and initiate further appropriate objectives.

The operational framework for this language curriculum goes across subject boundaries and emphasizes the importance, for example, of the child's social and emotional needs, as well as her creative, imaginative, literal and mathematical needs.

Helping Language Development

This approach (Cooper J., Moodley M. and Reynell J., 1978) was developed for parents and teachers to use with children from 2–5 years of age with impaired language development. It reflects a commitment to a developmental approach to the teaching of language skills.

The authors chose not to use the usual phonetic approach to the development of oral language which is mainly concerned with articulation and speech sounds, or a syntactic approach, which is mainly concerned with specific practice and drill in sentence patterns.

The rationale behind their scheme was that language development depends on a child being able to adapt to the language environment. This demanded a totally integrated learning approach where the ten-minute drill session would not be appropriate or meaningful.

The identification of their main aims for a language programme shows many aspects of the previous project. They considered there were seven main aims for language development:

1. Attention control
2. Concept formation
3. Symbolic understanding
4. Verbal comprehension
5. Expressive language
6. Intellectual use of language
7. Performance

Alongside the broad aims, specific developmental objectives are suggested and a criterion-referenced assessment grid is included (figure 2) within which the parent or teacher can monitor and evaluate the child's performance.

Schools Council Communication Skills Project

Tough (1973) suggested a rationale for the development of language skills that also demanded a framework of aims, objectives and assessment. The aims of this project had implications across all types of schools and classrooms, and focused not just on developing the pupils' language uses, but also on the use of language by the teacher. The seven broad language uses that Tough identified were:

1. Self-maintaining
2. Directing
3. Reporting
4. Logical reasoning
5. Predicting
6. Projecting
7. Imagining

Individual scoring sheet for checklist

Name   Date of assessment
Date of birth   First
Date of school entry   Second
                                  Third
                                  Fourth

SKILLS	RATING SCALE			
	Good to very good	Adequate	Below average	Poor or well below average
1 Listening				
2. Naming				
3. Categorising				
4. Describing colour				
shape				
size				
5. Denoting position				
6. Sequencing sequencing				
linking sequences				
using tenses				
7. Reasoning reasoning				
planning				
OPTIONAL				
Clarity of speech				
Comprehension—instructors				
Attentiveness—stories				

Place a cross in the appropriate square and join the crosses to form a profile. Several assessments can be plotted on the same scoring sheet, and a different colour can be used for each profile. The date of assessment and colour used to draw profile should be noted. If more than three of four profiles are drawn another scoring sheet will be needed.

Fig. 1 An objective checklist (from the Schools Council Project in Compensatory Education).

Within this framework of language development, specific aims and objectives mentioned, for example, in the two previous studies, can be included to provide resources for and complement this curriculum approach. Resource materials, although themselves originating from various backgrounds, can be usefully included to complement and extend this curriculum approach. (See Resources for list.)

Tough's identification of language use within the context of the classroom has allowed the teacher to build a bridge between educational theories and practices. She wrote (1973): 'The development and use of language must not only be an objective for early childhood education but as the major means through which other objectives for education may be reached.'

In the project she set a framework on which other studies and curriculum strategies could be focused.

NAME:													
D.O.B:					DATE:								
VERBAL COMPREHENSION													
Situational understanding													
VERBAL LABELS													
RELATING 2 NOUNS													
RELATING 2 CONCEPTS: NOUN, VERB													
RELATING 2 CONCEPTS: NOUN, ADJ.													
RELATING 3 OR MORE CONCEPTS													
EXPRESSIVE LANGUAGE													
Situational words and phrases													
VERBAL LABELS—NAMING OBJECTS													
RELATING 2 NOUNS													
RELATING 2 CONCEPTS: NOUN, VERB													
RELATING 2 CONCEPTS: NOUN, ADJ.													
RELATING 3 OR MORE CONCEPTS													
CODE: GRADES	COMMENTS
---	---
1. OCCASIONALLY	
2. MOST OF THE TIME BUT FLUCTUATING	
3. STABLE	

Fig. 2 A criterion-referenced assessment grid (from Helping Language Development).

Literacy studies

There is substantial evidence to imply a positive relationship bet
guistic competence and ability in literacy as researched, for exai
Francis (1973), Clark (1976) and Windeatt (1976).

Writing

In the writing process, Britton (1971), Doughty, Pearce and Thornton (1972),
Graves (1978) and Clay (1980) suggest that the child needs to be more
involved in his own learning and be given the opportunity to discuss, plan,
and revise his writing.

A model for the growth of competence in writing development identified
by Doughty, Pearce, and Thornton (1972) suggests four stages, known as
'Rehearsal'. The four steps are recognition, familiarization, hesitant command and fluent command. They suggest (1972) the following sequence
towards its promotion of growth:

1. Exploratory discussion to initiate a topic.
2. Work tasks carried out in groups involving collaborative discussion and
   planning.
3. The writing of some reports by the group.
4. Evaluative discussion by the class of the reports.
5. A final stage involving re-writing in the light of both the evaluative discussion and further group discussion of its implications for individual
   reports.

The implications for assessment in this form of organization raise many
issues. The teacher needs to identify what it is she is encouraging the pupils
to do, and how she can monitor and assess the outcomes. As Doughty (1972)
stated: 'Linking the exploratory talk to writing tasks which have clearly
defined goals that relates to the on-going work of the class is not merely
devised in order to produce a piece of writing for marking.'

Reading

Reading research likewise reflects the need to recognize the contribution that
a pupil can make to her own learning. Dixon (1967), D'Arcy (1973), Walker
(1974), Barnes (1978) and Richards (1978) have all suggested that flexible
grouping for discussion can be a successful model of organization.

Walker (1974) structured his groups to develop flexible reading skills
through the promotion of sequencing, predicting and cloze procedure activities, at an oral as well as written level and found it to be a successful strategy.

Richards (1978) wrote of her research findings: 'Group work provides
opportunities to talk freely and it is generally accepted that it improves the
pupils' language, but we need to be aware that the language used in the
group situation will tend to be that which comes most readily to the
participant.'

Barnes (1976) examined learning in small groups and provided evidence
of the effectiveness for learning such contexts provide. Barnes and Todd
(1977) went on to look at the social and cognitive strategies that occurred in

group discussion. Barnes (1976) suggested five factors that need to be taken into consideration when planning discussions.

1. *Feeling of competence*: This relates to the motivation and interest levels of pupils.
2. *Common ground*: This demands that the problem or materials are matched to pupil or group interests and levels of understanding.
3. *Focusing*: This relates to the structure of questions and intentions for the group to be made explicit.
4. *Pace*: The group has to measure and plan the outcomes and organize itself.
5. *Making public*: The end product has to be relevant and organized, clear, and communicated to an audience.

This framework, along with the other studies mentioned, provides the teacher with alternative and flexible management techniques for the promotion of language in the classroom. The principles of such approaches apply to any classroom context and to any pupils, irrespective of their language ability or disability. Clark (1976) suggested that:

'It is important to consider the extent to which it is possible to provide in school the necessary language interaction of children, otherwise the child deprived of the essential characteristics of language prior to and parallel to his school experiences might indeed suffer a deprived language environment at home and a deprived language environment at school.'

Dewhirst (1981) using the Barnes framework in a reading situation, investigated how the context of group discussion, with or without a teacher, influences the manner and level at which the pupils organize and communicate their thoughts. It was concluded that there is a place for pupils to have balanced experiences of both these settings. On the one hand, pupils need to be given structured opportunities with a teacher to develop methods of response and learn how to question texts, and on the other hand being allowed the freedom to take on roles in a group, without the teacher, and to develop and organize group response and understanding. It was found that the quality of the teacher's language, or perhaps her concept of her role in the dialogue, influenced her group's performance.

As Francis (1977) wrote: 'Teaching styles may be more important than methods of instruction.' Researches suggest that a teacher must be open to new forms of management and be willing to take varied roles in the development of her pupils' language and learning skills. She must also recognize the important principle of time: time for reflection, time for rehearsal, time for discussion.

Summary

Language researches and language curriculum projects will, of course, present different perspectives on the communication process. However, basic to all of them is the commitment to the concept that the teacher is the crucial factor in the development of the full potential in the child's communication experience and abilities. The teacher, therefore, must take professionally balanced and informed judgments about how he can best plan and implement a language curriculum, using a variety of resource materials and contexts appropriate and relevant to the needs of his pupils. A teacher can then, as a result of placing his pupils in a variety of language learning contexts, begin to build up a picture of their performance with regard to their attitude, response and capabilities.

This, then, supplies a positive basis on which the teacher can plan realistic experiences that can extend the children's language.

References

Barnes, D. *Communication to Curriculum*, Penguin, 1976.

Barnes, D. and Todd, F., *Communication and Learning in Small Groups*, Routledge and Kegan Paul, 1977.

Bereiter, C. and Englemann, S., *Teaching Disadvantaged Children in Pre-School*, Prentice Hall, 1966.

Beveridge, M. and Jerrams, A., 'Parental involvement in language development: an evaluation of a parental assistance plan' in the *British Journal of Educational Psychology*, Nov. 1981.

Britton, J., (1971) 'What's the use?' in Wilkinson, A., (ed.) 'The context of language' in the *Educational Review* 23, No. 3.

Clark, M. M., *Young Fluent Readers*, Hodder and Stoughton, 1976.

Clark, M. M., *Pre-School Education*, SSRC, 1979.

Clay, M., (1980) in 'Reading and writing for the Child with difficulties', in Clark, M. M. and Glynn, T. (eds), *Educational Review* Occasional Publications 8.

Cooper, J., Moodley J., Reynell J., *Helping Language Development*, Edward Arnold, 1978.

D'Arcy, P., *Reading for Meaning*, Vol.2, Heinemann, 1973.

Dewhirst, K. W. (1981), 'Comprehension in reading of eight- to nine-year-olds as revealed by language use and levels of thinking in different learning situations' (unpublished MEd dissertation, University of Birmingham).

Downes, G., (ed.) *Language Development and the Disadvantaged Child*, Holmes McDougall, 1978.

Dixon G., *Growth through English*, OUP, 1967.

Doughty T., Pearce J., Thornton G., *Exploring Language Growth*, Edward Arnold, 1972.

Francis, H., *Language in Teaching and Learning*, London University Press, 1977.

Graves D., in *Bullock and Beyond: Research on the Writing Process in Teaching for Literacy*, Davis, F., and Parker, R., (ed.), Ward Lock, 1978.

Hewison. J. and Tizard, J., (1980) 'Parental involvement and reading attainment' in the *British Journal of Educational Psychology*, Vol. 50, No. 3.

Richards, J., *Classroom Language: What Sort?*, London University Press, 1978.

Tizard, B., *Involving Parents and Teachers in Nursery Schools*, Graw McIntyre, 1981.

Tough, J., *Focus on Meaning*, Ward Lock, 1973.

Tough, J., *Development of Meaning*, Allen and Unwin, 1977.

Walker, C., *Reading Development and Extension*, Ward Lock, 1974.

Windeatt, S. (1976), 'An investigation of the relationship between oral and language skills and reading ability in junior-school children' in the *Register of Reading Resources*, Centre for the Teaching of Reading, University of Reading.

Resources

ILEA, *Language for Learning*, Heinemann.
Tell-Tales, Evans.
Storyboards, ESA.
Learning Development Aids publications

Further reading

Bindley, W. and Griffiths, R., *Listening and Speaking*, NARE, 1976.

Clay, M. M., *Reading: The Patterning of Complex Behaviour*, Heinemann, 1971.

Hoey, A. M. (1977), *Listening and Learning*, Dominie (available from Holmes McDougall).

Hunter-Grundin, E., *Language: A Systematic Start*, Harper & Row, 1979.

Mackay, D. *et al.*, *Breakthrough to Literacy*, Teacher's Manual, Longman, 1978.

McNicholas, J. and McEntee, J., *Games to Develop Reading Skills*, NARE, 1973.

Reid, J. and Low, J., *The Written Word*, Teacher's Manual for *Link-Up*, Holmes McDougall, 1973.

Sandwell Child Psychology Service (1979), *An Approach to the Acquisition of Basic Skills*, Child Guidance Centre, 12 Grange Road, West Bromwich, B70 8PD.

Somerset Education Authority, *Ways and Means 2*, Globe Education, 1981.

Southgate, V., Arnold, H. and Johnson, S., *Extending Beginning Reading*, Heinemann/Schools Council, 1981.

Walker, C., *Teaching Pre-reading Skills*, Ward Lock Educational, 1975.

5
Mathematics for primary-school children with learning difficulties

BARRY PINFIELD

The mathematics curriculum

In all schools, an attempt should be made to provide a 'balanced' curriculum. The definition of what constitutes a 'balance' is wide open to discussion, and has been under observation for many years. A balanced curriculum would also have a beneficial effect on the subject of mathematics. Within the subject, balance relates to its major components — number, measures, spatial and graphical. Surveys in the past decade have shown clearly that, in general terms, this balance is over-weighted for all children towards number, and even more over-weighted when we consider the mathematical diet of children with learning difficulties.

We, as a profession, alongside the general public, can readily see a utilitarian purpose for doing sums. However, reasons for including the other aspect of mathematics are not as readily apparent to us. Thus number work is not neglected, but again the *Primary School Survey* (1975) and the recent Assessment of Performance Unit report (1980) gave evidence of areas of concern. Perhaps we might spend less time on number, which could be more profitable for our pupils too. A later section in this chapter will hopefully provide some useful ideas which may assist in achieving this objective.

Measures

The topic of measures is often neglected. Measurement can often mean just length, but we must remember that area, volume, time, capacity, weight and money also fall into this category. Money and time often have a utilitarian appeal. On the subject of time, the aspect of passage of time is often bypassed. These topics are of course very practical indeed, and perhaps the practical and often very messy nature of the work provides organizational problems. If you have 20 children in your class, heaven help you if all 20 are involved in water-play and the associated 'development of capacity' activities. Some classrooms do not have water readily available. If the topic is weight, not many schools (if any) will have 20 pairs of scales. When effective curriculum planning within a school is lacking, then these topics which represent organizational problems may well be avoided by a succession of teachers. Suddenly a child reaches the secondary stage of education with no experience of one or two of these curriculum areas.

The topics under the umbrella of measures also gives considerable scope for language work. Consider the following expressions: heavier than, lighter than, longer, shorter, taller, tall, short, higher, less than, more than, the same as, day, month, year, minute, hour, metre, litre — and so on.

Each individual in today's society should also be able to make estimates and, if a child has a wide experience of measurement activities, he or she will eventually be able to estimate with some degree of accuracy. All too often people attempt to purchase goods, and find that their estimate of their cost is inaccurate, which leads to embarrassment and eventually to a lack of confidence. Lengths in metres, and capacities in litres are now fairly commonplace, and often estimations are needed instead of precise mathematical decisions — e.g., how much electric flex is needed to make an extension, so that the hi-fi can run from a plug at the other end of the room? Of course, accuracy must be interpreted very broadly for 'our' children, but it is nonetheless a worthwhile venture.

Spatial work

Spatial work is not usually seen as having direct utilitarian application. However, we all live in space, and need to be aware of our position in relation to other objects. Fitting shapes into a larger shape is part of all our lives, and experience in these related activities in school can often prove useful. I am often reminded of a boy at my first school, who painstakingly made a rabbit hutch, but then discovered that he needed to dismantle it in order to take it from the workshop and then home. Above all, some children may find success in the practical approach needed for spatial work, and may well become motivated. This may be very desirable when balanced with number work and its constant reminder of failure. Space and space-fitting, picture-making, pattern-making are all worthwhile activities.

Graphical work

Graphical work is another must. It is well known that children with learning difficulties have problems with extracting information from newspapers or from public notice-boards. Skills in collecting information, displaying it, and then reading from that information are important life-skills. The background to acquiring these life skills should be formed in the primary school. Once again, this work can be directly related to the child's own environment, hence motivation should again be provided by the material used.

Precise details of a balanced mathematics curriculum are not within the scope of this chapter — indeed, it warrants a book of its own. However, I hope to suggest that what is needed is a balanced diet, including areas of mathematics which are perhaps less fashionable, but nonetheless equally valuable.

Thought needs to be given to planning, let us say, half a term's work, trying to show development and variety within that short period. It is no good saying 'We'll go on to work on shapes when they've mastered subtraction,' because some will never move on to shape-work under that system. Short-term, and reasonably easy targets must be part of effective planning and thus of the effective curriculum.

Possible reasons for failure

There are most certainly various factors which contribute to children's failure with mathematics. When looking diagnostically at each child, there will be differing elements, which have contributed in varying degrees, to the failure which you are trying to overcome. Below are listed twelve reasons to consider. This list is not exhaustive, and you may add to them. Also, several reasons are closely interlinked, and you may feel that the twelve could be further condensed. The order of priority is not suggested in this random list.

1. Large numbers used

'There is an enormous wealth of number work using numbers 0 to 100. It can give full reign to all number concepts and number skills, which would be considered suitable for slow-learning primary age children.' (Biggs, 1981.)

HM Inspectorate have suggested that the infant stage for 'normal' children should not proceed beyond numbers up to 20, indeed even up to 10 in some cases (HMSO, 1979). However, the curriculum of some schools suggests that numbers up to 1000 be taught at this very stage! I feel strongly that children should have some idea of the size of numbers before operating with them. Often, however, children are busy operating with numbers that they cannot explain — e.g., 253 — not recognizing the component parts of the number itself. Frequently, in order to prove to ourselves that children *can* explain 253, *we will phrase questions in such a manner as to invite the answer we require*. Think carefully about that statement — the author has also been guilty on many many occasions of falling into this trap.

For example, if questions such as 'What is the 2 worth?' bring no response, we ask 'How many hundreds are there?' instead. No response again, so the frustration builds up, the teacher's finger points to the 2 and the last question is repeated. The answer comes. '2, sir,' or '2, miss,' and we can be complacent and think that the child has understood the story of 253. Usually nothing could be further from the truth.

2. Lack of understanding

The previous example can also be used to illustrate this point. The presentation of place-value work and the complete idea of what a number is about can often be neglected by the teacher rushing to do sums, 'adds, take-aways, times and shares'. Some colleagues may say, indeed do say, that it is acceptable to teach the technique, and understanding will follow at a later date. I believe wholeheartedly that this is not so, and that it is also unnecessary. It is possible to teach with understanding, but it requires concrete materials, and a patient build-up of work. A later section on using structured apparatus is designed to support this argument.

3. Lack of concrete materials

The interlinking of reasons continues. Piaget has influenced much of the work related to the psychology of learning since the late 1950s. His stages of (i) pre-operational, (ii) concrete, and (iii) abstract are valuable reminders to teachers. Almost all of the children to whom this book refers will not reach the final stage, but teachers often ask children to work from abstract ideas.

65

There are problems with older children when a teacher attempts to re-introduce concrete materials, so a sensitive approach is needed. Very often, children can handle money with reasonable confidence, but cannot then translate that skill into an abstract form. The use of *Base 10* Dienes, and Tillich's material is vital to building understanding and hence a firmer foundation for later work. The same idea is very necessary at the secondary-school stage too, and for a far wider range of abilities than has normally been associated with 'practical' work.

4. Gaps in the linear build-up of knowledge

Mathematics is a subject which, when broken down into fine detail, comprises a range of concepts and skills which are highly ordered. If you consider, say, subtraction, there are over thirty stages in its development from 'I have 4 sweets, take 2 away, how many left?' to '3000 − 1436'. More-able children can take two, three or four of these stages during a short time, but the slow-learning child will need to spend longer on each stage. As a result of this sequence of development, gaps which occur are likely to cause problems.

Checklists produced by working parties in my LEA have itemized approximately 750 stages in primary mathematics, and that list was not compiled for children with moderate learning difficulties. Hence, the task is enormous.

5. Crutches not allowed or abandoned

In our society there is considerable pressure on teachers to achieve targets by the end of a stage of education. This is probably more true for 'normal' children, but probably is still evident at a lower level for slow-learning children. This pressure often tempts us to bring in short cuts and techniques without achieving understanding, in order to obtain the 'correct answer'. For example, a school may be adopting a system of using concrete materials to teach simple addition of two digit numbers, and using an extended form of recording:

$$
\begin{aligned}
25 &= 20 \text{ and } 5 \\
16 &= 10 \text{ and } 6 \\
\hline
&\ \ 30 \text{ and } 11 \\
&\ \ 30 \text{ and } 10 \text{ and } 1 = 41
\end{aligned}
$$

This may appear long-winded and laborious, and the move towards 25 + 16 becomes the more accepted one, 25 + 16, 1 down, carry 1, 2 add 1 add 1 equals 41. The move from the concrete stage to the abstract may be far too quick — indeed some children may never reach the abstract stage. The result may be a lack of success and a total loss of confidence.

6. Techniques forgotten or confused

This reason for failure is closely linked with the previous one. Here, technique has become the over-riding factor, and confusion can ensue. For example 32 − 15 done without concrete materials may create all sorts of problems: '2 take 5; I can't, so 5 take 2 equals 3; and 3 take 1 equals 2 —

answer 23 Or 5 take 2; I can't, borrow 10, 10 take 5 is 5; add 2 is 7; 3 take 1 is 2 — *answer 27.*

7. Wide range of notation used

Some commercial schemes use a wide range of notation within a short space, which can cause much confusion for the slow learner. Care is very necessary when introducing symbols and other notation. There must be a limit to the range in use. It is important to use words, both spoken and written, for long periods before symbols take over. It is interesting to note that children have been developing language for about three to four years, before we attempt to transfer to reading, which is in fact a symbol system. In mathematics the gap between experiences symbolism is often far shorter. I would recommend that you do not rush young children into using symbols.

8. Language

This section is related to all the previous sections. Language policy related to mathematics should be discussed by each school, and control should be exercised on the introduction and use of the policy. Just one word can cause a child to fail, and often we can unconsciously add an extra word, or re-arrange words so as to create problems.

Let us consider a small aspect of subtraction, e.g., '5 take 3'; '5 take away 3'; 'from 5 take 3'; '3 from 5'; 'take 3 from 5'. There is even more language relating to subtraction, but within these five examples confusion can, and often does, reign. A list of necessary words needs to be considered for each new topic which is being taught. Suitable language will often come better from a group discussion with colleagues, rather than from the attempt of a single teacher.

9. Reading levels inappropriate

Much of the mathematics taught at primary-school level will need to be given orally but, needless to say, pressures dictate that workcards, books and worksheets be used. Recent research was conducted at Charlotte Mason College of Higher Education (*Maths in School*, 1978) which analysed the reading levels of the most popular primary mathematics textbooks. These reading levels were found to be from one to four years above the chronological age for which the mathematics was intended. The discrepancy becomes even greater when we consider children with learning problems.

However, having raised the problem, it is not easily solved, and probably not solvable at all. My own experience, with this knowledge in mind, has been to produce pupil material with a minimum of language — in fact, so little that the child has insufficient information to enable him or her to progress. We can certainly improve on the current situation, but whether we can find an acceptable solution for all slow-learning children is another matter.

10. Need for motivating material

Material for children which is motivating can prove difficult to find. Often children are heard to say they are bored when doing practice work in any subject. Practice is important, but if we can provide that practice in an enlightened form, then a properly motivated child will learn more effectively. The value of games is included in a later section, and must rate as a motivator of the highest order.

11. Lack of application of skills

The *Primary School Survey* and reports by the Assessment of Performance Unit (1978 and 1979) have shown this topic to be a cause for concern. We appear to have concentrated on skill teaching, developing the algorithms for the four rules — forgetting to relate them to the *real* problem or issue which came first. The algorithm was devised in order to organize efficient addition, subtraction, division and multiplication. This now overshadows the original problem. One solution is to get children to either write or tell stories about sums that they are doing.

Teachers must remember that it is pointless developing skills which the child cannot then apply. How often has a child asked 'is it an add, a take, a times or a share, miss?' Our answer has been to dress up the sum in words, and this is not enough. The story-telling or writing must begin at a young age, and is obviously inextricably interwoven with the language development of each child.

12. Lack of suitable diagnostic tests

Diagnosis and suitable remediation must be key factors in the satisfactory development of slow-learning children. However, it is difficult to find tests in mathematics which diagnose in detail. Obviously, the wide range of the checklists mentioned earlier indicates that several tests would be necessary. Many of the tests would need to be given orally, and would need practical materials. Probably four or five tests would be needed in each basic topic, thus the four rules may need twenty tests to cover the complete range of skills which require testing.

Criterion-referenced tests are few and far between, so self-help may be the answer. Assessment, record-keeping and accountability are key words in today's educational scene, but we still have a long way to go in solving these issues. There are no easy answers.

Using structured apparatus

All sorts of materials, both commercial and environmental, should be used within the primary school, but as the child approaches the need to consider numbers beyond 20, then structured apparatus becomes more necessary. The following are considered suitable: *Unifix* (Philip & Tacey), *Multilinks*, *Stern* (ESA), Tillich's (E. J. Arnold), Dienes (ESA), Cuisenaire, *Colour Factor*, *Centicubes* (Osmiroid), *Base 10* (Nottingham Handicrafts).

The first three types of materials are slightly larger than the others and may therefore appeal more to pupils. *Multilink* is based on a 2cm cube, *Unifix* and *Stern* on a cube that is slightly less than 2cm. The other materials, with the exception of Dienes, are based on a 1cm cube. Dienes is slightly less than 1cm. Tillichs, Dienes and *Base 10* are what one might consider as being most suitable for our purpose. The others all need slight modifications, e.g.

(i) from *Colour Factor*, *Stern* and Cuisenaire only the 'ten' rods and 'one' rods would be needed.

(ii) *Unifix*, *Multilinks* and *Centicubes* would need 10s taped together.

Beware of the 1cm cubes, as these are small enough to be swallowed, pushed up noses and down ears.

Counting and place value

In dealing with numbers greater than 20, understanding of exchange and place value is absolutely vital.

As 'tens' and 'hundreds' are large numbers for children to work with, some preliminary experience with smaller groupings will be helpful.

These activities may be seen by the teacher as number base work, but that phrase should not be used with the children. Please note also that environmental situations are being used. This is preferable to the multi-base material provided by Tillich, Dienes and other suppliers.

Exchange activities involving addition

1. Grouping, using numbers less than 10

(a) To work in numbers up to six, a game using eggs, egg-cartons and boxes (holding six cartons) can be played. Use a die marked 1,2,3,4,5,4. The children will need to use the actual materials.

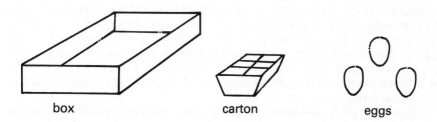

box   carton   eggs

The children take turns to throw the die and collect eggs according to the number thrown. As soon as they have six eggs, they take a carton. When six cartons have been filled, a box is taken *into which the cartons are placed*. The winner is the first to fill a box.

Recording can be done, but limited to either:

3 cartons and 4 eggs, or

cartons	eggs
3	4

Note: The largest denomination should be on the left — e.g., *cartons* are on the left of *eggs*.

(b) Similar activities and games can be thought out for other numbers. For instance, buttons (counters), cards and sheets of paper can be used for grouping in fours. Children, carriages and trains can be used for grouping in fives, and so on.

2. *Grouping in tens*

When children are familiar with *grouping* using numbers less than 10, then activities involving tens and ones can be introduced using the structured apparatus.

(a) Take a handful of *ones* and group into *tens*, and then exchange them. Record this as 3 tens and 4 ones, or as shown below:

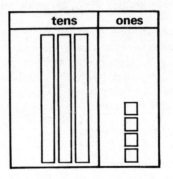

(b) *Race to 30*

The following apparatus is needed for two players: 6 tens, 25 ones, a die marked 1–6. Each player throws the die in turn and collects his or her score. The players will eventually run out of ones, and hopefully without prompting may exchange 10 ones for 1 ten (hence the limit of 25 ones). We should, hopefully, be guiding the child to discover that he or she can exchange, without presenting the situation in a didactic form. The winner would be the first player to reach or pass 30. Players do not need to throw sixes to start, or finish exactly on 30. These are unnecessary frustrations.

The 'second grouping' of 100 (1 flat) is difficult to achieve immediately, as 100 will be too large a number for many children to handle — hence 30 as the initial target.

Recording of this activity should follow, using, in turn, a number strip and number line. Both 'strip' and 'line' should be the same size (e.g., with spaces of 1cm) as the structured materials. A 100 square, blank 100 square and hexagonal snake should follow (figure 3).

Note: There is a *structured* progression in this activity which needs careful thought and plenty of practice. The hexagonal snake is really the abstract stage. The pictorial presentations help to bridge the gap between the concrete and the abstract.

Variations should include the following: die marked 2 to 7, 3 to 8, 4 to 9, cards marked from 1 to 9. These will speed up the exchange process, which is fundamental to the activity. Targets can be extended beyond 30 up to 100, where the 'second exchange' can take place. Another alternative is to start at 50 and collect materials — the winner being the first to reach 100.

Other activities should include:

(c) Use counting materials (such as acorns, pebbles, bottle tops) and dice.

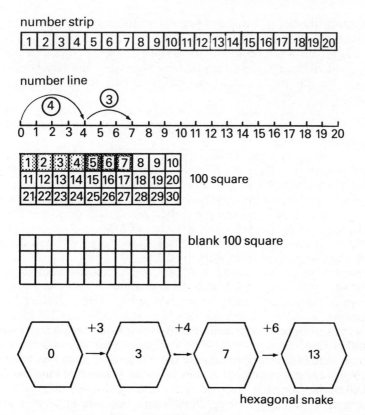

number strip

| 1 | 2 | 3 | 4 | 5 | 6 | 7 | 8 | 9 | 10 | 11 | 12 | 13 | 14 | 15 | 16 | 17 | 18 | 19 | 20 |

number line

100 square

1	2	3	4	5	6	7	8	9	10
11	12	13	14	15	16	17	18	19	20
21	22	23	24	25	26	27	28	29	30

blank 100 square

hexagonal snake

Fig. 3 Five ways of recording number activities.

Let children take turns to throw a die and collect the appropriate number of objects. After a specified number of throws (5 each or 10 each), each child will group his or her counters in tens and say how many he or she has.

(d) Repeat the previous activity using selected apparatus, in the following order, to prepare the children for operating on two-digit numbers:
Cubes (*Unifix, Multilink* and others) that can be laid along a number track for comparing.
Cubes — fastened or taped in tens before counting along a track or number line.
Cubes — loose, to be exchanged by children for rods of ten before counting.

(e) For recording the numbers scored, cards can be prepared for exchanging with rods and cubes. For rods, write numbers from 10 to 90 (10, 20, 30, etc.). On each card, draw a line down between the units and the tens. For cubes, number the cards from 1 to 9. The 'tens' cards must be twice

71

as wide as the 'units' cards and in a different colour. By placing the 'unit' card on top of the 'tens' card, the total number is formed.

These cards can be widely used at a later stage. It is important that the children understand which number represents the largest amount of cubes. For instance, a child looking at 19 may see it as more than 21 because 9 is a 'big' number.

Note: It may help some children if the numbers are represented in pictorial form on the back of the cards using pictures of the Tillich's material.

(f) Give a child two different dice (distinguished by colour or size). One, when thrown, will represent 'tens', and the other 'ones'. The child collects the appropriate material and states the number.

This could be competitive when two or more players take part, the winner being the player with the highest number. A change of rule could make the winner the one with the lowest number.

Other variations are to use a different die, e.g., numbered 4 to 9, 3 to 8, etc., or playing cards numbered 1–9.

(g) A game in which two numbers are compared is another valuable activity. Write each number, from 1 to 99, on a separate card, or use commercially available tablets, and put them in a box or bag. Two children take a card each and compare their numbers. This can be done by forming the numbers with 'tens' rods and 'ones' along a track, or finding them on a number line.

This could be used as a game, the children keeping the score to see who gets the larger number in, say, 10 turns. (Later, the smallest number could be the winner.)

(h) To teach that it is the 'tens' digit that is the more important in determining the size of the two-digit numbers, the following activity is suggested.

0–9	10–19	20–29	30–39	40–49
50–59	60–69	70–79	80–89	90–99

Place ten labelled containers in order, as above. Give the children cards numbered 0–99 to sort into the correct containers.

(i) For this activity, put two sets of numerals, 0–9, in different colours, into separate bags. The child selects a *blue* card ('tens') and a *yellow* card ('ones') and makes a number, using concrete materials if necessary.

This activity can be extended by providing two sets of numerals, 0–9, all one colour. Now the child takes two cards and writes down the pair of numbers formed from the two digits — e.g., 1 and 4 would make 14 or 41.

The child is asked which is the larger number, and records them in a table. Many children will need concrete apparatus to decide which is the larger.

Note: With two sets of cards, numbers such as 22, 66, etc., will occur.

41	is larger than	14
53		35
63		36

If one of the cards selected is 0, then the numbers will be, for example, 50 and 05. Children should be encouraged to read the second number as 'no tens and five'. They should understand that this number is the same as 5, and using concrete apparatus will help the understanding.

Understanding the use of zero as a place-position-holder is important, especially at a later stage.

(j) A game requiring two-digit numbers to be sorted with a decade is also valuable. The child is given a set of ten cards with numbers from 10 to 19, and is asked to put them in order.

This may be turned into a game, as follows. Each child requires his or her own set of cards, which are placed face down, at random, in front of him or her. The players take turns to select a card and turn it over. If it is 10, the card is placed face up away from the other cards. If not, it is replaced face downwards. The next card required is 11, followed by 12, etc., until the sequence is complete.

Ordering numbers from 20 to 29, 30 to 39, etc., can be done in the same way, using appropriate cards. A different colour is recommended for each set.

If desired, the game may be played with each child using a different set of numbers.

The place-value activity in (e) can now be extended, with the child having two sets of cards (rather than a die) marked 0 to 9, selecting two cards, and deciding on their position in relation to the given target. Suggested targets are as follows:

> Make the largest number.
> Make the smallest number.
> Make a number nearest to 50.
> Make a number nearest to 25, to 75, etc.
> Make an even number.
> Make an odd number.
> Make a number greater than 40.
> Make a number less than 60.

There will not necessarily be a winner or a loser in the last four 'targets'. Observation by the teacher will be very worthwhile. Decisions and thinking are being used in this game, and watching can tell the teacher a great deal about the understanding or otherwise that the child has achieved.

3. Exchange activities involving subtraction

Subtraction is a difficult concept and skill for nearly all children to handle. Its introduction therefore is important. The use of structured apparatus has considerably strengthened the case for *decomposition* as a suitable method of subtraction, and likewise weakened the method known as *equal addition*. Many adults do use the latter method, but very rarely do they understand what is happening. Technique is displayed by them, but understanding of the process is certainly missing.

The following activities, together with their various variations, are fundamental to basic understanding.

Take 29 in the form of 2 tens and 9 ones. Throw a die marked 1 to 6 and 'take away' the score on the die. After two or three throws with a score of 22, a problem will occur. A child throws, say, 4, so 4 needs to be taken away, but only 2 ones are available. Hopefully, with plenty of exchange practice in the addition activities, the child may see, or may be led to see, that 1 ten can be exchanged for 10 ones, hence this is the material now available:

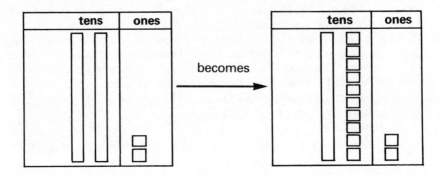

Now 4 can be 'taken away'. The winner is the first child to remove all his or her materials. Remember to tape together those *Unifix*, *Multilink* and *Centicubes* — if not, just 2 will be taken from the 10 and *exchange will not take place*.

There should be no recording in the first instance. Recording could then follow a progression similar to the exchange and addition activities, using the number strip, line, 100 square, blank 100 square and hexagonal snake, as shown in figure 3.

Note: In both addition and subtraction activities, the skill of counting on, and counting back, is being considerably enhanced.

Twenty-nine was purposely taken as the first experience, so that the problem of exchange did not arise instantly. By starting at 31, exchange will almost certainly be needed immediately. Once again, no six is needed to start, and the players do not need to get rid of the last 2 or 3 ones precisely — 2 left and a 5 thrown is acceptable. Starting points can increase in size, and varying dice, numbered 2 to 7, 3 to 8, 4 to 9, or playing cards with tens, and pictures removed, can provide plenty of variety.

In order to consider 100 and its breakdown, a game taking away from 100 until you have 50 or less left can be used. Again observation by the teacher is vital.

These addition and subtraction activities should be used with money, where we are constantly having to exchange large amounts in order to give correct money for goods, fares, etc., instead of receiving change. However, when using money there is no *physical* equivalence (e.g., of size) when exchanging. One 10p coin is equal in *value* to ten 1p coins!

Some mathematics textbooks suggest the use of an abacus, using counters identical in size, but of different colours. However, when 10 blues (ones) are exchanged for something identical in size — 1 red (ten), then the child needs to have abstracted the whole idea of place value and exchange. My advice at this point is to beware of the abacus when dealing with children who have learning difficulties.

Skill teaching is a vital part of our work and, in order to make progress, a developmental scheme is needed. Decomposition is based on the idea of re-grouping. Thus 22 was shown as 20 add 2, but after exchange it became 10 add 12. This is fundamental to later work. Hence practice of this type is very worthwhile. Here are some examples:

$$22 = 20 \text{ add } 2 = 10 \text{ add } 12$$
$$31 = 30 \text{ add } 1 = 20 \text{ add } 11$$
$$45 = 40 \text{ add } 5 = 30 \text{ add } 15$$

4. Addition and subtraction using structured apparatus

Much work with answers of less than 20 must be assumed before we embark on these activities. It is also felt that both addition and subtraction work using concrete materials with answers below 20 will not have involved the idea of place value, although the numbers used will fall between 10 and 19. The use of boards marked as shown on page 74 is worthwhile.

When adding, both numbers are placed on the board and then combined to provide the answer.

In subtraction, it is suggested that the larger number is placed on the board and the number to be removed is taken from the first row and placed in the bottom row. Therefore the answer is the number remaining in the top row. The 'take away' aspect of subtraction is therefore being used.

The following is suggested as a suitable progression for addition. No answers should exceed 50 at first, then 100.

(a) Double digit + single digit with no exchange.
(b) Double digit + double digit with no exchange.
(c) Double digit + single digit with exchange (no units left over).
(d) Double digit + single digit with exchange.
(e) Double digit + double digit with exchange in *ones*.

Here is an example for (e):

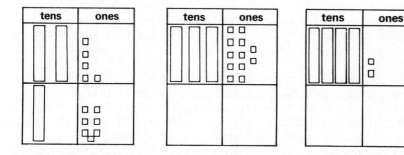

Recording might follow as shown:

$$25 = 20 \text{ add } 5$$
$$+$$
$$17 = 10 \text{ add } 7$$
$$\overline{}$$
$$30 \text{ add } 12 = 30 \text{ add } 10 \text{ add } 2 = \mathbf{42}$$

Later, recording can be done in columns:

25	25	25
+	+	+
17	17	17
	2	42
	1	1

This might be considered an *intermediate* stage:

$$25$$
$$+$$
$$17$$
$$\overline{}$$
$$12$$
$$+$$
$$30$$

A progression for subtraction would follow a similar development.

(a) Two digits subtract one digit with no exchange.
(b) Two digits subtract two digits with no exchange.
(c) Two digits subtract one digit with exchange.
(d) Two digits subtract one digit with whole tens and exchange.
(e) Two digits subtract two digits with exchange ones.
(f) Two digits subtract two digits with whole tens only in first numbers exchange needed.

Once again early numbers should not exceed 50, and later 99 (100 creates other problems.) Here is an example for 62 − 35. (Use a 'tens' and 'ones' board.)

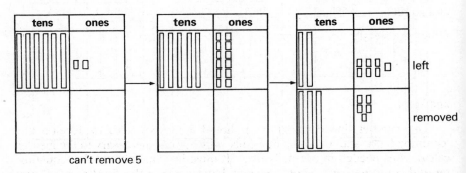

Therefore, 27 is the answer.

Recording could follow this progression:

$$62 = (60 \text{ add } 2) = (50 \text{ add } 12)$$
$$\underline{35 = (30 \text{ add } 5) = (30 \text{ add } \underline{5})}$$
$$20 \text{ add } 7 = 27$$

5. Recording

Other methods of recording are possible, although they need to be carefully controlled. The matrix method is suggested in order to familiarize children with the use of a grid from which information is taken, as this is widely used in our society — reading timetables, charts for cash benefits, etc.

Both addition and subtraction activities necessitate the use of the number line, which is a very important resource for all children, since it bridges the gap between the structured apparatus and the eventual abstract presentation of 'sums'.

Here is an example of a matrix grid:

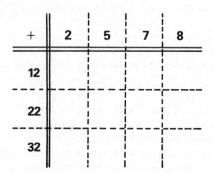

This matrix grid is also showing a significant pattern:

$$12 + 2$$
$$22 + 2$$
$$32 + 2$$

and so on.

Other grids could show the pattern which emerges from:

$$18 - 3$$
$$28 - 3$$
$$38 - 3$$

and so on.

The number line (see figure 3) should again be used, to develop the 'counting back' and 'counting on' skills, which are so necessary to the mental calculations needed in our daily lives. It must be remembered that counting on and counting back across the tens barrier is not the first stage of such activities.

This chapter does not permit a detailed approach to multiplication and division, using the same material. However, if these ideas bear fruit, it should be easy to develop extensions to cover the remaining two operations.

The value of games in the classroom

Many of the suggested activities listed in the previous section are in the form of games. More game activities will be suggested in this section too, but first there needs to be some justification for such an approach.

One of the reasons for failure was concerned with 'boring subject matter', which led to a need to motivate the child. One of the major ways of achieving this objective, and making mathematics into an enjoyable pastime, is through the use of games.

The word 'games' can be emotive. We need to consider the games we use, and ensure that their educational value is worthwhile. The games suggested so far are very much related to concept formation, skill practice, decision-making and thinking. Games will not generally be a feature of many homes from which our children come, and yet many teachers would probably lay claim to their own arithmetic development through games during their childhood — Ludo, Snakes and Ladders, dominoes, card games, Monopoly, and so on.

Games can also provide purposeful practice, and chance can remove the more unpleasant aspects of competition. Some games can be revealing to the teacher, when careful observation has taken place. The social training which permeates all our work will also benefit: learning to follow rules, accept decisions and lose graciously. It is important that instructions are given orally — this is so much quicker and clearer than writing them down.

It is advisable that not too many children play in each game. Too many players cause too much interaction and also too much inactivity. It is also not advisable to let all the class play at once. A game can be used as a reward too but, like the time-filling aspect, it must be used in its own right. If not, the credibility of games will suffer. Obviously we shouldn't over-use games — balance is vital, as with all things within the curriculum.

Dominoes

The vast majority of people have seen and used sets of dominoes, but almost certainly they will be one type — a double-six set, with each number shown by its own identical arrangement of dots. Dominoes with differing arrangements, but still in double-six sets, are easy to make using thick card 10cm by 5cm and different-coloured sticky spots readily available from major stores. It is suggested that sets with three arrangements be made: number bond, random and normal:

In the number bond and random sets, 6 is represented in different ways which are not repeated. The same is true of 5, 4, 3, and so on.

The games suggested should be played first with the normal set, then the number bond, then the random set. The degree of difficulty within these three sets is quite extensive.

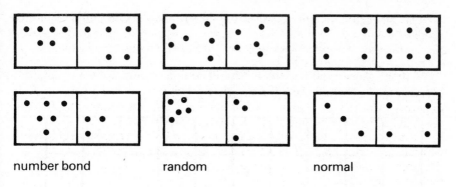

number bond   random   normal

Instructions

Two players take seven dominoes each and play the usual game of matching, drawing from the 'wood' if unable to go. The winner is the first player to play all his or her dominoes ('chip out').

Variations

(a) Use dominoes only up to double 4, matching as in the previous game, but adding the dots at each end. Each player should record his or her progressive total on a number strip using counters.

(b) Play the game as in (a), but start at 20 and subtract the end dots from 20, using a number strip and counters.

(c) The same game as in (a) and (b) could be played, with the score being recorded in different ways, such as on a number line, 100 square, hexagonal snake, (see figure 3), or with tally marks.

(d) Use the full set of dominoes. Match as in previous games, scoring one point if the ends *add up to an even number*.

(e) Variations on (d) could include: odd numbers, numbers less than 6, numbers more than 7, and so on.

(f) Another variation on games in (d) and (e) could be to find the *difference* between the ends, and score points as before.

Nought often causes problems for children, but it is not easy to deal within a more formal setting. Thus its use is deliberately included in the ensuing activites.

Snakes and Ladders

Equipment

Number strip from 1 to 20 for each player. Die marked 0,1,1,2,3,3. Counters.

Instructions

Each player takes turns to throw the die and then records his or her progressive total on the number strip with a counter. The winner is first to score 20.

(a) Play the game as above, but use clue cards instead of the die — e.g., Count on 3; Move on 2; Add 4; + 1, and so on.

(b) Play the game as above, but start at 20 and use the clue cards to involve subtraction.

Please note the role of language in these activities.

(c) *Hazard and bonus game*

Play the game as above with a die, but certain squares are *bonus* squares, and others are a *hazard*. Here is an example:

1	2	3	△4	⑤	6	7	8	⑨	△10
									11
21	20	△19	18	17	16	△15	⑭	13	12
22									
23	24	25	26	27	28	29	30	31	32
									33

◯ means *count on* 2;   △ means *count back* 2.

This strip would also work for *move on* 3 and *move back* 3. It will not work for 4 (5 *move on* 4 = 9).

Note: Other strips could be used, but thought must be given to where the hazards and bonuses are placed.

Problems of language and communication

Language development in mathematics is usually a source of concern. The vocabulary used in the whole range of mathematics is very considerable, and consequently great care is needed to structure situations which will enable certain language to be developed. For example, various kinds of play will help develop a wide range of language. The brick-building corner can bring forth vocabulary such as: tall, taller than, short, shorter than, long, longer than, various numbers, how many, more, less, same as, wide, narrow, high, large, big, larger than, and so on.

However, in planning his or her work the teacher must know the words she or he intends to introduce during the week. She or he should not attempt to introduce too many words at any one time, but rather to structure the learning situations to emphasize the few chosen words.

As each new topic is introduced, a list of suggested vocabulary should be developed, and then suitable planning can be arranged so that effective language development takes place. Reference has already been made to problems of language in the section dealing with failure, and below is a list of words which might be considered when dealing with the whole subject of subtraction.

take	find the difference between
take away	remove
from *n* take *n*	less
take *n* from *n*	what is *n* less *n*
from	how many more
subtract	count on (complementary
subtraction	addition is used
minus	particularly when giving
deduct	change)
decrease	
count back	
move back	

This list is not exhaustive, but nonetheless it represents a wide use of possible language — all of it related to that dreaded topic of subtraction. The idea of difference in subtraction should receive special emphasis, as in the real world we rarely 'take away', but we often compare amounts. Many adults then tend to use complementary addition as a means of achieving their answer. Perhaps the reasoning behind this lies in the fact that addition is easier to handle than subtraction.

Compare the pocket money of two children, say 50p and 75p. Who has the most and by how much? The problem can be looked at as $50 + ? = 75$, rather than $75 - 50 = ?$.

This is a possible method of recording:

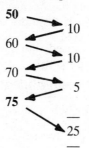

The answer is given by addition.

The whole problem of communication requires great patience. Very experienced educationalists, when giving instructions to groups of fellow educationalists, often fail to communicate successfully. My own experience of trying to describe a mathematical game on several occasions is that I have never been completely successful. We are often aware of the problems, but cannot then solve them successfully. Perhaps it is a reminder for us to bite our lip, count to ten, and try again, with better-chosen words.

Conclusion

When planning a mathematics curriculum for children with learning difficulties, we must consider several points as basic guidelines. These are fundamental to each stage, and need to be considered as a child progresses from class to class. As such, these points need to be considered by all teachers, so that uniformity of approach and action will at least help to eliminate the usual problems of transfer, even within the same school.

1. Language development within the mathematics curriculum must be carefully planned, instead of the teacher adopting a haphazard approach. Where possible, precise language should be used, with much support during its introduction, and then constant reference should be made to it during future work. Where possible, visual displays can aid the language development. The approach from class to class needs to be consistent and carefully planned, limiting the words which could be introduced to a manageable number.

2. The linear development of concepts and skills, including the finer points necessary for children with learning difficulties, is essential if progress is to be made. Reference has been made in the Appendix to a checklist for subtraction which has 38 points, and it is very probable that this is not complete. When you consider the differing aspects of mathematics — addition, subtraction, length, fractions, time, plane shapes, graphs, etc — this clearly indicates a complex planning programme to ensure that all the fine details are not overlooked.

3. Considerable attention must be focused on the use of concrete materials and, later, structured apparatus. All children will need these aids if the mathematics attempted is to be meaningful. Techniques and skills are of no value unless understanding has been achieved. Our eventual aim is the application of these skills in the child's own world, and evidence from various HMI reports shows clearly that many children cannot apply their own skills in everyday life.

4. Whenever children are asked to do work which involves reading, then great care is needed. As has already been illustrated, hardly any commercial texts are anywhere near correct in their reading levels. This aspect needs to be extended towards notation too. The notation used should be carefully planned within the school, and the use of symbols should be viewed with caution.

5. Within the mathematics curriculum, each school should try to provide a balanced diet. Number is bound to be predominant, but it must not overshadow selected work in measures, spatial and graphical work. Wherever possible, the child's own environment should be used in all of this work, which means a reliance on home-produced materials, rather than on commercial texts.

6. If number is to predominate, then a plea must be made for plenty of work on what one might call the 'concept of number'. It is absolutely vital that ideas on sequencing numbers, place value and exchange are fully developed, before we rush headlong into operations in addition, subtraction, multiplication and division. In all this work, structured apparatus is very,

very necessary, it should then lead into the use of pictorial forms, and the wide use of the number line.

7. Consideration should be given to games which will provide a motivating influence and help to provide a positive attitude towards mathematics. It should be remembered that mathematics ought to be practical, purposeful, positive and pleasurable. Finally, practice is very necessary, and games can be an acceptable way of achieving that objective.

Appendix

A checklist for subtraction

1. Concrete objects to 'take away' – numerals 1 to 5.
2. Pictorial representations – numerals 1 to 5.
3. Both of the above aspects for numerals 6 to 10.
4. Number bonds 1 to 5 to 10 linking addition and subtraction, e.g:

$$4 \text{ add } 2 = 6$$
$$6 \text{ subtract } 2 = 4$$
$$6 \text{ subtract } 4 = 2$$

5. Counting back in ones for numerals 1 to 10.
6. Comparisons — difference — using numerals 1 to 5.
7. Comparisons using numerals 6 to 10.
8. Difference — using numerals 10 to 20.
9. Take away — using numerals 10 to 20.
10. Counting back — use of the number line from 10 to 20.
11. Consecutive subtraction, e.g., $12 \,^{-2}\, 10 \,^{-3}\, 7$
12. $16 - 6$, $15 - 5$, $14 - 4$, etc. (all answers to be 10).
13. Partition of numerals from 10 to 20. Linking addition and subtraction, e.g:

$$? - 4 = 13$$
$$13 - ? = 6$$

14. Value of 0 in subtraction, e.g: $5 - 0$, $7 - 7$, etc.
15. Pattern work, e.g: $9 - 4$, $19 - 4$, $29 - 4$; patterns should be horizontal, matrix form, number line, vertical.
16. Decomposition games — counting back and exchanging.
17. Subtraction involving exchange, using concrete materials.
18. Subtracting in tens: $50 - 20$, $60 - 10$, etc.
19. Regrouping numbers involving exchange e.g:

$$32 = 30 \text{ add } 2 = 20 \text{ add } 12$$
$$25 = 20 \text{ add } 5 = 10 \text{ add } 15$$

20. Subtraction of two digit-numbers — no 'carrying' — using structured material, e.g:

$$42 - 21 \quad \begin{array}{r} (40 + 2) \\ - (20 + 1) \\ \hline (20 + 1) \end{array}$$

83

21. Subtraction of two-digit numbers involving decomposition, e.g. 32 − 17:

$$
\begin{array}{rl}
30 \text{ add } 2 = & 20 \text{ add } 12 \\
10 \text{ add } 7 = & 10 \text{ add } 7 \\
\hline
& 10 \text{ add } 5 = 15
\end{array}
$$

22. The concept of complementary addition should be introduced using the numerals learned so far. Use of money or structured apparatus is essential. E.g: 50 − 23; 23 + ? = 50.
   Note: It is important that children be introduced to other language which involves the process of subtraction, e.g., count back; less than; fewer than; difference between; take away; more than; move back; minus, etc. Problem work should be encouraged to help develop this language.

23. Subtraction of units (U) from hundreds, tens and units (HTU) — counting back — e.g., 157 − 5 = 152.
   Note: HTU should be less than 200.

24. Subtraction — TU from HTU — no decomposition, e.g:

$$
\begin{array}{rll}
136 = & (100 \text{ add } 30 \text{ add } 6) \\
- 23 = & \phantom{(100 \text{ add }} (20 \text{ add } 3) \\
\hline
& (100 \text{ add } 10 \text{ add } 3) & = 113
\end{array}
$$

25. Subtraction — TU from HTU — decomposition of tens only, e.g:

$$
\begin{array}{rlll}
142 = & (100 \text{ add } 40 \text{ add } 2) = & (100 + 30 + 12) \\
- 35 & & (30 + 5) \\
\hline
& & 100 + 0 + 7 & = 107
\end{array}
$$

26. Subtraction of 10s from multiples of 10>100 and <200, e.g., 120 − 30, and 100 − 40.

27. Subtraction — TU from HTU — decomposition of H and T, e.g:

$$
\begin{array}{rll}
123 = & (100 + 20 + 3) = & (120 + 3) \\
- 41 = & (40 + 1) = & (40 + 1) \\
\hline
& & 80 + 2 = 82
\end{array}
$$

28. Subtraction — TU from HTU — decomposition of H and T, e.g:

$$
\begin{array}{rll}
134 = & (100 + 30 + 4) = & (120 + 14) \\
- 57 = & (50 + 7) = & (50 + 7) \\
\hline
& & (70 + 7) = 77
\end{array}
$$

29. Development of short methods of notation to replace the extended form.

30. Subtraction of TU from 100 (breaking down one hundred into *tens* and *units*):

$$
\begin{array}{rll}
100 = & (100 + 0 + 0) = & (90 + 10) \\
- 53 = & (50 + 3) = & (50 + 3) \\
\hline
& & (40 + 7) = 47
\end{array}
$$

31. Subtraction of TU from multiples of 100, e.g:

$$
\begin{array}{rcll}
300 & = & (300 + 0 + 0) & = & (200 + 100 + 0) \\
- 78 & = & (70 + 8) & = & (70 + 8) \\
\hline
& & & = & (200 + 90 + 10) \\
& & & = & (70 + 8) \\
\hline
& & & = & (200 + 20 + 2) = 222
\end{array}
$$

32. Development of points 30 and 31 above to:

$$
\begin{array}{r}
100 \\
- 46 \\
\hline
54 \\
\hline
\end{array}
$$

33. Complementary addition — change-giving from £1 or £5 could be used as an alternative method of subtraction from 100 and multiples of 100, e.g:

$$£100 - 43p = 43 + ? = 100$$

34. Subtraction of U from HTU — involving decomposition, e.g:

$$
\begin{array}{rcll}
176 & = & (100 + 70 + 6) & = & (100 + 60 + 16) \\
- 9 & = & (9) & = & (9) \\
\hline
& & & & (100 + 60 + 7) = 167
\end{array}
$$

35. 'Double' decomposition, e.g:

$$
\begin{array}{rcll}
204 & = & (200 + 0 + 4) & = & (100 + 90 + 14) \\
- 7 & = & (7) & = & (7) \\
\hline
& & & & (100 + 90 + 7) = 197
\end{array}
$$

Note: The process of subtracting U from HTU need not be presented formally; it is a 'counting back' operation, e.g., $176 - 9 = 167$.

36. Subtracting HTU from HTU to follow a similar progression.
37. Linking subtraction with addition, e.g., $114 - 99$ being represented as 'counting on' $(99 + ? = 144)$ and 'counting back' $(114 - ? = 99)$.
38. Other methods of subtraction should be tackled, e.g., $53 - 29$, using the number line:

$$53 \xrightarrow{-20} 33 \xrightarrow{-9} 24$$
$$53 \xrightarrow{-9} 44 \xrightarrow{-20} 24$$
$$53 \xrightarrow{-30} 23 \xrightarrow{+1} 24$$

(Manchester Education Committee, 1975.)

References and further reading

Assessment of Performance Unit, *Primary Survey Report* No.1, HMSO, 1980.

Brennan, W. K., *Curricular Needs of Slow Learners*, Schools Council Working Paper 63, Evans/Methuen, 1979.

Checklist for Number, Measures, Spatial and Graphical Work, Manchester Education Committee, 1975.
DES, *Mathematics 5–11*, HMSO, 1979.
DES, *Primary School Survey*, HMSO, 1975.
DES, *Trends in Education*, HMSO, 1975.
Mathematics in School, Vol. 7, No. 4 (1978).
Skemp, *The Psychology of Learning Mathematics*, Penguin, 1971.
Turnbull, J., *Maths Links*, NARE, 1982.
Williams A. A., *Basic Subjects for the Slow Learner*, Methuen, 1970.
Williams, and Shuard, *Primary Mathematics Today*, Longman, 1970.

6

Achieving the significant difference in reading

PAULA HODSON

For the small number of pupils who do not appear to improve their reading skills despite exposure to a number of different teaching strategies, it may be necessary to break learning tasks into very small steps before teaching can take place. It is suggested that an objectives approach is a particularly effective method of tackling this problem.

When a pupil is experiencing difficulty in learning to read, teachers usually try a range of strategies. This range often includes the following considerations.

Would more practice solve the problem?

More practice usually involves more frequent opportunities to read to an adult and more experience with materials at one level, either supplementary materials or, in some cases, more than one attempt at a certain page or section. The strategy has obvious advantages: immediate feedback is available for the pupil, the teacher can provide incidental relevant teaching sessions and there is an opportunity to practise skills already mastered, so that skills can be used effectively when reading. The strategy is a popular one and is successful with many pupils.

However, this strategy may not be sufficient for some pupils. These pupils may not be able to master new material while they are trying to read, even when the teacher is available to correct and explain the mistakes. They need to have the material they have not mastered identified and then specifically taught, before they can benefit from practising it.

Would a different scheme solve the problem?

When giving the pupil more practice has not solved the problem, teachers often try to find more appropriate materials. Goodacre (1969) reported that when many teachers found that a pupil could not read a book aloud fluently they gave the child a book of similar difficulty from another scheme. Like the above strategy, this may be a successful approach with many pupils. The new materials may be more appropriate with regard to the language used, the interest level and the rate at which new words are introduced, for example. A pupil might also benefit from a change from a scheme based on the principle of few and frequent words, for example, to perhaps a scheme with a greater emphasis on developing word attack skills. However, some pupils fail to benefit from this strategy because, even when there is some consideration of the factors likely to be causing the problem in the original scheme and the new scheme selected with care, there is unlikely to be a perfect scheme that will actually teach the pupil to read. Even when the most appropriate scheme has been discovered, many pupils need specific teaching to benefit from it.

Would checking the pupils' sub-skills solve the problem?

This type of strategy represents a more specific attempt to isolate and then overcome a deficiency in some of the sub-skills thought to contribute to the process of reading. The analysis of the skills involved now tends to centre on the actual reading process, rather than on reading readiness type skills, so that there is a greater probability that an improvement in these skills will lead to an improvement in reading itself. Analysis can vary from a consideration of letter discrimination and sight work acquisition in the early stages, to an analysis of phonic and comprehension skills in the later stages of reading. Pupils are usually assessed in a particular area, often on published check-lists and then given direct teaching, workbooks or games to learn the skills they do not have.

This strategy is a popular one, particularly in the area of phonic skills. The validity of teaching phonic word attack skills has received experimental support in that Williams (1974) was able to demonstrate that a mastery of most phonic rules preceded a sudden and dramatic spurt in word recognition. The isolation of sub-skills makes the task of teaching more specific, easier to structure and simple to evaluate. This strategy used with the two strategies described above, or slight variations on them, is successful in helping many pupils to learn to read.

However, there are possibly two reasons why certain pupils who need a level of specific teaching may not benefit from this strategy. Firstly, a pupil may not be able to master a specified sub-skill and secondly, a pupil's mastery of a sub-skill may not lead to an improvement in the pupil's actual reading.

Using a framework of objectives

There are therefore a number of pupils for whom the range of strategies outlined above is not adequate. These pupils require the most appropriate materials available and frequent opportunities for immediate feedback from adults, but they need to be taught far more specifically than other pupils. Each learning task therefore needs to be precisely defined. Furthermore, these pupils need the task of learning to read broken down into much smaller steps than they have been presented with so far and some of these steps may involve aspects of reading which are usually learned incidentally by more fortunate pupils.

A programme of objectives has been suggested as a successful strategy for teaching pupils with learning difficulties (Ainscow and Tweddle, 1979). An objective precisely defines each task in terms of what the pupil would be observed to do if he had mastered the task, in what circumstances and to what degree of success. The philosophy is that, in a hierarchy of objectives, the attainment of each objective makes the following one easier to achieve. The framework can be extended to include as many small steps as necessary and can be written to teach the learning of any skill.

An example of a hierarchy of objectives based on a fairly traditional phonic sequence see (Jackson, 1971) might be:

(a) When reading a passage containing 25 unfamiliar words, each starting with a different letter (circumstances), the pupil can suggest a word beginning with the appropriate sound and consistent with the context of the passage (behaviour to be observed) with 100 per cent success (degree of success).
(b) When reading a passage containing 15 two or three-letter, phonically regular, unfamiliar words (three for each short vowel), the pupil can identify each word with 100 per cent accuracy.
(c) When reading a passage containing 11 four-letter phonically regular unfamiliar words (one with each of the following endings: mp, st, nk, it, nd, nt, sp, ng, sk, lp, ld) the pupil can identify each word with 100 per cent success.

The precise definition required for an objective may reveal that the pupil's task had not previously been specifically defined, taught or tested. In this situation a pupil can be set appropriate tasks and may then be able to achieve the proficiency required. However, the framework can easily be extended for pupils who cannot master a particular skill, even when it has been precisely defined. These pupils need the task broken down into smaller steps. Some pupils may, for example, have mastered objective 1 above but may not be able to attain objective 2. In this situation, intervening objectives or short-term objectives, also referred to as finer-grained objectives (Leach, 1980) or the result of second order task analysis (Gardner and Tweddle, 1979) can be written to bridge the gap between the two original objectives. Once the intervening objectives have been mastered, it is only a small step to master the original objective and this is now possible to achieve. For example, intervening objectives between objective 1 and 2 above might be:

1. When reading a passage containing 10 two or three letter phonically regular words with a short 'a' sound in the middle (as in bat), the pupil can identify the words with 100 per cent accuracy;
2. As above for words with 'i' in the middle (as in bin);
3. As above with words with 'o' in the middle (as in hop);
4. As above with words with 'e' in the middle (as in pet); and
5. As above with words with 'u' in the middle (as in fun).

However, although the use of an objectives framework can, in this way, help pupils to master previously unattainable skills and there are several manuals available to help teachers write objectives (see for example Mager, 1962 and Gronlund, 1970), objectives have not been widely used in Britain to teach reading to pupils experiencing considerable difficulty. It may be that the approach has not been more widely adopted because of the difficulty of deciding what the hierarchy of objectives should be written to teach. In other words, using an objectives approach means it is possible to teach most skills in time, but the real success of the approach necessitates a clear formulation of which skills need to be learned by a particular pupil. This problem in identifying the appropriate sub-skill to teach an individual pupil in the area of reading is summarized by Moyle (1974) 'If there is a perfect linear order in which reading skills should be presented to the pupil, we do not know what it is . . . Children at the same general level of reading ability display a wide variety of levels of development in the various sub-skills of reading'.

Very experienced teachers of reading may know, intuitively, which skill to teach next but, for the majority of teachers, it is by no means obvious which sub-skill a particular pupil would benefit from learning next. This is less of a problem in the very early stages of reading when a pupil needs to be able to discriminate between letter forms and have a basic sight vocabulary. Beyond this stage many pupils benefit from learning phonic word attack skills and, where this is proving beneficial, it is relatively easy to increase the complexity of the rules the pupil is asked to apply. However, there are some pupils beyond the first reader stage of reading who would not benefit from more advanced phonic knowledge, pupils who already over-use phonic cues or pupils with a serious difficulty in another sub-skill area, for example. It is for pupils in this situation that it is difficult to identify the important sub-skill to teach next. The following strategy represents a tentative attempt to specify the sub-skills a particular pupil may benefit from learning and then to teach these skills using an objectives framework.

Identifying the problem

A possible solution to the dilemma of which sub-skill a pupil needs to learn next may be to examine what is causing the problems for the individual pupil. Pupils may be able to compensate satisfactorily for an apparently important skill that they do not have, but they may be lacking a skill that so many pupils develop incidentally that it is not usually considered a skill. For this reason the emphasis is shifted from an investigation of which skills the pupil does or does not have to a consideration of which skills the pupil needs. In this way it is likely that mastery of a needed sub-skill will result in an improvement in actual reading.

A type of error analysis similar to that suggested for the oral informal reading inventory (IRI) (see Pumphrey, 1976) may reveal a pattern of errors and it may then be possible to teach a sub-skill to overcome them. The author has found the error analysis from two levels of fluency to be useful for this purpose: one at the instructional level (95 to 98 per cent accuracy) and one at about 90 per cent accuracy level. The advantage of using two levels of fluency for analysis is that the instructional level reveals the more elementary errors that occur in a relatively easy passage, whereas the passage with the greater number of errors is more likely to reveal a pattern of errors in the time the teacher has available. A tape-recorder is useful since, even if the precise notation suggested for the IRI is not adopted, it is imperative that all errors and the pupil's suggestions are recorded. Both passages should be from books/cards available for the pupil to read and the more difficult passage from a book the pupil would like to progress to.

For each error, an attempt is made to identify the skill or skills that, if applied, would have prevented the error. This involves an analysis beyond the classification of errors into categories such as substitution, no response, etc. since the lack of one specific sub-skill can result in errors in more than one category, and errors within one category can reflect the absence of very different sub-skills. An error classified as mispronunciation, for example,

Instructional level passage (not quoted in full):

Text	Pupil's attempt	Possible causes in terms of sub-skills weaknesses
1. This is a tale of a man . . .	This is a table of a man . . .	(i) Failure to use backward-acting context cue. (ii) Incomplete phonic analysis – 'b' not analysed.
2. He loved climbing up and down . . .	He loved climbing by . . .	(i) Very common word not instantly recognized. (ii) No letter analysis. (iii) Failure to use backward-acting context cues.
General fluency. phrasing, etc.	satisfactory	
Comprehension.	satisfactory	

Passage read with approximately 90 per cent accuracy (NB: self-corrected mistakes are not counted as errors). Passage not quoted in full:

Text	Pupil's attempt	Possible causes in terms of sub-skills weaknesses
1. A young man was walking in Sherwood Forest	→	
2. His	He	(i) Very common word not instantly recognized. (ii) Initial letter only analysed. (iii) Backward-acting context cues not utilized.
3. clothes	cl-cloak	(i) Morpheme 's' not utilized in identification. (ii) Incomplete phonic analysis 'th' not analysed. (iii) Backward-acting cue for word form not utilized.
4. were green like the trees	were green like a tree	(i) Very common word not instantly recognized. (ii) No letter analysis. (iii) Morpheme 's' not utilized.
5. in the forest . . .	→	
6. He heard	He had	(i) Common word not instantly recognized. (ii) Incomplete letter analysis, 'e' and 'r' and total length not analysed.
7. the cry	a cry	(i) Very common word not instantly recognized. (ii) No letter analysis.
8. of a child	for a, from a child	(i) Very common word not instantly recognized. (ii) No phonic analysis.
General fluency, phrasing intonation, etc.	satisfactory	
Comprehension (fact recall, vocabulary inference)	satisfactory	

Fig. A Identifying the problems.

could be the result of a lack of skill in using context cues (convict, noun, pronounced as convict, verb, for example), a failure to identify the correct morpheme, a faulty phonic analysis, a failure to adjust the phonic/morphemic cues to actual words and so on. It is important to note at this point that error here does not only refer to misidentified words, but would include any faulty aspect of the reading process, such as a failure to answer comprehension questions satisfactorily or the reading of a passage with incorrect phrasing.

For each mistake, a list is made of the sub-skills which, if they had been utilized, would have increased the chance of a correct response being given. In some cases the mastery of one sub-skill would have prevented the mistake, for example, when a very common sight-word is confused with another or when the morpheme 's' is ignored and a singular word suggested. However, in other cases the correct response would only have been achieved if more than one or a combination of sub-skills had been used. It is important to list all the sub-skills that have apparently not been used, even if the mastery of one of them would have solved the problem, since this data is important when a pattern of errors is identified. A consideration of the responses given elsewhere in the passage will then suggest the particularly weak sub-skills.

Deciding on a priority problem

When the error analysis has been completed, it is unlikely that the lack of one sub-skill is responsible for all the errors. As mastery of an increased proficiency in one sub-skill may take a pupil some considerable time, it is of some importance to decide on priorities. A serious weakness in the ability to monitor meaning should certainly receive some priority, since a pupil who is failing to understand the meaning of a text is failing to understand the purpose of the whole exercise. Where the cause of errors seems likely to be a failure to monitor meaning, such as the suggestion of words inconsistent with the meaning of the text, or the failure to answer comprehension questions at the factual recall level, sub-skills in monitoring meaning need to be taught.

Apart from sub-skills in monitoring meaning, priorities have to be selec-

The following priorities for sub-skill mastery were listed	
Sub-skill	**Level of sub-skill to be learned at this stage**
1. The immediate identification of very common words.	Pupil can immediately identify the 20 most common words according to McNally and Murray (1962).
2. The use of backward-acting context cues.	Pupil can correct errors he has made earlier in the sentence, without prompting, when he has read the phrase which contains a backward-acting cue of meaning or syntax.
3. The recognition of the morpheme 's'.	Pupil suggests a plural noun where the morpheme 's' occurs.

Fig. B Selecting the priority problems.

ted on the basis of the pattern of errors made. The frequency with which a mastered sub-skill will be used is an important factor to consider. Some sub-skills are important to teach either because they refer to a specific situation which occurs frequently such as the distinction of 'were' and 'where', for example, or because they can be applied to a variety of situations or words, such as the ability to blend sounds to produce a word. Provided the passage is reasonably representative of what the pupil will be reading, the number of times a sub-skill is listed as a possible cause of an error will give some indication of how frequently the sub-skill might be used.

A second factor it is useful to consider is the level of the sub-skills listed as possible causes of errors. Pupils are more likely to develop an efficient reading strategy, with an appropriate balance of speed and accuracy, if they can use a range of skills. It is therefore probably better to select as a priority a sub-skill which was not applied at a low level rather than attempting to achieve a high level of proficiency in only one sub-skill area.

Writing the objectives

Having decided on the priority sub-skill, a sequence of objectives can then be written. Objectives at this level should specify a degree of proficiency in the sub-skill that will be effective when the pupil is trying to read in an unsupported situation. For example, a pupil is often considered to have mastered the single letter sounds if he can produce the sound or key word when presented with a letter. This level of skill would not be useful to the pupil when he is unsupervised, and this failure to specify a useful level of proficiency is one factor that can account for the failure of reading to improve following the 'mastery' of a sub-skill. The degree of proficiency specified in the objective needs to be increased so that the pupil can suggest a word beginning with the sound and consistent with the context of the passage. On the other hand, the most difficult objective in the sequence would probably not specify complete mastery of the sub-skill, such as the ability to apply all phonic rules, but would define a proficiency level the teacher considered appropriate and realistic for the pupil to aim for at that particular stage.

Writing the intervening objectives

Intervening objectives or short-term objectives are then written to help the pupil attain the easiest objective. At this level it is not usually possible to identify an independently useful skill that, if mastered, would make the original objective easier to obtain (tasks that would precede objective (a) below, for example), so objectives of a slightly different type are written. Intervening objectives usually make the objective task easier by modifying the requirements for pupil behaviour, the degree of success and/or the cir-

---

1. When the word 'of' occurs in a passage, Simon can identify it without hesitation and 100 per cent accuracy.

2. When the 20 commonest function words occur in a passage, Simon can identify them without hesitation and 100 per cent accuracy.

Fig. C Writing the objectives for the priority sub-skill.

	Started on	Mastered	Checked
1. In a passage in which 'of' occurs 4 times, with the 'o' and the upper section of the 'f' coloured, Simon can identify 'of' without error. (Starter objective.)	20.9.79	20.9.79	
2. In a passage in which 'of' occurs 5 times, Simon can read 'of' without error, when he has a cue card with the 'o' and the upper 'f' coloured for comparison.	20.9.79		
3. In a passage in which 'of' occurs 4 times, Simon can read 'of' without error when he has a cue card with 'of' on it for comparison.			
4. When the word 'of' occurs in a passage, Simon can identify it without hesitation and 100 per cent accuracy. (Original objective.)			

Fig. D Writing a programme of short-term objectives to attain the first objective.

cumstances of success. These modifications are often well-known teaching methods. The circumstances, for example, could be made easier by restricting the choice of responses available or by highlighting the key features. The pupil's behaviour could be made less demanding by only asking the pupil to say whether his teacher's reading of a word is correct or not, or to pronounce a word when the teacher has isolated the morphemes. The specified degree of success can, of course, be reduced. Short-term or intervening objectives therefore differ from main objectives because a teaching method is usually implied and because the level of proficiency is not usually sufficient for a pupil to utilize the skill effectively in an unsupported situation.

The objective (a): when reading a passage containing 25 unfamiliar words, each starting with a different letter, the pupil can suggest a word beginning with the appropriate sound and consistent with the context of the passage. This could be preceded by the short-term objectives:

1. For each of the 25 letters (excluding x) presented in random order, when the teacher gives the sound, the pupil can say a key word with 100 per cent success.
2. For each of the 25 letters, presented in random order the pupil can give the sound, the key word and a further word starting with the sound with 100 per cent success.
3. When the pupil is presented with 25 unfamiliar words the pupil can suggest a word beginning with the appropriate sound.

The first short-term objective in the sequence should be one that the pupil can already attain. The number of short-term objectives required depends on the difference in proficiency between the first short-term objective and the original objective.

94

When the first main objective has been attained, short-term objectives to reach the second main objective, if they are needed, are then written.

Summary

To summarize, the strategy suggested here is:

1. Identify the problems (Figure A).
2. Select the priority problems (Figure B).
3. Write the objectives for the first priority problem (Figure C).
4. Write the short-term objectives for the first main objective (Figure D).

Evaluation of the strategy

The strategy outlined in this article is certainly not an easy method of teaching poor readers to read in a short period of time. It is suggested as a strategy when less specific approaches have failed.

The disadvantages are obvious:

1. Programmes of objectives are not easy to write. Furthermore, the investment of time involved is considerable and the programme achieved may not be useful for more than one pupil.
2. Once-written programmes of objectives, particularly at the short-term level, need to be used experimentally. A pupil may need more short-term objectives than was originally estimated but, in other cases, progress may be more rapid than anticipated and several short-term objectives may be superfluous. It is essential that frequent checks are made to ensure that the achievement of short-term objectives are contributing to the attainment of the original objective and that the attainment of the objective results in an improvement in the pupil's reading.

The advantages for a pupil with serious difficulties are, however, considerable.

1. Objectives can monitor the achievement of very small amounts of progress. Progress becomes apparent and therefore significant which is encouraging for both the pupil and the teacher.
2. When pupils are discovered to have forgotten a previously mastered skill, because the criterion level for success had been specified, it is easy to modify the objective for a higher degree of mastery. Similarly, a failure to generalize a skill to a particular context can be remedied by altering the circumstances specified.
3. A pupil can master a skill that was previously unobtainable.
4. The pupil knows exactly what he is required to learn and he can work towards it at a rate he can cope with. He is, in fact, using time very efficiently.

Some pupils learn to read almost incidentally and many others become fluent readers with very little systematic instruction. It would be pointless to use a pedantic framework for these pupils. For the unfortunate pupils who fail to learn to read so easily, the use of an objectives framework provides an alternative strategy in which they can make significant progress.

Acknowledgement

The influence of the work of David Tweddle, Senior Educational Psychologist, Sutton Coldfield, is gratefully acknowledged.

References

Ainscow, M. and Tweddle, D. A., *Preventing Classroom Failure: An Objectives Approach*, Wiley, 1979.

Gardner, J. and Tweddle, D. A. (1979), 'Some guidelines for sequencing objectives' in the *Journal of Association of Educational Psychologists*, Vol. 5, No. 3.

Goodacre, E. J. (1969), 'Published reading schemes' in *Educational Research*, Vol. 12.

Gronlund, N., *Stating Behavioural Objectives for Classroom Instruction*, Macmillan, 1970.

Jackson, S., *Get Reading Right*, Phonic Skill Tests, Gibson, 1971.

Leach, D. (1980), 'Assessing children with learning difficulties: an alternative model for psychologists and teachers' in the *Journal of Association of Educational Psychologists*, Vol. 5, No. 3.

Mager, R. F., *Preparing Instructional Objectives*, Fearon, New York, 1962.

McNally, J. and Murray, W., *Key Words to Literacy*, Schoolmaster Publishing Company, 1962.

Moyle, D. (1974), 'Sequence and structure in reading development' in *New Horizons in Reading*, Vienna, Fifth IRA World Congress on Reading.

Pumphrey, P. D., *Reading: Tests and Assessment Techniques*, Hodder and Stoughton, 1976.

Williams, P. (1974), 'Early reading: some unexplained aspects' in *New Horizons in Reading*, Vienna, Fifth IRA World Congress on Reading.

from *Remedial Education*, Vol. 16, No. 4 (1981).

7

The contribution of drama

GORDON PIDGEON

Drama teachers and specialists are usually convinced that drama is a vital factor in educational development. Despite a wealth of information and suggestions for lesson activities which act as pervasive agents, there is still a reluctance by other teachers to incorporate the natural activity of children into the learning programme. Drama has become far more integrated into the curriculum, but its exploitation for all children, especially those we unfortunately label remedial, is still tragically ignored.

Evidence based upon statistical analysis to support the tenets concerning the value of drama in education are extremely rare. However, some conclusions from two statistically-based investigations into children's drama may help to substantiate the generalized claims.

Reasoning and drama

In the initial experiment designed to test maturity of judgement it was found that children's reasoning was significantly improved following involvement in dramatic activity. The significance at the 5 per cent level indicated that children did benefit from inter-actions in group dramatic activity. Their reasoning and logical conclusions made as a result of 'experiencing' situations were significantly better compared with children who had no dramatic experience. It can be concluded from this experiment that dramatic activity is an essential prerequisite for the development of logical thought. It would seem that many of our remedial children need opportunities which will help develop and strengthen their immature level of causal relationships. The importance of the acquisition of experiences in the formulation of concepts should be the central core in the educational programme for remedial children. This investigation provides evidence to support the claim that drama is a way of providing these experiences, a way of enriching the vocabulary of life.

Literacy and drama

The second investigation into children's dramatic story composition revealed considerable data to support the dogma that drama is a natural activity in the campaign for literacy. This investigation into children's dramatic play was carried out in a number of primary schools and resulted in the analysis of data concerning story content, character, movement, dialogue and symbolization. The principal aim of this study was to compare possible stages of development in drama with stages of developmental psychology. Apart from the hypothesized stages of development in dramatic work, the analysis of data indicated suggestions for the possible content of reading books as well as other ways in which the creative elements could be harnessed in the fight to establish literacy. A detailed description would be out of place here, but perhaps a brief outline of some of the findings might point to the opulent material contained in children's dramatic stories. The outline may also indicate the gulf between existing reading material and children's interests. Children were asked to create a story in a group situation and then to improvise their story in the open space of the hall. The collection of story titles included: Snow White, The Magic Horse, Commandos, Cops, Robbers and Charlie Chaplin, Cinderella, Matches, The Titanic, Bank Robbery, Dr Frankenstein, Lost in Space, A Home Situation.

Stories were initially classified according to the source material used; this classification was:

1. Traditional story: those stories which were based upon previously heard material.
2. Original story: those stories which had not been heard previously, stories which the children had completely made up for themselves.

Fewer than 30 per cent of the stories were classified as traditional or based upon borrowed material. This analysis meant that a vast proportion of stories were original. The children who made these stories were not exceptionally gifted. Drama had not been a regular feature of their programme. The children, from mixed backgrounds, had learning difficulties: retardation and emotional problems were common features, yet children were all able to contribute in a group story situation.

Differences in story content

First-year children (7–8 year-olds) would appear to rely upon the traditional story, and the analysis revealed a gradual abandonment of the traditional material as the children became older. A further classification of stories was based upon content. Many of the stories were germane to fairy-tale material, and the classification between fairy-tale and non-fairy-tale material revealed a greater use of fairy-tale vocabulary in the stories created by the younger children. Seventy-three per cent of the first-year stories were related to the fairy-tale world, compared with 14 per cent of the fourth-year stories. Within the four story classifications, several story themes appeared with regularity. The themes included those of: robbery, war, hunting, ghosts, disaster, holidays, space, monsters, dreams. The stories made by girls throughout the four age divisions were overwhelmingly directed towards fairy tales and also included such themes as monsters, robbery, dreams, injustice, and confused identity. Boys' themes were mainly related to robbery, space, war and monsters.

An analysis of *dramatis personae* resulted in an extensive list of characters relevant to children's stories. The distribution of characters seemed significant in relation to age and sex. A sample from the survey includes a dog, Cinderella, brontosaurus, King Harold, witch, ballerina, cowgirl, Frankenstein and pantomime horse. In some group plays, characters had such ordinary names as Bill, Tom, and with them such incongruous individuals as Coffee, Sugar Plum and Markus. In another play, Pinky, Perky and Gluko accompanied an old woman. Sometimes a child's surname was used for the name of a character and this produced Corporal Jones, Sergeant Smith, P. C. Bloggs. It may seem that the incongruous, the mundane or the commonplace names used for characters were of little importance and of no significance. However, characters were chosen seriously by the children and, although the characters presented as types, there were logical balances within groups. The factors of tension, fear and dominance were closely related with the characters, even if they were merely outlined by the children's own names. Characters, whatever their name or the related plot, clearly belonged to four main groups:

(a) the hero;
(b) the dark or evil character;
(c) the oppressed;
(d) roles supportive of either (a) or (b).

Animal characters were included in each of the age-groups, but the younger children included more animalistic characters than the older children. Characters outside human form, but not animal included the witch, geni, Dalek and space being. The most popular animal character was the monster. The characters outside human form: witch, ghost, devil, etc., were always associated with the antagonistic forces within the story.

The study of story plot, themes and character groups brought about the tabulation of story ingredients which the children used in their composition. These included the following factors:

1. The evil character, or the powerful force, usually the witch, devil, monster or robber.
2. The good character, those that oppose the characters in 1.
3. The confrontation. This develops because
   (a) 1 attacks 2;
   (b) 2 sets out to find 1.
4. A journey.
5. The conflict or fight when evil is matched against good.
6. If 1 overpowers 2, then an escape avenue is provided.
7. Good overpowers evil in the end.
8. Need for supportive roles for both groups, evil and good.

Many of these content factors may appear to be synonymous with the content of fairy tales, but this would not suppose that reading material should be exclusively orientated around folklore material. Many of the stories were masked by modern situations and were relative to the real world, but they were not concerned with the events centred around the suburban family. A great deal of children's reading material lacks vitality and imaginative development, two factors which characterized the dramatic stories. Children were not presenting a picture of their own world. A number of their stories were analogous to the epic with its vitality and spirit of adventure. The essential chase, or the battle between weak and strong created tension and elongated suspense. Incongruent character groups were acceptable, and it was not illogical for a detective, after being turned into a frog, to rescue his comrades from prison. These may seem to be illogicalities of a fairy-tale world, but for the child they were the means of communicating ideas. The communication of ideas was divorced from the adult sense of intellectual logic which so often stifles imaginative conception.

Remedial education

Many of the findings would seem to be of great importance to those concerned with remedial education. One of the main justifications for including drama in remedial programmes is based upon drama's role in the struggle for literacy and the opportunity it offers to slow learners for the expression of their own ideas or the ideas of others. Children learn to read and write in order to function in a system based upon literacy, but the key to this functionality is enjoyment. Reading should be an enjoyable pursuit in its own right. The struggle to break the symbolization barrier has to be overcome, but parallel with this confrontation is the necessity to build a love for stories.

This stage in the development of literacy can be achieved through dramatic activity. It commences with the development of oracy which becomes the anacrusis to literacy. If language skills are to develop, then reading aloud by an adult is paramount, but children also need to contribute to stories and eventually create their own. Ideally, these activities should be the nucleus of our pre-school language development programmes, but there is also a developmental path for the stages of education which follow. Drama becomes a functional factor in the education of children, as well as being an art form which is essential for their natural development. Dramatic activity stands in silent silhouette against the conglomerate mass of paraphernalia which often symbolizes remedial programmes designed to develop literacy.

Reading for pleasure

A great deal of the material created by or used by the remedial specialist is concerned with the mechanics of the reading process. There are an appalling number of unimaginative and senseless reading and writing activities which constitute the main diet for those children who have failed in the system of reading. Eventually, some children will cope with the easiest publications from Fleet Street, but what of reading as we the élite know it — reading for enjoyment, for the mystical marriage of the emotions with the imagination? This would seem to be our prerogative — or is it? Do we in fact read for pleasure? The capacity for imaginative satisfaction has to be developed at an early age through the interactions of dramatic play. For the realization of this need, the philosophy of pedagogy needs to veer from the present edict that reading is the key factor in academic growth, where the accumulation of correct opinions is a mark of success, to the view that reading is the key which unlocks our other world. If we are to be successful readers, we need not only the acquisition of skills, but a love for reading. Reading must therefore be concerned with subject matter which complements and satisfies the heterogeneity of our personalities.

Children make up stories when they play, and there would seem to be an affinity between this natural expression of the child and the activity we term reading — both are vehicles for the story. Unfortunately, the term 'play' has emotional overtones for a number of adults, including teachers. The importance of play is, like the story, often misunderstood and sadly misinterpreted. Creative play or story-making is part of that 'emotional' discipline, drama. This discipline is often regarded flippantly, yet when children are given the space and time to participate in dramatic activity, they are provided with an opportunity to develop oracy and basic language skills through the motivation of their own story themes.

Some of the themes outlined in the investigation could be used in the development of literacy either as reinforcement by the teacher or as reading-scheme material. It would seem from some of the experimental conclusions that the children with learning difficulties could be better employed in a more active environment which uses drama as the link with academic, aesthetic, emotional, creative and therapeutic needs of the children.

The fact that dramatic activities are not universally accepted and used as a main source for learning can only result in impoverished education. The fecundity of dramatic activities need not be itemized in these columns, but three salient features of drama require tabulation:

1. Drama is pragmatic rather than theoretical.
2. It incorporates the use of all facets of the personality.
3. Dramatic activity is concerned with communication and relationships.

These features alone should justify the inclusion of drama in education. Details of the side benefits and cross-references with other subjects can be found in numerous volumes on the subject. However, the main justification for including drama in remedial programmes is based upon drama's role in the development of language skills, logical thought and concept formulation, a factor which is fundamental in the extension of learning.

Children and creativity

The investigations into children's drama brought about the endorsement of these features as well as a structured evaluation of dramatic symbolisms in their ontogenetic order of appearance. Drama is concerned with creation, it is an activity in which the child reveals and eventually offers part of himself. Parallel with this aspect is the value which drama has in terms of being a therapeutic experience and also as a cathartic activity, although some authorities regard this aspect as of little importance.

All children, especially those we term remedial, need to be given the chance to develop their own 'wonderful ideas'. Piaget sees the essence of intellectual development as 'the having of wonderful ideas'. Wonderful ideas were displayed in the children's dramatic stories. Perhaps these stories could have been incorporated into the reading system or used to replace some of the present less imaginative material. Reluctant readers — there were many in the investigation — were able to create stories. They indicated an innate desire to build and coalesce story ideas. Perhaps the expertise of authors could use the material for 'tailor-made' stories?

Involvement in story-making may bring teachers to realize that it is the content of reading material which is important. Much of the hard work in reading is concerned with techniques. Techniques are necessary. For some they develop too slowly or not at all, but without the spirituality implicit in 'a love for reading', even the well-established technique is meaningless.

101

Drama can provide the key, the key to story creation which is so often withdrawn from our poor readers. Although drama is included on timetables, its potential has not yet been fully harnessed.

Child drama can be regarded as the mirror of life, the outward manifestation of life's environmental struggle as well as the symbolization of the conflicts within the inner self. Slade maintains that this art form is 'the doings of life'. It may be the child's counterpart to many forms of adult expression. Drama is not the panacea for all educational problems, but it could be incorporated into educational programmes and so extend and develop literacy for those children who are reluctant readers, as well for as those with special learning difficulties. It may fulfil the exigencies of the remedial unit. It may not only bring a form of expression, but a form of relief from the continuous mono-chromed landscape which frequently encapsulates our children. Involvement in dramatic story-making may be the precursor to an appetite for the adult novel from which we ought to learn so much.

References and further reading

Baldwin, A. L. *Theories of Child Development*, John Wiley, New York, 1967.

Coggin, P. A., *Drama in Education*, Thames and Hudson, 1956.

Courtney, R., *Play, Drama and Thought*, Cassell, 1968.

DES, *Drama, Education Survey 2*, HMSO, 1968

Flavell, J. E., *The Developmental Psychology of Jean Piaget*, Van Nostrand Reinholdt, New York, 1963.

Griffiths, R., *Imagination in Early Childhood*, Routledge and Kegan Paul, 1935.

Haggerty, J., *Please Miss, Can I Play God?*, Methuen, 1967.

Hodgson and Richards, *Improvisation*, Methuen, 1966.

Hodgson and Banham, *Drama in Education*, Survey 1 and 2, Pitman, 1972.

Isaacs, S., *Social Development in Young Children*, Routledge and Kegan Paul, 1946.

Jennings, S., *Remedial Drama*, Pitman, 1973.

Millar, S., *The Psychology of Play*, Penguin, 1968.

Opie, I. and P., *The Lore and Language of School Children*, Oxford University Press, 1959.

Opie, I. and P., *Children's Games in Street and Playground*, Oxford University Press, 1969.

Peel, E. A., *The Pupil's Thinking*, Oldbourne, 1960.

Piaget, J., *Play, Dreams and Imitation in Childhood*, Routledge and Kegan Paul, 1951.

Piaget, J., *The Language and Thought of the Child*, Routledge and Kegan Paul, 1926.

Piaget, J., *The Child's Conception of the World*, Routledge and Kegan Paul, 1929.

Piaget, J., *Judgement and Reasoning in the Child*, Routledge and Kegan Paul, 1928.

Piaget, J., *The Child's Conception of Space*, Routledge and Kegan Paul, 1956.

Pidgeon, G. D., *Children's Judgement and Child Drama*, Educational Drama Association, 1975.
Slade, P., *Child Drama*, University of London Press, 1954.
Slade, P., *Experience of Spontaneity*, Longman, 1968.
Way, B., *Development Through Drama*, Longman, 1967.

from *Remedial Education*, Vol. 10, No. 1 (1975).

Section 2
Subject areas

The challenges facing curriculum planners are not restricted to any one aspect of the curriculum, but permeate the whole of pupils' learning experiences. Mention has already been made of communication skills and mathematics, and both of these will be further developed by subsequent contributors. Similar evidence could be found in a much wider sample of the educational diet which is offered to pupils. Humanities, fine arts, moral education, design technology, environmental sciences and recreational studies are but some of the labels found on school timetables, and all pose problems for both teacher and child. In moral education, for example, there is no one generally accepted code of values to be passed on to pupils who live in a pluralist and multi-cultural society. It can be argued that it is not the school's task to attempt to pass on particular attitudes and values, but rather to foster in the pupils the ability to think for themselves, to form their own hypotheses and to test them out before drawing their own conclusions. Such flexibility and adaptability of thought may well be beyond the powers of many during their school years, but progress is more likely where the emphasis is on understanding rather than rote learning.

Three areas of study — science, geography and history — have been chosen in this section, because they illustrate a wide range of demands in the middle years of schooling. In addition to language and mathematics, these subjects comprise a substantial portion of the basic academic curriculum, whether taught separately, or combined under such titles as integrated studies of environmental studies, or as components of a project. Investigations quoted in subsequent chapters demonstrate that science, geography and history are heavily burdened with technical vocabulary (Richards, 1978); involve texts requiring high levels of reading proficiency (Lunzer and Gardner, 1979); require a high proportion of transactional writing (Martin et al., 1976), and frequently display a mismatch between pupils' cognitive development and the cognitive demands of curricula (for example, Shayer and Adey, 1981, Boardman, 1979, Schools Council *Social Studies Project*, 1981). All four factors pose problems for children with learning difficulties. Even so, history, geography and science have much in common in that they provide opportunities for discussion, vocabulary development, improvement of reading and writing skills, as well as promoting the exchange of views and the growth of creative thinking.

A common characteristic of pupils with learning difficulties is their limited ability to generalize from one situation to another and, consequently, they are prone to compartmentalize their thinking skills. It is essential that they are given ample opportunity for regular reinforcement and are frequently shown the relevance of their skills in a much wider context. Throughout the three chapters which follow, it will be made clear that pupils learn more readily where they are given active encouragement to develop their powers of observation and prediction, also when they are given the opportunity to discuss the wider application of these powers with both peers and teachers.

8

Science

MIKE HINSON

The ideal of 'science for all' came a little closer to realization with the publication of *The School Curriculum* (1981). This important statement regards science as an essential component of 5–16 education for all children.

Over the last twenty years, a variety of curriculum development projects have been initiated and, due to the dedication and determination of science educationists, the overall opportunities for children to study science have greatly improved. Nevertheless, the provision of curricula successfully geared to the needs of children with learning difficulties is inconsistent.

An overview

Primary schools

Despite substantial expenditure of time and money, the ideas and materials emanating from national curriculum development projects have been slow to influence the quantity and quality of science teaching in the majority of primary schools. Teachers often lack a working knowledge of elementary science appropriate to the needs of primary-school children. HM Inspectors report (1978) that, as a result, only a minority develop activities requiring careful observation and accurate recording beyond a superficial level. Nevertheless, examples of good practice suggest that all children between the ages 5–11 benefit from contact with scientific ideas.

Secondary schools (11–14 years)

It is generally accepted that pupils should be offered a common experience in science during their first two or three years in the secondary school. It is here that national projects have made a sustained impact on science teaching. However, in many schools, science lessons are still over-concerned with the acquisition of knowledge: science as a collection of facts to be communicated and remembered. Syllabuses are likely to comprise of topics which teachers regard as essential learning, based on their own higher academic training, rather than those more suited to the pupils' levels of cognitive development. This is not to the advantage of less-able pupils. Teaching resources abound, yet it is only recently that authors and publishers have paid closer attention to the linguistic difficulty of the materials which they produce.

Secondary schools (14–16)

Aspects of Secondary Education in England (1979) focused on the education of secondary-school pupils in their fourth and fifth years. Not one school in the 10 per cent sample was found to provide a full range of balanced science courses for all pupils up to the age of 16 plus. However, about one third of all schools made some form of science compulsory for every pupil in this age-range. Those of below-average ability usually studied general science.

Whatever the type of school, it was the work of the less-able which gave the greatest cause for concern. In 10 per cent of the schools, a lack of any real objective to the science courses gave rise to apathy and inattention. This was compounded by topics and concepts beyond pupils' understanding and with little relevance to their lives.

Special schools

Brennan (1979) reported that successful work was mainly based upon modern primary-school science teaching methods which had been adapted to the needs of pupils in the senior classes of special schools. Perception, observation and language were well exploited. However, much of the content of science curricula took the form of useful knowledge, e.g., knowing how to wire a plug. Such knowledge is not particularly scientific unless pertinent questions are asked which lead to the investigation of the principles and laws involved. Brennan concluded that the science curriculum failed to go beyond the level of fact or skill in most special schools. Significantly, this trend was also noted in some secondary schools where the remedial department was responsible for organizing science teaching.

Benefits of science education

These days, progressive science teachers build their courses around a backbone of meaningful practical experiences which they share with their pupils. This approach can benefit children with learning difficulties in a number of ways:

1. Careful observation is central to scientific method, yet children with learning difficulties are not always good at noticing things. Science lessons provide tangible situations in which they can systematically improve their powers of observation: seeing the obvious and the less obvious, the expected and the unexpected, in a new light.
2. Children experience a variety of activities which characterize science (looking for patterns, classifying, accurate measurement, and so forth) in the process of obtaining scientific data. The interpretation of this involves a series of cognitive processes: considering facts, predicting, experimenting, attempting to explain and drawing conclusions. Science therefore helps children with learning difficulties to organize their thoughts.
3. Both primary and secondary-school science involves the handling of unfamiliar materials, the observation of fascinating demonstrations, carrying out exciting experiments and, from time to time, sharing that sense of 'glorious adventure' experienced by other scientists on the verge of discovery. Potentially, science has a unique motivational value, especially for pupils who might have become disillusioned with other aspects of the curriculum. It can also provide a more palatable medium through which those with learning difficulties can improve their progress in the basic skills of numeracy and literacy.

4. Practical work is frequently organized on a co-operative basis with pupils in pairs or groups. These arrangements are of considerable benefit to those who need to learn the social skills of sharing. They also generate valuable opportunities to strengthen relationships with adults.
5. Effective sharing and decision-making depend upon communication. Group learning in science can help pupils to shape their own understanding through discussion. Even the shy child is more likely to talk in a small group with friends.
6. Integrated approaches to science such as rural science and environmental studies can give less-able pupils a greater awareness of the ways in which science and technology contribute to the worlds of work, citizenship, leisure and survival.

The aims of science education

As the result of widespread debate by science teachers, the Association for Science Education (1981) outlined six main aims which, in its view, should be embodied in all pupils' education through science. These can be summarized as:

(a) To learn and understand a range of scientific concepts, generalizations, principles and laws;
(b) to acquire the skills and processes of practical science;
(c) to develop the ability to use a scientific approach in problem solving and then to communicate these results to others;
(d) to develop some understanding of advanced technological societies and the importance of science in our everyday lives;
(e) to be aware of the contribution which science makes to our cultural heritage;
(f) to realize that science helps in the process of establishing a sense of personal and social identity.

The Association believed that, by presenting a set of goals to be achieved by the end of compulsory education, it created a framework within which the specific aims and objectives of different courses or stages of the educational process could be determined.

Planning Effective Progress accepts the assertions of the Warnock Report (1978) that the purpose and goals of education are the same for all children. It is feasible, therefore, to utilize an authoritative set of aims such as these as a framework for specific objectives when designing science courses geared to the needs of children with learning difficulties.

Curriculum objectives

Brennan (1979) regards increased precision in defining curriculum objectives (outcomes of behaviour) as essential in effective curriculum planning. Skills must be established before they can be elaborated, integrated and generalized. This is necessary if the learner is to acquire the conceptual insights which are part of generalization and the link between perceptual-motor activities and the cognitive process. The curriculum model proposed by Wheeler (1967) is one which has particular advantages for children with learning difficulties in science, because it is both suitable for skills learning and consistent with the psychological principles which should be applied to their teaching. The stages can be summarized as:

1. Statement of educational aims
2. Translation of aims into statements of objectives
3. The selection of learning experiences
4. Selection of content
5. Organization of interaction of experience and content
6. Evaluation
7. Feedback.

Prestt (1976) explains that scientific skills at the primary stage can often be developed by using content that is normally not thought of as science. Teachers need to bear in mind that the skill being learned is the criterion for development, rather than the material used in the process. A rigorous analysis of the basic facts, concepts, techniques and the sequential development of a scientific discipline is necessary in framing curriculum objectives for pupils in the 11–16 age-range. Such reasons as 'Well, every child ought to know that' should be viewed with some caution. Schofield (1969) recommends a closer look at pupils' perceptions of the science we teach: 'We have too often thought of the problems we face in terms of our own perception, often idealized, of the science we place before our pupils'.

The Practical Curriculum (1981) exhorts teachers to monitor pupils' experiences when establishing an effective curriculum. This is further developed in *Science 5–13, Objectives in Mind* (1972), *Match and Mismatch* (1977) and Shayer and Adey (1981), all of which are worthy of closer scrutiny. However, before determining the content of effective science courses for children with learning difficulties, there are three areas where problems occur which must be considered.

Attitudes

Attitudes to school which are acquired and developed during a child's school years may become permanent, remaining long after the subject matter has been forgotten. Negative attitudes to learning are more likely to influence success or failure in a school subject than a child's actual ability. If she cannot do something, then this is likely to over-ride her ability to do it, thus creating a lack of self-confidence, an unwillingness to try new activities and a general air of disillusionment. Unfortunately, this is all too often the case with those who have special educational needs.

Newton (1975) found three main components in children's attitudes to science:

(a) *Belief-disbelief*, e.g., logical reasons for believing that science is, or is not, of personal and/or social value.
(b) *Like-dislike*, e.g., 'science is boring', 'science is a good hobby'.
(c) *Behaviour*, e.g., 'I would like to be a scientist'.

He found that, once a child had learned these three aspects, they became long-lasting. Formed early in life, they could prove difficult to change once incorporated and overlaid in a child's personality.

Pupils' negative attitudes towards science often stem from the unfavourable attitudes and limited aspirations of their teachers. One remedial teacher wrote, 'It seems a pity that this book only contains materials for remedial reading. Is it because it is not possible to do any science with the lowest ability? I suspect that this is the case.' A biology teacher reported in NARE *Guidelines* No. 3 (1978):

> 'The attitude to mixed ability teaching in science is basically determined by the teachers' view of the subject in terms of their scientific training and is therefore academically rigorous. They have high-level aims which the majority of less-able children will not attain, i.e., the "block" is on before the children ever start.'

Here is evidence of a self-fulfilling prophecy whereby children live down to the teachers' lowest expectations. Several topics in *Match and Mismatch* (1977) explore the effects of attitudes on learning. The book suggests guidelines for teachers' positive action, besides describing behaviours which emerge as being harmful. Checklists are outlined as a way of looking at the opportunities provided in the classroom. They can be used to monitor the development of certain attitudes and behaviours in even the youngest children.

Language

In a study of the language demands of major school subjects, Richards (1978) found that physics, biology and chemistry were the ones most heavily burdened with specialist vocabulary. Language becomes complex when used in any situation geared towards specialist teaching. Pupils need to be helped to acquire the vocabulary and correct phraseology that is appropriate to their development if they are to succeed in science. On the other hand, premature use of a science register of language may become a hindrance to learning. Pupils require adequate time for specialist words to acquire meaning. Many secondary-school teachers still remain unaware that they need to modify the language of their adult world in order to make contact with pupils. They are not the only guilty ones. Difficult terms such as 'evaporate', 'vapour' and 'condense' have been noted in science textbooks for quite young children.

Primary-school teachers have long recognized that children learn by doing and that they use talk to interpret their observations. More recently, there has been a growing awareness in the secondary school of the importance of pupils' talk, and the value of classroom discussion in science lessons. In his helpful book, Carré (1981) poses three questions:

(a) Why should our pupils talk in class?
(b) If they are reluctant to do so, does that give us licence to dominate classroom talk?
(c) Should we concern ourselves with creating a range of activities in science which helps develop the language skills of listening and talking?

He maintains that the search for answers to these questions will tell us important things about how pupils learn the science we try to teach them. Two other publications which discuss these aspects in depth are: *Language in Science*, (ASE, 1979) and the in-service pack entitled *Language in Chemistry* (Scottish Curriculum Development Service, 1980).

111

The Effective Use of Reading (1979) has demonstrated the excessive demands made of children in the lower years of the secondary school by science textbooks currently in use (mean reading level of 13·5 years). Mac-Gibbon (1978) admitted that it is only recently that authors and publishers have begun considering which topics may have to be modified, postponed or deleted, however, scientifically desirable, because most children cannot be expected to cope with the essential language. Another publisher, Hawkins (1980) suggests that in the preparation of more easily read texts, the way ahead lies not simply in strict vocabulary control, but through the introduction of harder words which will enrich a child's vocabulary, provided that their contextual meaning is clear. Even though publishers are now more aware of this major problem, schools are frequently dependent upon teacher-produced worksheets and similar materials whose linguistic level can be just as complex. Much useful guidance is to be found in *Readability in the Classroom* by Harrison (1980) who stresses that improving the readability level for slower readers is only profitable when the course material itself is worthwhile.

The Schools Council Project, *The Development of Writing Abilities, 11–18*, distinguishes three broad categories of function, namely expressive, transactional and poetic. Many science teachers believe that the impersonal style of transactional writing helps pupils to remember what they have done and that it will provide a framework for revision. Writing is seen by them as a way of assessing progress, knowledge and performance. Impersonal writing often creates a barrier for younger children and the less-able, who feel unable to cope with its alien style *and* specialist vocabulary at the same time. Therefore, they attempt very little.

The expressive category of language function is rather like speech recorded on paper and is more typical of the accounts written by these children. Whilst acknowledging the necessity for some for of structure helpful to pupils in writing scientific reports, Carré (1981) sees this as a more effective form of writing. Initially, it encourages pupils to write in a personal way about things they know, using words with which they feel comfortable whilst still including facts, data, scientific terms and ideas. In this way, writing will become part of learning and a means by which children are able to sort out their ideas and absorb knowledge for themselves. Both Carré and Head (1974) collected together examples of pupils' writing in science.

Cognitive development

There is a growing realization that effective science education depends upon developmental stages rather than chronological age. Much of this thinking has been influenced by the basic research of Piaget and his associates (1958), whose experiments involved the solving of scientific problems. Peel (1964, 1966) has shown that their findings provide an invaluable account of pupils' growth of learning and thinking when applied to school subjects.

Everyone is familiar with Piaget's four main stages: sensori-motor; pre-operational; concrete operational and formal operational thought. Each stage extends and builds upon the one before, forming the necessary foundation for the next one. Children pass through these stages in the same order, but at a rate which varies from child to child. 'The principal data of childhood thought are the concrete realities and tangibles of the immediately present situation.' (Peel, 1960)

Science 5–13 (1972) adopts a developmental approach and concludes that, during the stage of concrete operations, children can best be helped by investigations based on experience of their environment. Attitudes of enquiry, objective judgement, personal responsibility, the ability to work independently and to organize one's own work can be established at an early age. This view is supported by such authors as Barber and Hayes (1973) and Showell (1979). *Match and Mismatch* (1977) is also concerned with the age range 5–13. It is an in-service project which aims to help teachers decide about activities and approaches which are best suited to a particular child at a particular stage of his or her development.

Secondary science often requires pupils to pose a hypothesis and then to examine the facts systematically to see if they fit. Even those of average ability have not reached this stage of cognitive development early in their careers and this has obvious implications for their rate of success. Nevertheless, science specialists show reticence in accepting this psychological evidence. In a survey of a large representative sample of the secondary school population, Shayer and Adey (1981) reveal a significant mismatch between pupils' cognitive development and the cognitive demands of the curricula taught in schools. Results also confirm that younger children and less-able pupils are limited to the use of concrete operational thinking. Shayer and Adey have developed *Science Reasoning Tasks* (SRT) which teachers can use to assess the cognitive levels of their pupils. They have also formulated a *Curriculum Analysis Taxonomy* (CAT), helpful to science teachers with no specialized knowledge of Piagetian psychology in analysing the level of difficulty of any science activity. Such analysis can lead to the successful choice of an approach to a topic and to the creation of a balanced curriculum suited to the developmental needs of a particular group.

Content

Establishing a framework for the curriculum

Curriculum 11–16 (1977) suggests that all pupils should leave school with a usable understanding of certain fundamental scientific topics. These can be summarized as:

1. The human body and how it functions.
2. Plant and animal nutrition. Matter and energy cycles.
3. Cells and cell specialization.
4. Multiplication, replication, checks and balances, both in individuals and communities.
5. Inheritance and evolution.
6. The concept of a pure substance. Its properties. Analysis.
7. Metals and non-metals.
8. New substances from old. Synthesis.
9. The significance of analysis and synthesis to the quality of life.
10. Chemical change and energy.
11. Atoms and molecules. Particles more fundamental than atoms. Introduction to the use of formulae and equations.

12. Localized and widely dispersed substances. Man the disperser. Recycling.
13. Uses of energy. What energy can do for matter. How energy is transmitted.

One guiding principle in establishing a framework for the science curriculum and its content must be that it should be applicable to pupils' everyday lives.

In her reappraisal of science education, Prestt (1976) outlines a two-stage framework for the study of science based on the work of Hirst (1965). Prestt contends that it provides a firm basis for knowledge, gives a valid description of science in our society and enables appropriate objectives to be pursued:

Primary stage (5–11)

(a) the development of scientific skills;
(b) beginning an understanding of how the scientist works — testing statements against experience — scientific method;
(c) scientific facts as they arise from the child's experience and interest;
(d) a beginning of simpler scientific concepts.

Secondary stage (11–16)

(e) fuller development of the scientific skills;
(f) increasing experience of using scientific method;
(g) basic scientific facts and concepts arising from their use as illustrative material in (e) and (f);
(h) development of structures relating concepts;
(i) social and economic implications of the application of science;
(j) science as an activity of the community at large.

Different components of the framework can be stressed, depending upon the stage of cognitive development, intellectual ability and interests of the children. For example, in primary schools (a) might be regarded as more important than (d), whereas particular emphasis could be laid on (i) and (j) in some secondary courses. Prestt quotes a detailed study undertaken by the American Association for the Advancement of Science. Its analysis of scientific skills distinguishes the simpler, basic skills from those more complex, or integrated skills, which develop from them. At the primary stage, emphasis must be laid on the basic skills of: observing, communicating, classifying, predicting, inferring, measuring, using numbers and space-time relationships. The integrated skills which develop later are: interpreting data, formulating hypotheses, controlling variables, defining operationally and experimenting. This identification of skills is somewhat similar to that expressed in the broad aims of *Science 5–13* (1972). Such a framework would prove valuable in establishing behavioural objectives for a science course suited to the needs of children with learning difficulties, using the guides discussed earlier in the chapter.

Early years (5–7)

Science with infants is virtually indistinguishable from other normal class-room activities, being primarily concerned with gathering experience. Almost any work or play which involves the exploration of the natural environment results in learning with understanding. The basic skills of science are the infants' natural way of exploring their world. Natural curiosity dictates that they will use these methods with or without our help — but fare more effectively if teachers also recognize these principles and offer guidance and encouragement.

However simple, the information given to young children must be accurate. All studies, even the simplest, should have an aim and a reasonable outcome. Showell (1979) advises that we should never underestimate children's knowledge. They are used to watching television and the amount of information retained, even by the youngest child, can be very surprising.

Middle years (8–13)

Children in this age-range are still building up background experience which will eventually lead to a more structured and analytical approach to science. They still need to explore and learn about the physical environment. Squires (1976) summarizes ideas which are fundamental to science in the middle years under three headings: the nature of earth's materials, forms of energy, and living things. The haphazard selection of concrete activities is not advisable if pupils are to make some sense of the world. 'Interest' and 'usefulness' are two criteria which can be used in choosing areas of study.

The major curriculum projects listed at the end of this chapter provide admirable source material for 5–13 science. In many instances, teachers will find it necessary to manufacture their own learning materials. Although a time-consuming process, it has the advantage of giving closer control over linguistic and cognitive levels.

Not long ago, an in-service course for remedial advisory teachers addressed itself to the task of formulating a set of criteria which could be used in assessing the potential value of published resources:

Presentation

(a) The overall impact and attractiveness of the format should motivate children to explore the text further.
(b) Diagrams need to be clearly drawn and meaningfully labelled. Diagrams and pictures should be well positioned in order to give maximum assistance in decoding the text.
(c) The use of coloured illustrations or print should not make a page visually confusing.
(d) Size and clarity of print are important, also the spaces between words and lines. Pages should not be overloaded with text.

Content

(a) What knowledge and experience does the author assume that children possess prior to reading the text?
(b) What is its level of conceptual difficulty?

(c) Is the information accurate?
(d) Will children be able to understand the outcome of a particular section?

Communication

(a) Preferably, the reading level of the materials should enable them to be used by poor readers. Alternatively, the materials should be capable of adaptation.
(b) Information should be clearly and simply expressed.
(c) Is there a simple glossary explaining scientific terms?

Practical

(a) Do the materials fit in with the scheme?
(b) Are they durable?
(c) Do they lend themselves to easy storage and retrieval?
(d) Taking all factors into consideration, are they value for money?

Older pupils (15–16)

Curriculum planning for low-achievers in this age group has its difficulties. Classes tend to include not only the less-able, but also more-able pupils who are poorly motivated, sometimes aggressive and frequently disillusioned.

The ways in which science teachers attempt to overcome these problems are exemplified by Clegg and Morley (1980), who developed a course for 14–16-year-old low-achievers in an urban comprehensive school. Amongst their criteria, the syllabus had to: be interesting and demonstrably of use to the pupils; have a practical basis; provide a sense of achievement; carry a certain prestige, i.e., not be regarded as a 'dumping ground' for those who could not manage any other science course; embrace all branches of science; help to improve literacy skills; and recognize the range of interests and abilities of the pupils.

Modules were designed to last for approximately half a term, although each pupil was allowed to carry a project to its natural conclusion. There was equal access to specialist equipment. Topics included:

astronomy	corrosion	detergents
dyestuffs	electronics	evolution
food	genetics	paper
photography	plastics	pollution
pond life	taxidermy	weather studies

Wherever possible, pupils were involved in making something, so that the end product was not simply a written account but consisted of concrete objects: photographs, a stuffed animal, a sectioned engine, and so forth.

Peck and Williams (1978) also selected topics seen by pupils to be of interest and relevance, at the same time stressing the underlying objectives of the course.

Both projects found that pupils enjoyed their work. This resulted in an encouraging improvement in motivation, behaviour and attendance. Those who entered for a CSE examination gained a higher grade than would have been likely in a more conventional course. The courses also attracted able pupils who wanted a relaxation from more rigorous academic programmes.

116

It was generally felt that pupils left school with a greater awareness of the scientific world and some recognition of their achievements in science.

Kershaw (1978) also outlines alternative forms of modular courses. In recent years, three major projects have published resources which can be utilized: *LAMP*, *Open Science* and *Science at Work*.

Future perspectives

1. If 'science for all' is to be successfully implemented, increased provision of in-service education must be regarded as an urgent necessity, whatever the financial stringencies. Primary-school teachers require courses which will give them a sound background for teaching science to younger children. Non-specialists responsible for science with less-able pupils in the 11–16 age-range would benefit from courses geared to special curricular needs. In line with the recommendations of *Education in Schools* (1977), science staff need to improve their professional competence to recognize pupils' learning difficulties and to 'counter them as far as possible'.
2. There is scope for science specialists to become more involved with language across the curriculum (*A Language for Life*, 138). Without becoming teachers of English, it is suggested that they could enhance pupils' understanding of scientific knowledge by developing their confidence and skills in talking, reading and writing.
3. Science teachers and remedial specialists need to work together more closely in the future. The curricular expertise of the subject teacher will ensure a balance when courses for low achievers are planned. Remedial teachers have a deeper understanding of child development, expertise in identifying children's learning difficulties and skill in adapting curriculum materials to special educational requirements. Therefore, they can be of help to each other. Team teaching arrangements are enhanced when a remedial teacher is included among the personnel.
4. Curriculum projects have provided an abundance of resource materials, not all of which are suited to the needs of children with learning difficulties. Considerable advantages would accrue if science and remedial teachers would set up local groups to select, evaluate, adapt and match appropriate resources to pupils' interests and learning requirements.
5. The value of practical work in maintaining a high level of motivation amongst pupils was evident in *Aspects of Secondary Education in England* (1979, para. 12.10), and enjoyment of practical science was frequently mentioned by pupils. Future planning should ensure that they all have equal opportunity to use specialist facilities during science lessons. The motivational value of courses linked with applied sciences, technology and environmental studies should not be underestimated, especially for the 14–16 age-group.
6. Very shortly, the Association for Science Education, in liaison with the Schools Council, will undertake a rigorous appraisal of all science teaching. It is hoped that researchers will give as much emphasis to the curricular needs of children with learning difficulties as they do to those of their more able peers.

In a technological age, our lives are inextricably enmeshed with the handiwork of scientific ingenuity. Science can no longer be limited to what happens in science lessons, for it is one way in which we can relate to our everyday surroundings. Therefore, science curricula must encourage *every* child's sense of wonder, healthy curiosity and enthusiasm for discovering his or her physical environment.

References and further reading

Association for Science Education, *Language in Science*, Study Series No.16., 1979.

Association for Science Education, *Education Through Science*, 1981.

Barber, H. M. E. and Hayes, J. Y., *Exploring the Physical World with Children of 5 to 9*, Dent, 1973.

Brennan, W. K., *Curricular Needs of Slow Learners*, Schools Council Working Paper 63, Evans/Methuen, 1979.

Bullock, Lord (Chairman), *A Language for Life*, HMSO, 1975.

Carré, C., *Language Teaching and Learning 4, Science*, Ward Lock Educational, 1981.

Carré, C. and Head, J. (eds), *Through the Eyes of the Pupil*, Science Teacher Education Project, McGraw-Hill, 1974.

Clegg, A. S. and Morley, M. (1980), 'Applied science — a course for pupils of low educational achievement' in the *School Science Review* 61, 216.

DES, *Education in Schools: A Consultative Document*, HMSO, 1977.

DES, *Curriculum 11–16*, HMSO, 1977.

DES, *Primary Education in England*, HMSO, 1978.

DES, *Aspects of Secondary Education in England*, HMSO, 1979.

DES, *A View of the Curriculum, HMI Series: Matters for Discussion*, 11, HMSO, 1980.

DES, *The School Curriculum*, HMSO, 1981.

Harlen, W. *et al.*, *Raising Questions*, Leader's Guide to *Match and Mismatch*, Schools Council *Progress in Learning Science Project*, Oliver and Boyd, 1977.

Harrison, C., *Readability in the Classroom*, Cambridge University Press, 1980.

Hawkins, R. (1980), 'How can publishers help?' in *Remedial Education*, Vol. 15, No. 2.

Hirst, P. H., *Philosophical Analysis and Education*, Routledge and Kegan Paul, 1965.

Inhelder, B. and Piaget, J., *The Growth of Logical Thinking from Childhood to Adolescence*, Routledge and Kegan Paul, 1958.

Kershaw, I. L., 'Science 14–16' in Hinson, M. (ed.) *Encouraging Results*, Macdonald Educational, 1978.

Lunzer, E. and Gardner, K., *The Effective Use of Reading*, Heinemann, 1979.

MacGibbon, H. (1978), 'A publisher's view' (paper presented at a COSTA/ EPC conference: 'School Books, Their Language, Presentation and Use').

National Association for Remedial Education, *Mixed Ability Teaching in Middle and Secondary Schools, Guidelines* No 3, 1978.

Newton, D. P. (1975), 'Attitudes to science' in the *School Science Review*, 47, 199.

Peck, M. J. and Williams, I. P. (1978), 'Science for the least able pupils leading to a CSE qualification' in the *School Science Review*, 60, 221.

Peel, E. A., *The Pupil's Thinking*, Oldbourne, 1960.

Peel, E. A. (1964), 'Learning and thinking in the school situation' in the *Journal of Resources for Science Teaching*, Vol. 2.

Peel, E. A. (1966), 'A study in the judgements of adolescent pupils' in the *British Journal of Educational Psychology*, Vol. 36.

Prestt, B. (1976), 'Science Education — a reappraisal', Part 1, *School Science Review*, 57, 201; Part 2, *School Science Review*, 58, 203.

Richards, J., *Classroom Language: What Sort?*, Allen and Unwin, 1978.

Schofield, R. (1969), editorial in the *School Science Review*, 51, 174.

Schools Council, *With Objectives in Mind, Science 5–13* Teacher's Guide, Macdonald Educational, 1972.

Schools Council, *Early Experiences, Science 5–13*, Macdonald Educational, 1972.

Schools Council, *The Practical Curriculum*, Working Paper 70, Methuen Educational, 1981.

Scottish Curriculum Development Service (1980), *Language in Chemistry*, Dundee College of Education, Dundee DD5 1NY.

Shayer, M. and Adey, P., *Towards a Science of Science Teaching*, Heinemann, 1981.

Showell, R., *Teaching Science to Infants*, Ward Lock Educational, 1979.

Squires, A., *Science in the Middle Years*, Study Series No. 6, Association for Science Education, 1976.

Warnock, M. (Chairman), *Special Educational Needs*, Report of the Committee of Enquiry into the Education of Handicapped Children and Young People, HMSO, 1978.

Watts, S., 'Children writing' in *Language in Science*, Association for Science Education, 1980.

Wheeler, D. K., *The Curriculum Process*, Hodder and Stoughton, 1967.

The following are articles in *Remedial Education* concerned with science for children with learning difficulties:

Wood, J. W. (1975), 'Curriculum design for ROSLA pupils — Part 2. A worksheet-based science course', *Remedial Education*, Vol. 10, No. 2.

Hinson, M. (1976), 'Do they break the glassware?' *Remedial Education*, Vol. 11, No. 1.

Beith, M. (1977), 'Science: its contribution to an integrated topic with a secondary remedial class', *Remedial Education*, Vol. 12, No. 1.

Kellington, S. H. and Mitchell, A. C. (1978), 'Integrated science for the less-able', *Remedial Education*, Vol. 13, No. 3.

Senior, P. H. (1979), 'Science for slow learners: some personal observations', *Remedial Education*, Vol. 14, No. 3.

Resources

Centre Science, Hart-Davis.
Insight to Science, Addison-Wesley.
Nuffield Combined Science, Themes for the Middle Years, Longman.

Science 5–13, together with *Learning Through Science*, Macdonald Educational.
Science Horizons, Globe Educational.
Steps in Science, Ward Lock Educational.
Teaching Primary Science, Macdonald Educational.
LAMP (Less Academically Motivated Pupils), Association for Science Education.
Open Science, Hart-Davis and Hutchinson.
Science at Work, Addison-Wesley.

9

Geography

MICHAEL WILLIAMS

Geography in England and Wales has a weak base in most primary schools, an established position in the early years in secondary schools, and stands in the forefront of the options available in the middle years of secondary schooling. Geography is taught either as a separate subject or as a constituent part of correlated or integrated courses to virtually all pupils at some time in their school career. When faced with pupils who have learning difficulties in geography, the inexperienced teacher commonly receives this working formula: keep your talking to a minimum; keep them active; try to capture their interest; tune in to their imagination and curiosity; and use a variety of approaches. At a more sophisticated level of pedagogical guidance this could be translated as: first of all, diagnose the pupil's learning difficulties. Afterwards introduce individualized, resource-based enquiry methods to studies which are both close to the learner's experience and appropriate to his or her level of understanding.

In this chapter, I propose to place this rule-of-thumb advice into the context of changes which are taking place in classroom geography, in the aims, content, methods of teaching and techniques of assessment employed in the subject. Reference will be made to the debate about the whole curriculum and the part played by geography teachers in that debate.

Geography in the curriculum

1. The early years

In a handbook published by the Geographical Association (Mills, 1981) a teacher, Melanie Harvey, summarizes the contribution which geography makes to the education of pupils in infant and first schools (5–7 year-olds). She points out that young children's investigations result from their innate curiosity. Their attempts to make sense of the world can be seen as a desire to order their environment. Geography can help young children in developing their abilities to observe, select, describe, measure, interview, assess and record. It enables them to present their findings in a variety of ways and to evaluate them. Harvey also stresses that language development is assisted by their attempts to describe and explain phenomena and through their discussion of personal reactions. Geography can extend beyond a description of places by encouraging a more personal response. It can also help to develop a more realistic understanding of the world and possibly counteract false impressions gained from the media.

'At the infant and first stage, children tend to accept what they are told;

they are very open and trusting. This means that value-laden topics such as birth, life and death, and the multicultural community in which they live can be discussed without inhibition. If they can be encouraged to seek both similarities and reasons for differences, this may contribute to the development of positive and friendly attitudes towards all people, including those from other cultures.'

Should the general reader conclude that the ideas and suggestions embodied in this list are over-optimistic and pitched at too high a level, then the author's subsequent paragraphs on vocabulary and mapwork will be more reassuring. Thus reference is made to the infant's difficulties of coping with words relating to position and location — up, down, over, under, on top, beside, next to, behind, etc. Teachers are recommended to use simple games and books, the singing of nursery rhymes and lessons in PE to overcome these spatial difficulties.

With regard to mapwork, it is suggested that this can be introduced at a simple level by posing such questions as 'How will Father Christmas know which is your stocking? Draw him a plan to go with your letter.' Melanie Harvey proceeds to three detailed sets of suggestions for topic work, outlining a study of transport, which includes mathematical work, with a reception class; a study of homes with six-year-olds, in which creative artwork is an element; and the study of pollution by seven-year-olds.

This account alerts us to the potential of geography for satisfying curiosity and arousing the interest of young children in their immediate environment. It highlights problems associated with language development and mapwork, problems which persist through to the time when pupils leave secondary schools, to which we shall return later in this chapter.

2. The primary years

The most authoritative recent source of information on primary-school geography teaching is the report *Primary Education in England* (1978). HM Inspectors' conclusions are based on evidence derived from 542 schools during the period 1975 to 1977. Although reference was made to good geographical work being carried out in some schools, criticism was expressed of two fundamental aspects: 'in the majority, essential ideas and skills were seldom given sufficient attention', and reference was made to 'the lack of progression and the amount of repetition in the work in geography'. This is in marked contrast to the optimism of the section (paras 635–646) on geography in the Plowden Report written a decade earlier (Central Advisory Council, 1966). The same optimistic spirit can be detected in a document (Geographical Association, 1981) written as part of the response to DES proposals for the school curriculum (DES, 1980):

'By the age of eleven, pupils should have been introduced to the principal aspects of the physical environment (weather and surface features), patterns of settlement, dominant occupations and forms of transport, and the leisure and recreational facilities of their home areas. They should also have been introduced to the variety of environments in which people live, both at home and overseas. In these latter studies teachers will seek to avoid any stereotyping of groups and nations and they and their pupils should have access to accurate, reliable and up-to-date sources of information.'

3. *The secondary-school years*

It is difficult to write authoritative generalizations about the place of geography in the curricula of secondary schools. For those pupils preparing for external examinations at ages 16 and 18, some order may be detected, but for the rest, and especially for non-examination pupils, there is a considerable variety in course provision. Guidelines for syllabus construction in geography have been published as books (e.g., Graves, 1979 and 1980, Marsden, 1976) and articles in the journal *Teaching Geography*. Further, as part of the Great Debate, the Geographical Association prepared curriculum papers (1977 and 1981) in response to requests from the DES and HMI, also the geographers in HMI have produced their own documents (1978 and 1981).

Most discussions of the place of geography in secondary education begin with an account of the changes which have taken place in the nature of the subject at university level. Simplistically, this may be seen as a shift from descriptive and regional approaches through to logical positivist and humanistic approaches to the study of geography. For the secondary-school teacher, this has meant

'a greater emphasis on the identification and explanation of significant spatial patterns, processes and relationships, both physical and human; a more rigorous analysis of man/environment relationships; a more scientific approach to explanation which may involve both generalization and prediction; a much greater concern with social issues and problems, for example, those of the inner areas of large cities and the siting of activities which may create disturbance, environmental pollution and social conflict; a growing interest in the way decisions are made concerning the location of certain phenomena.' (HMI, 1981)

Certainly, teachers of subjects other than geography who were taught geography before the mid-1970s will find in school syllabuses, examination papers and curriculum resources evidence of these changes. In particular, the publications stemming from the Schools Council geography projects (*Geography for the Young School Leaver, Geography 14–18* and *Geography 16–19*) show in detail the ways in which new ideas, content and teaching methods can be applied.

Throughout the changes taking place in the nature of the subject, the special contributions of geography to children in schools remain largely the same as they have been for more than fifty years. These have been summarized in a Geographical Association publication (1981) as graphicacy, world knowledge, international understanding and environmental awareness.

In introducing new approaches to traditional courses, geography teachers have been encouraged to evaluate, clarify and specify their aims, content, methods of teaching and techniques of examining. This has led to much discussion about the pupils' acquisition of knowledge, attitudes and skills in geography, and these have been explored in the context of a structure which increasingly takes account of themes, problems, places and concepts viewed at the following scales: 'micro' (local), 'meso' (regional, national and continental) and 'macro' (global) scales. These dimensions of curriculum planning in geography can be illustrated as a diagram (figure 4).

This diagram should help the non-specialist to understand the variety which is evident in geography syllabuses. Within the subject, there is a continuing discussion about the relationship between physical and human aspects and the linkage between traditional and modern emphases to the study. The teacher commences his or her career with these as part of a classroom personality, and to them must be added a variety of classroom approaches to teaching and learning. The diagram illustrates the range within which substantive choices must be made. Given the range, it is not surprising to find in any one school a mixture of 'geographies', with each teacher bringing unique approaches to the overall picture.

Running through the picture are two continuing threads evident in the learning difficulties experienced by pupils in geography: problems associated with *graphicacy* and *language*. These exist at all levels, from the primary school to the sixth form, and in all classes. In geography they are inescapable, though teachers vary in their ability to recognize the kind and significance of the problems and they differ in the solutions they adopt.

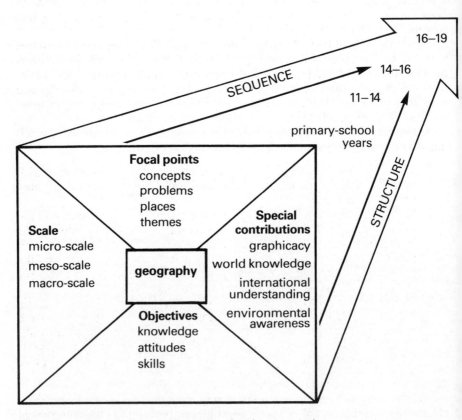

Fig. 4 Dimensions of curriculum planning in geography.

124

Graphicacy

The word graphicacy has been defined by Balchin (1972), the geographer who popularized the term, as 'the communication of spatial information that cannot be conveyed adequately by verbal or numerical means'.

Spatial information lies at the heart of classroom geography. It would be impossible to conceive of geography lessons which did not incorporate maps, photographs and diagrams presented in a variety of forms for children to study and use. Indeed, so commonplace are graphic materials in geography classrooms that the problems encountered by pupils working with them have frequently been overlooked.

In recent years, painstaking and thoughtful research has demonstrated that maps and photographs present many different problems for young learners and, unless teachers can cope with them, pupils are unlikely to achieve a great deal of geographical learning. For a detailed consideration of the learning problems associated with graphicacy, the reader is advised to turn to the publications of Boardman (1976 and 1979), Catling (1979, 1980, and 1981), Gerber (1981a and 1981b) and Sandford (1972 and 1978). Their studies have focused on maps and aerial photographs. They draw our attention to the range of skills required in the study of maps and the distinctions between map reading, map drawing, map interpretation and map use for problem solving.

That the introduction of maps into primary-school classrooms requires very careful planning is evident from Catling (1981), who lists nine aspects of map understanding: position and orientation, map symbols, map scale, map perspective, map purpose, map style, map drawing, map reading and map interpretation. He also shows how these may be developed in a sequential way for pupils from five to thirteen years of age.

Boardman (1979) concluded that the map-reading skills can be divided into three main groups according to their degree of difficulty.

1. The skills that appeared to be the most developed were those which involved judging the height of the land, following a route on the map and giving direction.
2. Skills that were less developed were the estimation of distance and the orientation of the map and the photograph. Transferring information from an OS map to a sketch map and visualizing the landscape also fell into this category, while identification of features on the map and the photograph appeared in this category for the O-level group only. For the other two groups, this appeared in the third category.
3. Skills that proved to be the least well developed included those relating features on OS maps to cross-sections. Descriptions of areas on the map or photograph and map interpretation also proved to be difficult. Caution must be used when including the last category of map interpretation, for many pupils did not complete the section of the questionnaire dealing with map interpretation.

What emerges from these studies is that map-reading is extremely complicated, requiring in the map reader literary competence and numerical ability. Children who have difficulty in reading text or working with simple mathematical concepts are certain to encounter difficulties with maps. To the difficulties of reading must be added the problems associated with scanning maps to find words and symbols, with converting words and symbols into images, with interpreting the association of lines, points and area signs presented in qualitative and quantitative forms.

For maps to come alive, pupils ought to engage in fieldwork which can begin, as Gerber (1981a) has demonstrated, in the school playground and continue further away from the school. Photographs, ground and aerial, should be introduced carefully, and lessons devoted to studying them in isolation and alongside maps. Pupils vary in their visual perception and teachers must be sensitive to these variations. Transforming information from maps to photographs and diagrams and to real landscapes assumes skills that must be acquired systematically. Only through the sequential structuring of exercises will pupils acquire these skills.

Certain publications have taken into account studies in graphicacy, and teachers with little background in geography teaching will find them invaluable as guides to appropriate content and exercises for young pupils. For older pupils the publications stemming from the Schools Council *Geography for the Young School Leaver* (*GYSL*) project are particularly relevant. A recent publication of the Geographical Association (Boardman, 1981) has focused on teaching selected *GYSL* topics to children with learning difficulties.

In the introductory chapter, Boardman picks out five strands which run through the seven studies in the booklet:

(a) the need to ensure appropriate reading levels in teaching materials;
(b) the need to provide practice in basic mathematical skills;
(c) the need for first-hand experience of the environment;
(d) the need to offer alternatives to written work, and
(e) the need to interest and motivate pupils.

Starting from a conventional local study of the urban environment, which focuses heavily on the careful description of houses, streets and urban zones, the reader is taken through detailed and very practical exercises on environmental evaluation, traffic enumeration and a study of leisure provision in a city. While these may be seen as mainstream geographical activities in classrooms, the last three studies are more novel. They focus on the playing of simple geographical games — 'Commuto' and 'Pick a Spot' — which focus on a city on the one hand, and a seaside resort on the other; changing attitudes and values in a study of third world problems, and the use of music and songs to arouse pupils' interests.

Language

Whereas graphicacy may be of special interest to geography teachers, language is a common interest of all teachers. Since the publication of the Bullock Report (1975) the expression 'language across the curriculum' has figured prominently in educational publications, especially those associated with the Great Debate about the curriculum. The applications of some of the guidelines derived from these publications to the teaching of geography has been attempted in a recent report (Williams, 1981) and in the introduction to it we read, 'In their geography lessons pupils talk, listen, read, write and think, and so do their teachers. The *language environment* of each classroom is essential to the teaching that goes on: teachers as well as pupils should learn geography together.'

In considering talking, writing and reading by teachers and pupils in geography lessons, we must acknowledge the difficulty of distinguishing between their general features and those that are specifically geographical. Geography lessons may be regarded as simply a change of context. However the claim which geography teachers make, that geography helps pupils to make sense of their world, points to the need for teachers to understand their pupils' private worlds and the way they perceive them. This simple assertion can be illustrated by two different ways of viewing geography.

View A

In the first view, the pupil is seen to be distanced from the world by the intervention of the subject, geography, mediated by the teacher. The logic of this is that only part of the world is studied by geographers and geography teachers select from the field those features which are considered appropriate for study by the pupil. The language by which the world is communicated to the child comes from the subject and from the teacher. In this view, the language of geography is seen to be distinguished by technical terms, sometimes described pejoratively as jargon. To understand geography, the pupil needs to understand the meanings of technical terms which contribute to the structure of geographical concepts.

We can anticipate many pupils experiencing difficulty in understanding and using the terms and associated concepts. It can be appreciated that some pupils will find that the language of geography makes the world a difficult place to understand and the subject may, if taught in this manner, lose its value in the overall education of pupils.

View B

A contrasting view of the subject is one where the pupil is seen to be in the world which he or she seeks to understand. In this search the teacher will contribute by trying to make sense of it in the pupil's own private terms. The language by which visual, tactile and other sensory experience of the world is assimilated is likely to be the vernacular of the pupil. This view suggests that the child turns to the teacher for help when difficulties are experienced and the teacher, as a geography teacher, then turns to the subject of geography for assistance. This is a useful reminder that geography is rooted in the real world of the child's experience and that there are several ways by which the teacher and the pupils may study it. It is in this view of geography-teaching that the Bullock assertion — 'language has a heuristic function: that is to say a child can learn by talking and writing as certainly as he can by listening and reading' — has particular relevance.

Listening to pupils talking about their world gives teachers insight into the meaning of the world for the pupils. It is through recorded speech that teachers can understand the depth and breadth of pupils' learning in geography. As a subject in school, geography provides opportunities for informed

127

talk in such activities as role-playing in games and simulations, in formal and informal discussions of local issues experienced at first-hand, and global issues seen through television programmes, books, comics and other media. In geography classrooms where teachers are aware of the gains from purposeful and orderly talk by pupils, the teachers are likely to be better informed about the difficulties encountered by slow learners. By creating situations where 'geographical talk' is normal, the sensitive teacher is likely to assist children with learning difficulties in giving expression to their thoughts, providing them with opportunities to describe their worlds. Such opportunities allow the teacher to intervene to encourage and praise good thinking and correct misapprehensions and misunderstandings.

Formal writing by the pupils is more commonplace than talking in geography lessons. Evidence shows that this writing often takes the form of responses to questions on teacher-prepared worksheets.

Worksheets

Perhaps the most important aspect of worksheets is the opportunity which they create for each teacher to teach in his or her own personal style, utilizing ideas or methods which are not usually found in conventional textbooks. *Language Teaching and Learning in Geography* (Williams, 1981) reminds us that worksheets most commonly require either a written or drawn response. 'Hardly any worksheets ask the child to discuss the answer with a neighbour, or with a group, or to verbalize the answer to the class or the teacher. Overwhelmingly, too, the answer is intended for the teacher and is expected to be written in a formal and impersonal style. The kinds of problems set on worksheets are usually 'well-formed', that is, having a clearly demonstrated solution.'

The worksheet has found its way into geography classrooms despite the abundance of geography textbooks available from publishers. Sometimes the worksheets supplement the textbook, sometimes they replace it. For many geography teachers, the worksheet is their response to the need to cope with the problems of teaching mixed-ability classes in comprehensive schools. Here the worksheet is seen as an attempt to permit individuals to work in their own way at their own pace, and it is not uncommon to find worksheets structured so that extra tasks are provided for the able, quicker learners and simpler tasks are set for the less able, slower learners. There is a real danger in geography that the latter will find themselves excluded from tasks requiring literary and numerical skills and instead they will be expected to do little more than copy, trace, draw and shade. It is too easy for geography teachers to divide pupils into three simple categories — gifted, average and less-able — and to plan their lessons accordingly.

Seeking guidance

For some geography teachers, the problems of the less-able lie at the door of the English department, defined as being responsible for improving reading and writing skills, and the mathematics department, responsible for improving numerical skills — assuming, of course, that remedial specialists are unavailable.

Nevertheless, teachers are generally aware that the less-able do not constitute a simple, single category. What geography teachers lack is clear evidence from research of the precise kinds of difficulties pupils experience in learning geography, together with explanations of the difficulties and guidance as to methods of remedying the most common problems. Books on methods of teaching geography are directed at some notional 'normal' teacher engaged in teaching 'normal' pupils. Geography teachers experience difficulty in finding positive guidance on how to teach their subject to children with learning difficulties.

Some assistance is available in articles by teachers recounting their own experiences. Three examples of recent articles are worth considering for the kind of advice they contain.

Kemp (1979) pinpointed the following strengths of the less-able pupil in geography: 'enthusiasm when motivated, good response to imaginative visual materials and ability in straightforward practical tasks'. The weaknesses were: 'short concentration span, poor comprehension skills, poor writing skills, little development of analytical skills and hesitant grasp of abstract concepts'. This led him to propose five teaching strategies:

'Avoid abstract concepts — base your ideas on concrete examples and use visuals to add substance.

Avoid overuse of purely written text — a strong link between written text and visual material is very important.

Avoid long, unbroken sentences of work — divide the work into limited objectives that contribute to an understanding of the whole.

Avoid material that is unstructured — in order to encourage analytical skills, pupils must be put into a position from which they can be expected to draw sensible conclusions; this is most effectively achieved by giving the work a well-defined structure.

Avoid prolonged periods when the pupil is not involved in practical tasks — imaginative, but straightforward practical tasks add to pupils' involvement and satisfaction and can be used to overcome analytical weaknesses.'

Booth (1980), writing about her low-ability pupils in a comprehensive secondary school, pointed to pupils' lack of interest and motivation, their low level of basic skills and their poor attitude to work in geography. After a discussion of appropriate teaching methods for teaching less-able pupils, she drew up two lists of activities which I have summarized in a table (figure 5) for the purposes of this chapter.

More recently, Pearce (1980) has described how he set about designing and teaching a new geography syllabus for 11–13 year-old pupils in mixed-ability groups. He exemplified his approach by quoting from a module on *Journeys between Towns* taken from a unit *Traffic in Networks*:

'1. It is "personalized" because it contains instructions, structured questions and open-ended tasks, so allowing the child to follow the learning route at his/her own pace in our mixed-ability setting.
2. It exposes the pupil to a variety of written, graphed and mapped resource materials.

Activities which seem to work with lower-ability children	Activities which do not work with lower-ability children
1. A short, clear snappy talk from the teacher to introduce the lesson	1. Prolonged teacher talk
2. Well-controlled class questioning and discussion (maximum ten minutes)	2. Dictation of notes
3. Class answering structured questions from the blackboard following on from discussion	3. Pupils reading large section of writing to themselves
4. Most non-writing activities (e.g., graph-drawing, statistical work, sketching, interpreting photographs, slides, etc., note-taking and worksheets based on television or movie films)	4. Unstructured written work
5. Listening to a teacher reading aloud	5. Listening to tape recordings
6. Map-work of all kinds	6. Making notes from books
7. Fieldwork	7. Writing up fieldwork
8. Solving problems	
9. Most work based on the local environment	
10. Worksheets which have a variety of activities	
11. Producing work for wall display	
12. Simulation exercises	
13. Role play	

Fig. 5 Dos and don'ts with lower-ability children: a summary of advice from Booth (1980).

3. It introduces the "primary concepts" of volume, distance, scale, number, sets, differentiation.
4. It introduces and reintroduces such "ideas" as networks, nodal points, traffic flow volumes.
5. It introduces such key "generalizations" as traffic congestion at nodal points in networks, the improvement of a network in detouring, the effects of re-routing on land use.
6. It aims to teach a number of geographical "skills" through activity rather than passive learning:
   thinking skills such as the analysis and transformation of statistics presented in tabular or graph form;
   the interpretation of traffic flow and land use maps and written material

study skills such as the proper use and retrieval of data from a variety
of resources;

communication skills such as the drawing of graphs and maps.

7. It introduces such "issue-based material" as the impact of a route
improvement scheme upon the local community.'

Pearce found that while children found his approach to geography enjoyable, it was necessary for him to devise firm monitoring strategies. He points
out that good habits of study, such as self-discipline, organization of approach, co-operative use of resources, intelligent reading of the instructions,
self-reliance and correct thinking procedures have to be taught.

In these three examples we find the kind of advice handed on by experienced geography teachers to others. To a large extent, the advice consists of
a series of strategies for coping, techniques of class management and the
organization of subject matter to enable the teacher confronted by thirty
pupils to achieve some progress for some pupils some of the time. What is
lacking in these accounts is an attempt to diagnose the learning difficulties
experienced by the pupils. Judgements are made on the general difficulties
they have, but what is lacking is an explanation for some of the more common
difficulties, and guidance on the most appropriate approaches to meet the
individual needs of pupils. The focus is upon the *teaching* difficulties of
teachers and how to resolve these rather than upon the *learning* difficulties
of *pupils* and how these may be reduced.

Teachers' accounts of their own classroom practice frequently distinguish
between those pupils who show no interest in learning geography and those
who are keen to learn but have difficulty in doing so. Geography teachers
are fortunate in having a variety of teaching methods and subject matter on
which to draw to motivate pupils. Watching films and television programmes,
field excursions, puzzles, games and simulations, drawing maps and pictures,
writing and doing sums are all part of the repertoire of the geography teacher.

Shifting the debate

How can this shift be achieved? Class teachers in primary schools and geography specialists in secondary schools are all too aware of the presence of
children with learning difficulties in their lessons. They appear to be relatively
unsuccessful in diagnosing the particular difficulties of individual children.
When they become more competent, they will be able to design appropriate
study programmes which match the needs of individuals. Changes need to
be initiated at three main levels: student teachers, assistant teachers and
heads of department in secondary schools.

Student teachers

There are two important balances which must be kept in the foreground for
student teachers: the balance in teaching practice between the teachers'
actual teaching and pupils' learning; and the balance between planning curricula for pupil success in examinations and curricula for non-examinees.
While the latter is seen to be most relevant in the secondary school, it also
has implications for the primary school.

Geography tutors in teacher education departments should strive to find

131

ways of involving educational psychologists and remedial education specialists in their geography curriculum courses in order to alert their students to
current principles and good practice in teaching children with learning difficulties. Through this, the interest of learning specialists may focus precisely
upon the ways in which pupils learn geography. It is unlikely that geography
tutors will be specialists either in primary education or in remedial education.
They will require the support of colleagues with experience in these areas to
improve the competence of their geography students.

Assistant teachers

Assistant teachers in secondary schools will find no shortage of authoritative
advice and guidance on the principles and practice of curriculum planning in
geography. There is, as has already been noted, a wide variety of books,
materials and journals, all of which are grounded in classroom experience.
There is a danger that the particular needs of individual pupils might be lost,
because they usually tend to focus on teaching strategies which originate
from curriculum planning models of an 'objectives–content–method–assessment' type.

Assistant teachers in primary and secondary schools need support both
from within and outside their schools. Within schools, the geography specialist and primary-school teacher require accurate and objective information
about the pupils they teach and guidance as to the ways in which they can
utilize such information.

Geography teachers do detect pupils who experience learning difficulties
in their lessons. They need to know more about the reasons why pupils have
these difficulties, together with more knowledge about strategies which have
proved successful with similar children. Teachers are unlikely to become
better informed without a deliberate attempt by others to provide information. Teachers from different subjects need to meet frequently in order to
exchange information about individual pupils, also to keep accurate records
which are available for consultation. They need access to experts from remedial departments to guide them in good practice. Detailed studies which
relate specifically to the learning experiences of individual pupils should lie
at the heart of school-based in-service activities. These changes do assume
that time and expertise is available in abundance, and this is unrealistic in
the schools of today. Increasingly, therefore, changes are likely to be initiated
from outside the schools.

We must emphasize that such outside expertise starts with the disadvantage of being distanced from teachers' immediate classroom problems. Nevertheless, there is evidence from LEAs with well-developed support services
that classroom teachers can benefit from the sensitive guidance provided by
specialist teachers who visit schools or provide in-service courses and work-
shops on basic skills in language and numeracy.

There is a need for much closer collaboration between geography and
remedial specialists within local authority advisory services. Unfortunately,
not all local education authorities employ specialist geography advisers and
many have insufficient remedial educationists. Help must therefore come
from other sources, such as the Geographical Association. However, much

more needs to be done to gather information and make it available in a suitable form for members to benefit from it.

Teachers' associations involved with subject specialists and special educational needs would benefit from closer collaboration at local, regional and national levels. Through individual associations, it should be possible to gather and disseminate evidence of good practice in teaching geography to children with learning difficulties. Associations have the potential for facilitating this, especially if they can engage in collaborative ventures such as conferences, courses, working parties and publications.

Heads of geography departments

One of the principal responsibilities of heads of geography departments in secondary schools is to assist in the formulation of whole-school policies for helping children with learning difficulties and the application of these within the geography department. Many geography departments meet formally to discuss their work. All such meetings should have 'learning difficulties of pupils' on their agendas. Not only does this alert all teachers to the importance of the problems, but it also contributes to exchanges of information about individual pupils and teaching strategies tried by teachers. The problems are less likely to be neglected if the teachers review their courses and resources in this way. The important message which the head of geography department needs to carry to all of the teachers in that department is that they are all teachers of children with learning difficulties and must regard themselves, to some extent, as remedial specialists.

References

Balchin, W. G. (1972), 'Graphicacy' in *Geography*, Vol. 57, Pt 3.

Boardman, D. J. (1976), 'Graphicacy in the curriculum' in the *Educational Review*, Vol. 28, No. 2.

Boardman, D. J., *Reading Ordnance Survey Maps: Some Problems of Graphicacy*, Teaching Research Unit, University of Birmingham, 1979.

Boardman, D. J. (ed.), *GYSL with the Disadvantaged*, Geographical Association, 1981.

Booth, M. (1980), 'Teaching geography to lower ability children' in *Teaching Geography*, Vol. 5, No. 3.

Bullock, Lord (Chairman), *A Language for Life*, HMSO, 1975.

Catling, S. J. (1979), 'Maps and cognitive maps: the young child's perception' in *Geography*, Vol. 64, Pt. 4.

Catling, S. J. (1980), 'Map use and objectives for map learning' in *Teaching Geography*, Vol. 6, No. 1.

Catling, S. J., 'Using maps and aerial photographs', in Mills (ed.) *Geographical Work in Primary Schools*, Geographical Association, 1981.

DES, *Primary Education in England*, HMSO, 1978.

DES, *A Framework for the School Curriculum*, HMSO, 1980.

DES (1978), 'Geography in the School Curriculum' in *Teaching Geography*, Vol. 4, No. 2.

DES, *Curriculum 11–16: Geography*, a working paper by the Geography Committee of HM Inspectorate, HMSO, 1981.

Geographical Association, *Geography in the School Curriculum 5–16*, Geographical Association, 1981.

Geographical Association's Education Committee (1977), 'Geography in the school curriculum: a contribution to the Great Debate' in *Teaching Geography*, Vol. 3, No. 2.

Gerber, R. (1981a), 'Young children's understanding of the elements of maps' in *Teaching Geography*, Vol. 6, No. 3.

Gerber, R. (1981b), 'Factors affecting the competence and performance in map language for children at the concrete level of map-reasoning' in *Geographical Education*, Vol. 4, No. 1.

Graves, N., *Curriculum Planning in Geography*, Heinemann Educational, 1979.

Graves, N., *Geographical Education in Secondary Schools*, Geographical Association, 1980.

Kemp, R. (1979), 'Teaching strategies for the less-able' in *Teaching Geography*, Vol. 5, No. 2.

Marsden, W. E., *Evaluating the Geography Curriculum*, Oliver and Boyd, 1976.

Mills, D. (ed.), *Geographical Work in Primary and Middle Schools*, Geographical Association, 1981.

Pearce, T. (1980), 'Teaching geographical "ideas" and "skills" to 11–13 year-olds in mixed-ability groups' in *Teaching Geography*, Vol. 6, No. 2.

Plowden, Lady (Chairman), *Children and their Primary Schools*, HMSO, 1966.

Sandford, H. A., 'Perceptual Problems' in Graves, N. J. (ed.) *New Movements in the Study and Teaching of Geography,* Temple Smith, 1972.

Sandford, H. A. (1978), 'Taking a fresh look at atlases' in *Teaching Geography*, Vol. 4, No. 2.

Williams, M. (ed.), *Language Teaching and Learning: Geography*, Ward Lock, 1981.

The following are articles in *Remedial Education* which deal with geographical studies:

Ciesla, M. J. (1979), 'Geography for slow learners in the secondary school', *Remedial Education*, Vol. 14, No. 2.

McKenzie, J. C. (1981), 'The teaching of geography to children with learning difficulties', *Remedial Education*, Vol. 16, No. 2.

10

History

ROY HALLAM

The nature of school history

For teachers, there is often a tension between the demands of their subject and the needs of their pupils. This is especially so with regard to children with learning difficulties where it might seem imperative to place their needs first. Yet in history teaching, there has recently been a strong movement of opinion in which it is argued that the starting point must be with the subject. 'History should be analysed before it can be taught in any credible manner to school children.' (Thompson in Burston and Green, 1972.)

In a most useful discussion, Rogers (1978), for example, contends that questions on history teaching remain unresolved through 'the failure to provide an adequate answer to the fundamental epistemological question — namely, "What is historical knowledge?" ' He continues that historical knowledge can be characterized in three ways — conceptual, propositional, and procedural. In other subjects, terms such as 'particle', 'angle' or 'contour' might have a precise meaning but, according to Rogers, history is 'conceptually non-esoteric. It does not contain extensive networks of concepts having little or no application outside itself . . . History is continuous with general human experience.'

However, historical concepts can surely be said to be specifically linked with time. In discussions with various groups of pupils, including those with learning difficulties, the writer found that they always instanced time as a crucial aspect of history. One third-year secondary boy gave the memorable statement that history for him was 'the past tense of mankind', a phrase which appeared to have meaning for him. Concepts such as 'feudalism', 'the manor', 'galleon', and so on, would surely smack of history to most people. Scott (1981) also reminds us that history contains organizing concepts such as 'cause', 'effect' and 'motive'. While not perhaps uniquely historical, these are essential if even the simplest historical narrative is to make sense.

Narrative forms the second of Rogers' (1978, *op. cit.*) three criteria. An area of knowledge such as history gains its coherence from its propositional character, or its 'know that'. In other words, 'History tells stories — but stories which seek to make intelligible the truth about events which have actually occurred.' This narrative is more than a description, since the historian has to select those events which are significant.

How can children be introduced to such an area of knowledge since they are manifestly not historians? Here we meet Rogers' third criterion, the procedural or 'know how'. This is concerned with appropriate ways of handling sources. An historical account depends on the historian's selection, understanding and treatment of his or her sources. We are in the world of evidence, its reliability, authenticity and adequacy. Again, this is surely a world for mature adults, not children? Rogers, however, considers that children can approach historical data in the manner required by Elton (1969), that is, without previous hypotheses, allowing history itself to suggest the questions which are to be asked. Children can do this precisely because of their lack of 'relevant bias and expectation'. Their saving ignorance makes children capable of attempting Elton's programme, provided of course that they are confronted with materials which interest them.

There is, however, a crucial difference between children and historians. The latter approach the evidence from a deep knowledge of the period. Children have to be 'confronted' with materials. The task of the teacher is to help mediate between the historical experience and the children, taking into account their cognitive development, social background and relevant affective experiences, as well as the nature of the subject. Langman (1978) reminds us: 'the classroom teacher has, in the final analysis, to teach the pupil history, not history to the pupil. It is an old maxim, nevertheless, it needs re-emphasizing.' This is the point at which developmental considerations make their entry into the discussion.

Developmental levels in school history

What capabilities in history can we expect from children with learning difficulties? This is an under-researched area (Cowie, 1979), far more work having been carried out with the general school population. Although it is under some critical revision at present, the most well-known developmental theory to start with is that of Piaget. Piaget recently claimed that he had: 'Laid bare a more or less evident general skeleton which remains full of gaps so that, when these gaps will be filled, the articulations will have to be differentiated but the general lines of the system will not be changed.' (Sinclair de Zwart in Modgil and Modgil, 1980.)

Early research work in school history based on Piagetian criteria (for example, Hallam, 1966, 1967) gave guidelines from which further investigations could develop (for example, Dickinson and Lee, 1978, and Hallam, 1979). That those guidelines appear to have some validity from the teachers' viewpoint can be seen in a recent publication by the Schools Council (1981). Over the period 1977–1980, a very large number of teachers in the London Borough of Merton examined ways in which children of different ages gained an understanding of the concepts and methods of work in history, geography and the social sciences. Their conclusions were as follows:

1. Until about 10 years of age, many children may still be at the pre-operational stage of thinking. Their thinking therefore tends to be 'inconsistent and unrealistic'. Such children answer 'with a tautology or irrelevance, or centred on one aspect of the data only'.
2. Children in the next stage can provide, from the available data, organized, detailed and co-ordinated explanations which may be limited, but are properly related to the question.
3. Only from about 13 years of age are many children moving towards formal

operational thinking. 'This is the stage they may not normally reach before about 15 years and which some seem never to reach.' Children at this level are able to form sound judgements, evaluate, edit and criticize.

4. The Merton group warns that incongruities will be evident among the general age levels. 'Some young children may show flashes of formal thought, while much older pupils have difficulty sometimes at the formal level.'

This study adds further confirmation to the general picture previously outlined by earlier researchers who based their investigations on Piagetian criteria (Stones, 1965, Hallam, 1966 and de Silva, 1969).

Children with learning difficulties are likely to be lagging behind their age-group. Gould (in Jones and Ward, 1978), reporting the results of a Scottish Working Party, states that the teachers' own classroom experience leads them to think that in each year-group there were likely to be a number of 'slow learners' who would find it difficult to read, write or converse at the level of most of the year-group. At the same conference, despite his generally optimistic findings, Scott (also in Jones and Ward, 1978) admitted that even in his experimental group, those pupils 'with a relatively low IQ, those who appeared reluctant to talk, those who appeared to have a limited verbal repertoire and fluency, tended to provide limited responses.' Yet as writers such as Cowie (1979) remind us, children have learning difficulties for a variety of reasons: emotional, linguistic, social, motivational and cognitive. As with the general school population, and because of this variety of difficulties, there is obviously likely to be a range of responses among a group of slower learners at any designated age level, as the following examples indicate.

'The Murder of Rizzio'

A class of primary-school children, aged between 9 and 10 years, worked on an amended version of Lord Ruthven's report of the murder of David Rizzio in Holyrood Palace (Hallam, 1975). The story of Mary, Queen of Scots, certainly intrigued the children, combining as it does romance, mystery, conspiracy, courage and death. After the general story had been told, we read and then acted the events described by Lord Ruthven. When the children had been divided into small groups, they tried writing their own plays. From their scripts, I compiled a class play which was acted by various groups, each group being recorded. A week later, the children were set questions on the account derived from Lord Ruthven. Most of the questions aimed at trying to discover whether they could make judgements. Two children with learning difficulties answered as shown in figure 6.

The girl appeared well cared for, attentive, precise, but scored low on intelligence tests. The boy was unkempt, from a broken home, was attending remedial sessions and failed to reach the score of 70 on a verbal reasoning test, though he was at the mean on a non-verbal reasoning test.

While the girl simply repeated words she had heard, usually without much relation to the questions set, the boy not only knew what had happened (concrete level) but was able to deduce motivation and bias from Lord Ruthven's tendentious language.

137

Questions	Girl	Boy
Why do you think the nobleman mentioned that David (Rizzio) had his cap on his head?	Because they did not no what to do	Becos he was il manad *(ill mannered)*
What do you think the nobleman meant Darnley to do when he said: 'Sir, take the Queen your wife to you'?	I do not no	Mov the Qene from Daved
What does the following sentence tell us about the Lord Darnley? 'But he stood all amazed and did not know what to do.'	He ignored them	he is stupid and he did not no wot to do
Which sentence tells us that Mary acted bravely?	She did ite braveley	She stod and prectid Daved
Can you find *two* ways in which the nobleman tried to put the blame for the murder on Lord Darnley?	I do not no	(a) Wen they sed it is all don (by)my lode *(Lord)* (b) Dornles wish becos his (Darnley's) dager was in his *(Rizzio's)* sid

Fig. 6 Written answers given by two primary-school children classified as having learning difficulties.

'Factory children'

In this second example, children from the remedial department of a large comprehensive school were asked questions on a father's replies to the 1833 Committee on Factory Children's Labour (Charles Edwards and Richardson, 1958). They also studied the reproduction of an 1840 picture from *Michael Armstrong, the Factory Boy* by Frances Trollope.

The pupils' chronological ages were above 13 years, all having a reading age of 10 years 6 months or below. There were notable differences among the answers of this superficially similar group. Two boys, for example, provided a strong contrast. The first boy (boy 1 in figure 7) was able to discuss the situation of the children with some degree of empathetic involvement. He had great difficulty, however, with such relatively simple measurements as the number of hours worked by the factory children. The second boy (boy 2) was very quick and accurate on time measurements, but often gave syncretic answers to the other questions. He confused the past and present through, seemingly, being over-influenced by his own experiences on a farm.

Such inconsistencies among the answers from children of a similar chrono-

138

Question 1
Why do you think the father allowed the children to work such (long) hours?

Boy 1
Maybe (*he had*) a big family and he wasn't bringing enough wages in himself.

Boy 2
So they'd get money and so they'd get food.

Why didn't the father get the money?
It would give the children a bit of experience.

Question 2
Do you think he was bothered – worried – about them?

Boy 1
Yes. It says they (*parents*) usually cry when they can't give enough to eat (*to the children*).

Boy 2
Probably – they did too much work and strained themselves.

Why do you say this?
Lifting heavy things and they might try to lift too much.

Question 3
Here is a picture from about the same time in history. What can you tell me about it?

Boy 1
There's no heating or furniture to have the coffee break. A child is cleaning stuff – going under when the machinery is working.

Have you anything to say about that?
Not very nice. I wouldn't like to do it – if you got trapped they wouldn't turn the machinery off.

So – what would happen?
They'd die.

Anything else?
The men look like they're holding a stick to hit the kids if they're not working hard.

Boy 2
Weaving and making jumpers and clothing.

What about the children?
They aren't doing much at the moment.

Anything else about the children?
They have top hats but most farmers have flat caps and they (*? farmers*) have a jacket instead of a long coat in case they got trapped. And women don't usually work on farms and if they did they should wear trousers and not dresses.

Question 4
What do we mean by the word 'evidence'?

Boy 1
Proof to show things happened. There really was the conditions.

Boy 2
Don't know.

Question 5
Can the picture describe more than the words?

Boy 1
It made me more determined that I like it in the times now.

Boy 2
I like to see what they used to do in the past.

Fig. 7 Spoken replies by two third-year secondary-school boys classified as having learning difficulties.

logical age have led to searching criticisms of the whole Piagetian stage model as applied to school subjects. The Genevan school has put forward the concept of *décalage* as an explanation, that is, children will 'lag behind' in different areas because of their previous, specific experiences, the demands of the content, and so on. This does not seem a strong explanation (*c.f.* Modgil and Modgil, 1979) and researchers have either tried to modify the model (*c.f.* Parcual-Leone in Tomlinson, 1981) or have looked to other ways of explaining the thinking of schoolchildren.

Bruner is strongly supported by Rogers (1978) as presenting the most potentially fertile theory currently available.

Bruner considers that children 'know' through three modes of representation — enactive, iconic and symbolic, that is, 'through doing it, through a picture or image of it, and through some such symbolic means as language' (quoted in Rogers and Ashton, 1977). Although Bruner initially seemed to view these modes of representation as related to ages, they are now used more as a means of organizing content and method. Through taking children to visit a castle, Rogers and Ashton showed how successfully Bruner's theories could be applied to the teaching of history. It is difficult to envisage, though, how those theories can present a comprehensive analysis of children's cognitive development.

As it can be argued that history requires thinking other than rational, Watts (1972) has provided his own model. He suggests that 'many, if not most, cognitive processes in both children and adults are of the nature of spontaneous associations of images and concepts . . . people think associatively.' He illustrates his ideas in a diagram (figure 8).

Just as there are developmental stages in R-thinking, so Watts postulates that A-thinking develops from 'daydream' to 'creativity'. Nicholls comments (in Nichol, 1981), that Watts does not specify or define these stages of development, nor does he define the meanings of the terms which he uses in

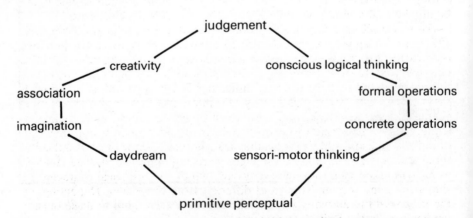

Fig. 8 Watts' model of thinking processes (quoted in Nichol, 1981).

his diagram. It would appear that more research is needed in order to verify the existence of Watts' 'A' stages.

Another developmental approach has been projected by Egan (1978 and 1979). Having argued that Piagetian-based research yields recommendations of little greater precision than an averagely sensitive teacher will already be practising, Egan outlines his own theory of development of historical understanding. This bears a resemblance to the innovative pattern recommended by Whitehead (1959), although Egan alters the age limits. During their school-years, children and young people will pass through three major stages, namely: *mythic* (approximately ages 4–5 up to 9–10 years), *romantic* (from about 9–10 to 15 years) and *philosophic* (from about 15 to the early twenties).

Mythic

Children begin to connect their feelings to history and develop concepts of historic time such as 'change' and 'otherness'. They should be encouraged to meet real heroes and villains rather than concentrate on the local environments, since 'the most engaging things to young children are not these prosaic studies, but rather the most bizarre flights of fancy.'

Romantic

This stage is marked by unsophisticated but servable concepts of historic time, change and causation. Romantic stories give the chance for children to identify with the most powerful and noble characters and forces, thus helping their developing egos. Such an increasing personal involvement in the past contains an element which is 'reflected in the interest in what was it like to live then?'

Philosophic

Interest is focused on 'the general course of history, the principles and laws of historical development'.

While Egan's theories could have most fruitful implications for the curriculum, they are not at present strongly supported as developmental stages through empirical work with children. As with research cited so far, it can be argued that a model is being applied to children's development.

However, Kelly's Construct Theory (quoted in Fransella and Bannister, 1977) can be applied in an attempt to allow the child to reveal her own constructions of 'reality'. As part of a more extensive investigation, methods derived from Kelly's theory were used with all types of pupils, including those considered to have learning difficulties. Groups were first asked what they understood by the term 'history'. From the range of answers, 'historical characters' was selected as an area which might be profitably investigated. Children were first asked to choose eight men and women whom they did, or did not, like and admire. Once they had chosen, often with great difficulty, three characters from among the eight were randomly listed. The children were next asked to decide how they saw two of the historical characters as similar in some way and the third different from those two. Depending on the nature of the answers, individual discussions were held to tease out the implications of the written statements.

Although the investigation is only in its preliminary stages, Kelly's construct theory might present another way of analysing developmental sequences in history. Primary-school pupils, aged 10–11 years and representative of a wide range of ability, gave constructs which were limited to roles (members of a royal family, explorers, writers); external characteristics ('wore glasses', 'smoked a pipe') and simple traits (good, bad, helping). On the other hand, boys aged 16–17 showed an ability to construct at a more abstract level. For example, some rulers took 'ill-advised actions' while others put 'their country on the map through worthwhile measures'. Children with learning difficulties in the third year of secondary comprehensive schools gave constructs which, in the main, resembled those of primary-school children. Occasionally, however, an individual pupil among this group replied at a more abstract level. For example, one boy wrote that Hitler was different from two other people since he 'wanted power for the third right' (*sic*).

The history syllabus

The generally held contention that, *on average*, pupils with learning difficulties are functioning at a level which is two years below that of their age group is supported by evidence that 13–14-year-old pupils were replying in a similar manner to primary-school children. While it is claimed persuasively that history can be taught successfully to infant children (Blyth, 1978), with these particular pupils formal history should perhaps start in their third year in the primary school (9–10 years). As most secondary-school pupils enter a fourth-year option system, which might or might not include history, the present consideration of the history syllabus will end in the third year of secondary schooling (13–14 years).

What could be the content of history for children with learning difficulties over this period of five years? In the first place, certain fundamentals must be considered:

(a) The nature of the subject must not be violated (*c.f.* Rogers, 1978), though this comment should be noted: 'The only statement about history which does seem to command common agreement is that it is about the human past and that it involves the concept of time past. Beyond this, it is difficult to isolate any other common attributes of history.' (Schools Council *History 13–16* Project, 1976)

(b) The syllabus should relate as closely as possible to what is known of children's developmental levels.

(c) A judicious modification of the all-too-prevalent chronological syllabus is needed, since the poor consumers can pass from skin-clad cavemen to industrious Victorians twice in their school careers, once at the primary and subsequently at the secondary level.

(d) History is about change and continuity over time so, in view of these pupils' well-attested difficulty with time concepts (Jahoda, 1963), it appears advisable that at least part of the syllabus should be placed along the conventional time continuum in order to help them develop their appreciation of time.

(e) Essentially, history is concerned with evidence.

From a deal of valuable advice on the construction of history syllabuses in general, (see Reeves, 1980, Partington, 1980), the following two sources seem particularly helpful for our present purposes. Hodgkinson (1979) considers that 'at root, we are trying to introduce children to the core of a discipline, its knowledge, skills and insights, so that children's personalities and intellectual development will be advanced in educationally significant ways . . . we need a blend of what is 'important' in history and what is 'suitable' for children.' While there may be some reservations about his divisions, Hodgkinson then presents a useful table of aims associated with content possibilities, from which these are selected:

Aims	*Some content possibilities*
1. Knowledge of	
(a) a common heritage;	British or European or world history.
(b) personal background.	Family, local and regional history
2. Understanding of	
(a) process of change and development;	Lines of development e.g. homes, transport through the ages.
(b) current social and political problems;	Contemporary history e.g. the 'Third' world.
(c) the conventions of time and periodization.	Chronological sequence.
3. Development of historical skills — enquiry, analysis and reconstruction.	Handling primary evidence, field studies.
4. Development of attitudes towards other people — sympathy, empathy, imagination.	Patches e.g. Tudor England; contrasting societies.

Hodgkinson in his 'content possibilities' refers to what are probably the three most common ways of dealing with content: a chronological survey of a particular part of the world; a study in depth of a fairly circumscribed period ('patch'); the investigation of a particular topic over long eras to show change and development, e.g., homes. Hodgkinson concludes with the intriguing comment that a blend of narrative and mysteries is probably the most advisable diet for enquiring but inexperienced young minds.

A powerful influence on syllabus construction for examination candidates in the upper years of the secondary school has been exerted by the Schools Council *History Project 13–16*. Surprisingly for many, the Project team's entry point was from a consideration of pupils' needs. The success of the project might be thought to have indicated this approach.

'What then are the needs of adolescents which history might meet?
1. The need to understand the world in which they live.
2. The need to find their personal identity by widening their experience through the study of people of a different time and place.
3. The need to understand the process of change and continuity in human affairs.
4. The need to begin to acquire leisure interests.
5. The need to develop the ability to think critically and to make judgements about human situations.' (Schools Council, 1976)

In the subsequent discussion, the team quotes tellingly from the Newsom Report (1963) in relation to the second of these needs:

'(Children need) an ability to enter imaginatively into other men's minds . . . It is important to keep good company and great company. People count . . . It is an enlarging of the spirit for our boys and girls to meet great men. It is important, too, to know bad company and to avoid it.'

With regard to this need to find personal identity, history can also show pupils examples of societies with values and life-styles quite distinctive from their contemporary world.

The Project team spell out the implications of the rather generalized fifth need — for, as they say, which subject is not going to develop critical thinking? — by explaining that history involves the comprehension and analysis of evidence about people. The evidence studied is inevitably varied and may be conflicting. 'In history they will see men and women hesitant about the way they should go, having to take decisions in situations where there was no right answer and having to live with the consequences.'

Their contemplation of presumed adolescent needs directs the project into a syllabus covering four major areas:

Studies in modern world history
Depth study of some past period
A study in development
History around us

With these two specific examples of construction behind us, and remembering the earlier stipulations, the following syllabus is therefore suggested (figure 9). In each year, five major areas are presented. Obviously, it might not be either possible or feasible to try to teach each area in one year. Teachers might need to be very selective, omitting some or choosing other areas from different years.

The content of this syllabus was more than slightly influenced by conversations with pupils. What children with learning difficulties saw as 'history' can be related to the views of writers already cited. For the children, history was firmly about people. Although they often had but a shaky comprehension of their lives and activities, the names in figure 9 are selected because, on the whole, they appeared to have made a vivid impact on the children (c.f. the Newsom Report, 1963, Egan, 1979, Fines, 1981). If, instead of trying to cover a great range, the teacher concentrated on such a limited number of people, then historically worthwhile narratives, rich in detail, could be developed.

Secondly the question of evidence appeared frequently. When a pupil suggested that a character such as Goliath or Robin Hood was historical, it was usual for another child to argue, 'That's not history!' In the ensuing discussion (or onslaught and counter-attack!) questions were asked about the nature of evidence. The children were able to respond sensibly to such questions. Pupils also showed interest in their local environments, especially when it involved their families.
'Why are there cholera graves outside the station?'
'What about our castle? Who lived there?'

144

Ages	Evidence	People in history	Local studies	Other peoples or conditions	Line of development
9–10 years	The story of the Wooden Horse Stories in the Old Testament, such as The Flood, Joseph, Goliath An Iron-Age farmhouse in Britain	Alexander the Great Hannibal Caesar, Cleopatra, Claudius	A study of the immediate environment of the school	Ancient Egypt or the Roman world	Homes or transport
10–11 years	Arthur Alfred Robin Hood	Mohammed Alfred William of Normandy Thomas à Becket Joan of Arc	A local church – the graveyard and the parish	The Vikings or aspects of the medieval European world	Plagues and diseases
11–12 years	The 'Princes in the Tower' Guy Fawkes	Leonardo da Vinci Martin Luther Henry VIII, Mary Queen of Scots and Elizabeth I Shakespeare	Family history	The Aztecs and Incas or New England settlements in the seventeenth century	Explorers
12–13 years	The use of primary sources such as parish registers, trade directories, census returns and parliamentary reports	Bonnie Prince Charlie Napoleon Nelson John Wesley George Stephenson Florence Nightingale Livingstone	An institution dating from the late eighteenth or early nineteenth century, for example, a school, hospital, workhouse, or factory	Moving westward in the USA or The South until the 1861–1865 Civil War	Crime and punishment
13–14 years	The death of Kennedy The Bermuda Triangle	Madame Curie Edith Cavell Amy Johnson Captain Scott Hitler Churchill Neil Armstrong	Pupil's own choice, with teacher guidance	Living in war-time conditions, World Wars 1 and 2 or pre-revolutionary Russia	Fashion or entertainments (to include sports)

Fig. 9 A history syllabus for children with learning difficiulties.

'We've been learning about our names and the names of our villages — it's good.'

One group of twelve-year-olds showed transparent joy in their learning about ancient Egypt. They were eager to talk about pharaohs, pyramids, frescoes and 'the thing to lift water', obviously having benefited from the study of a society so strikingly different from their own.

No child mentioned — or could perhaps be expected to mention — the 'line of development' approach. Nevertheless, the interest shown in the Schools Council's *Medicine* (1976) and the possibilities inherent in such areas as 'plague and disease' or 'fashion' should mean that the pupils could gain a worthwhile historical perspective from such a study, if it was properly treated.

The proposed syllabus can be criticized on a number of grounds, especially the concentration on 'western' history and the probably too conventional chronological framework. This was organized so there could be cross-relationships made, but a teacher might prefer to provide a complete contrast, say with 'nineteenth-century factory conditions' at the age of 9–10 years. The contents should allow, however, for many of the desiderata recommended earlier: narration, investigation of evidence, introduction to concepts such as 'change' and 'empathy', the use of primary sources and, in Fines' phrase (1981), knowing 'how men tick'. In the space afforded by one chapter, the implications of this syllabus have been dealt with only fleetingly. A book, or a series of books, devised specifically for children with learning difficulties is needed, as was requested at the 1978 Historical Conference on the teaching of less academic pupils.

As the area of 'evidence' is probably the most exacting part of the proposed syllabus, yet potentially fascinating, especially with these particular pupils. It will monopolize the remaining space.

Evidence

The Wooden Horse — the ground sweep of the legend combined with Schliemann's excavations in his attempt to discover the facts (see Magnusson, 1972).

The Old Testament — the most colourful stories which appeal to children can be shown to relate to archaeology and history — for example, Woolley's excavations at Ur for the Flood; the history of Egypt about 1700 BC for Joseph; the fight to establish one nation in Palestine against the Philistines. (See Grolleburg, 1950, Parrott, 1955, and Thompson, 1973.)

Iron-Age farmhouse — on the south downs of Hampshire, such a farm was built, Peter Reynolds (1979) spending six years as an Iron-Age farmer. His experiences can be tested against generally accepted theories of the Iron Age. There is also a BBC TV series. (See also Mace, 1959.)

Arthur — did he exist? If so, where and when? How and why did the stories develop in the Middle Ages? Nichol (1979) has a stimulating two-page spread and Ashe (1969) gives a most thorough explanation.

Alfred — The story of the cakes being burnt exemplifies how stories — which might have a basis in fact — accrue around a famous figure. (See Birley, 1955.)

Robin Hood — a BBC television programme 'Read On' sets the scene well

146

and traces the development of the legend through documents held at Nottingham Castle Museum.

The 'Princes in the Tower' — the Schools Council *History 13–16* Project's presentation of this murder mystery will need careful editing and selection, but all the material is there for an exciting series of lessons.

Guy Fawkes — John Hull, Head of Humanities at Bransholme School, Hull, has prepared this story as a detective investigation, helping the pupils to realize the inconsistencies in the generally accepted tale. For example, he asks the following questions:

'Isn't it amazing that they (the conspirators) were able to rent a cellar *right under* the House of Lords?'

'The barrels were left in the cellar for seven months. No one discovered them. Why not?'

'Four of the plotters were shot before they could be arrested. Was this a way of shutting them up for ever?'

The use of primary sources — Jones (1973) emphasizes introducing children to the bases of an historian's knowledge. Parish registers have been used most successfully with primary-school children and groups of older less-able pupils. For example, a range of activities can be developed from the entries for one year: occupations, ages of death, causes of death, and where people lived. If the local medical officer has a recent account of causes of death, then interesting comparisons can be made.

The death of Kennedy — two recent articles in *Teaching History* (Hodgkinson and Long, 1981; Blake, 1981) give valuable introduction to how this tragedy can be treated as an historical detective exercise. The former article is specifically concerned with children with learning difficulties.

The Bermuda Triangle — the unexplained disappearance of planes in the area between Miami and Grand Bahama Island allows the presentation of evidence, speculation and mystery. (See Samuda, 1978.)

Teaching methods have been comprehensively discussed by such writers as Hull (1980), Reeves (1980), Hagerty and Hill (1981), Kerry (1982), as well as others cited earlier in this chapter. If the enthusiasm and imaginative approaches shown in their books and articles can be related to teachers' knowledge and planning, then there seems little doubt that children with learning difficulties could and should benefit from a study of history during these vital years of their school life.

References and further reading

Ballard, M. (ed.), *New Movements in the Study and Teaching of History*, Temple Smith, 1970.

Bannister, D. and Fransella, F., *Inquiring Man*, Penguin, 1977.

Blyth, J. (1978), 'Young children and the past' in *Teaching History*, Vol. 21.

Burston, W. H. and Green, D., *Handbook for History Teachers*, Methuen, 1972.

Charles Edwards, T. and Richardson, B., *They Saw It Happen 1689–1897*, Blackwell, 1958.

Cowie, E. E., *History and the Slow-Learning Child*, Historical Association, 1979.

de Silva, W. A. (1969), 'Conceptual formation in adolescents with special reference to history material' (unpublished PhD thesis, University of Birmingham).

Dickinson, A. K. and Lee, P. J., *History Teaching and Historical Understanding*, Heinemann, 1978.

Dix, B. and Smart, R. (1981) 'Down among the dead men — graveyard surveys' in *Teaching History*, Vol. 30.

Dorner, J., *Fashion*, Galley Press, 1979.

Dunning, R., *Local Sources for the Young Historian*, Muller, 1973.

Elton, G. R. *The Practice of History*, 1967.

Egan, K., (1978), 'Teaching the varieties of history' in *Teaching History*, Vol. 21.

Egan, K., *Educational Development*, OUP, 1979.

Fines, J., 'Exploring in the open' in *The Times Educational Supplement*, 6.11.1981.

Fransella, F. and Bannister, D., *A Manual for the Repertory Grid Technique*, Academic Press, 1977.

Hagerty, J. and Hill, M., (1981), 'History and less-able children' in *Teaching History*, Vol. 30.

Haigh, G., *Teaching Slow Learners*, Temple Smith, 1977.

Hallam, R. N. (1966), 'An investigation into some aspects of the historical thinking of children and adolescents' (unpublished MEd thesis, University of Leeds).

Hallam, R. N. (1967), 'Logical thinking in history' in the *Educational Review*, Vol. 19, No. 3.

Hallam, R. N. (1975), 'A study of the effect of teaching method on the growth of logical thought with special reference to the teaching of history' (unpublished PhD thesis, University of Leeds).

Hallam, R. N. (1979), 'Attempting to improve logical thinking in school history' in *Research in Education*, Vol. 21.

Heater, D., *World Studies*, Harrap, 1980.

Hodgkinson, K., *Designing a History Syllabus*, Historical Association, 1979.

Hull, J. (1980), 'Practical points in teaching history to less-able secondary pupils' in *Teaching History*, Vol. 28.

Jahoda, G. (1963), 'Children's concept of time and history' in *Educational Review*, Vol. 15.

Jones, G. and Ward, L., (ed.), *New History, Old Problems*, University College of Swansea Press, 1978.

Jones, R. B. (ed.), *Practical Approaches to the New History*, Hutchinson, 1973.

Kelly, G. A., *A Theory of Personality*, Norton, New York, 1963.

Kerry, T., 'The demands made on pupils' thinking in mixed-ability classes' in Sands, M. and Kerry, T. *Mixed Ability Teaching*, Croom Helm, 1982.

Langman, T., 'History', in Hinson, M. (ed.) *Encouraging Results*, Macdonald Educational, 1978.

Modgil, S. and Modgil, C. (eds), *Towards a Theory of Psychological Development*, NFER, 1980.

Nichol, J. (ed.), *Developments in History Teaching*, University of Exeter School of Education, 1980.

Partington, G., *The Idea of an Historical Education*, NFER, 1980.
Peel, E. A., 'Some problems in the psychology of history teaching' in Burston, W. H. and Thompson, D. (eds) *Studies in the Nature and Teaching of History*, Routledge and Kegan Paul, 1967.
Reeves, M., *Why History?*, Longman, 1980.
Rogers, P. J., *The New History*, Historical Association, 1978.
Rogers, P. J. and Ashton, F., (1977), 'Play, enactive representation and learning' in *Teaching History*, Vol. 19.
Routh, C. R. N., *They Saw It Happen, 1485–1688*, Blackwell, 1965.
Schools Council, *The New Approach to Social Studies*, 1981.
Scott, J. (1981), 'Contents and concepts' in *Teaching History*, Vol. 31.
Shemilt, D., *History 13–16*, Holmes McDougall, 1980.
Stones, S. K. (1965), 'An analysis of the growth of adolescent thinking in relation to the comprehension of school history material' (unpublished DCP dissertation, University of Birmingham).
Tomlinson, P., *Understanding Teaching*, McGraw-Hill, 1981.
Whitehead, A. N., *The Aims of Education*, Benn, 1959.

Resources for history as evidence

Ashe, G., *All About King Arthur*, Allen, 1969.
Birley, R., *The Undergrowth of History*, Historical Association, 1955.
Blake, A. (1981), 'Who was John F. Kennedy?' in *Teaching History*, Vol. 30.
Grollenberg, L. H., *The Penguin Shorter Atlas of the Bible*, Allen Lane, 1959.
Hodgkinson, K. and Long, M., (1981), 'The assassination of John F. Kennedy' in *Teaching History*, Vol. 29.
Jones, R. B., *Practical Approaches to the New History*, Hutchinson, 1973.
Lines, C. and Bolwell, L., *Exploring the Past, Life in the Past, The Past around Us, Town and Around* series, Macdonald Educational, 1981.
Nichol, J., *The Saxons*, Blackwell, 1979.
Magnusson, M., *Introducing Archaeology*, Bodley Head, 1972.
Parrott, A., *The Food and Noah's Ark*, SCM, 1955.
Place, R., *Prehistoric Britain*, Longman, 1959.
Reynolds, P. J., *Iron-Age Farm*, British Museum Publications, 1979.
Samuda, M., *Unsolved Mysteries*, Edward Arnold, 1978.
Schools Council, *History 13–16 Project*, Holmes McDougall, 1976.
Thompson, J. A., *The Bible and Archaeology*, Paternoster Press, 1973.

Section 2—Conclusion

In the past, over-directed teaching, dictated notes and vigorous uniformity have frequently been major features of science, geography and history lessons. For the majority of pupils, geography was long associated with descriptive factual material. Nowadays, it is regarded as having a much wider perspective. For example, the wealth of stimuli in urban geography or the study of poverty and overcrowding can be geared to a wide range of ability, thereby promoting discussion and the formation of values which can be supplemented in other lessons. In history, pupils can be encouraged to explore feelings as well as facts, relating them to their own experiences and life-styles. Modern science teaching now emphasizes active enquiry rather than the more passive amassing of factual content. Teaching strategies must encourage the search for alternative explanations rather than concentrating upon one fixed solution. Basic principles of good practice are relevant across the curriculum, and evidence suggests the urgent need for the pooling of expertise by subject specialists, remedial teachers and those researching into the nature of learning difficulties.

Although teachers can do much to ameliorate the situation, it would be unrealistic to deny that many problems remain. Topics and assignments beyond the pupils' comprehension are frequently found in schemes of work. Pupils are often unable to explain from information given to them, experiencing difficulty in relating the question to the relevant content. There has been an improvement in the availability of teaching materials, but only recently has there been any real attempt to consider the question of readability.

The Schools Council has been active in curriculum innovation for many years, and some of the materials produced have applications to children with learning difficulties. This was firmly established in Curriculum Bulletin 5, *Teaching Materials for Disadvantaged Children* (Gulliford and Widlake, 1975). Examples of good practice, based directly or indirectly on Schools Council initiatives, can be found in many schools. Unfortunately, however, it appears that the majority of teachers are still insufficiently aware of the work carried out by the Schools Council or of the curriculum materials and publications which it has produced. It has recently initiated a further review of current experience and practice entitled *Curriculum Materials for Pupils with Learning Difficulties*. The present Project involves teachers in small-scale investigations into the use of existing Schools Council materials, after which they report their findings. Information will also be gathered concerning adaptations of such materials, or alternative materials derived from them, together with reports on techniques developed by specialist teachers who are working with pupils with learning difficulties in a particular area of the curriculum. It is envisaged that the results of the Project will be published as a series of short booklets embracing the main subject areas.*

NARE's Curriculum Studies Sub-committee has been formulating a set of guidelines which are intended to help teachers in the evaluation of curriculum materials. Attempting to analyse the educational worth of books and materials without some form of guidance can be a daunting task. Once information is available, however, teachers can successfully match resources to particular circumstances and purposes. The guidelines pose pertinent questions regarding format, content, interest, motivation, suitability, effectiveness and decision-making. The information gathered by this approach enables informed, professional decisions to be taken in the effective classroom use of curriculum materials. Entitled 'Choosing Curriculum Materials', the guidelines are now undergoing a final evaluation prior to publication (1982).

Harrison (1980) has produced a valuable practical guide for teachers anxious to improve their assessment of the readability of school materials. Earlier chapters describe the nature of readability, what can and cannot be measured, how the data is best used, and the difficult relationship between comprehension and readability. Harrison then gives a realistic appraisal of several readability measures, together with all the details necessary for their application.

Such authoritative information is vital when evaluating the wide selection of published materials which purport to be suitable for the educational needs of children with learning difficulties. Inevitably, gaps will become apparent and, with characteristic enthusiasm, many remedial teachers will then set about producing their own materials in order to complete a learning programme.

Elsewhere in this book, reference has been made to the injudicious use of worksheets. These can have the advantage of enabling the teacher to develop a more personal style, free from the constraints associated with some textbooks. Worksheets can allow for a diversity of challenges and might cater for a wide range of ability but, unless great care is taken, they do little to improve the lot of the less-able. Questions need to be well thought-out and cover a range of comprehension levels, thus enabling pupils' cognitive abilities to be extended without them becoming disillusioned. Problems should be sufficiently open-ended to cater for a variety of response, encouraging creative thinking rather than the regurgitation of set answers.

Harrison (op.cit.) gives a set of simple and easily remembered guidelines for those wanting to write some readable prose. He warns that it can be futile to write to some strict formula, also that the total curriculum context cannot be ignored. Further helpful advice is given by Hartley (1978) in his guidelines for the writers of instructional materials, also by Hartley, Morris and Trueman (1981) who describe their investigation into the use of headings in texts intended for less-able children. Davies (1978) has produced a prac-

---

* For further information contact the Schools Council, 160 Great Portland Street, London W1N 6LL.

151

tical introduction to the problems of initiating various forms of individualized or resource-based work.

In conclusion, the evidence from science, geography and history suggests that, where there are clear objectives, flexible strategies, appropriate content and regular monitoring, pupils with learning difficulties will make better progress. Many of the conclusions drawn have important implications for other areas of the curriculum.

References and further reading

Davies, W. J. K., *Implementing Individualized Learning*, Council for Educational Technology, 1978.

Gulliford, R. and Widlake, P., *Teaching Materials for Disadvantaged Children*, Schools Council Curriculum Bulletin 5, Evans/Methuen, 1972.

Harrison, C., *Readability in the Classroom*, Cambridge University Press, 1980.

Hartley, J., *Designing Instructional Text*, Kogan Page, 1978.

Hartley, J. Morris, P. and Trueman, M. (1981), 'Headings in text' in *Remedial Education*, Vol. 16, No. 1.

National Association for Remedial Education (1982), *Choosing Curriculum Materials, Guidelines* 5, NARE, Lichfield Road, Stafford, ST17 4JX.

Section 3
Secondary and post-school education

Evidence from national surveys suggests that, in most secondary schools, both teachers and pupils work hard and their efforts achieve solid results. The great majority are 'orderly communities where much thought and effort is given to promoting the well-being of individual pupils' (*Aspects of Secondary Education in England*, 1979).

However, the spectre of examinations still haunts secondary education. Even though recent curricular exorcism might have initiated some welcome changes in syllabus content and lesson presentation, there remains a high proportion of children for whom the academic goals represented by public examinations are inappropriate. *The School Curriculum* (DES, 1981) charges schools with the function of preparing children and young people for all aspects of adult life (para. 53). Secondary schools are expected to build on the foundations laid in primary schools, ensuring that this foundation is reflected in the whole of the curriculum. The eight areas of experience: aesthetic and creative, ethical, linguistic, mathematical, physical, scientific, social/political and the spiritual have far-reaching implications for the secondary curriculum offered to children with learning difficulties. Measured against these, the present options available to many less-able pupils pay only lip-service to their real needs. Discriminating use of such criteria when translating general principles into practice will help schools to achieve a more realistic balance in future.

Contributors to this section discuss not only the important grounding in the language arts and mathematics, but also current attempts to gear curricular development to the needs of adult life.

11

Language in the secondary school

—————————— MIKE HINSON ——————————

In the foreseeable future, the unrelenting advance of the micro-processor will enable most people to possess their own computers. Enthusiasts forecast that world-wide networks, via satellites, will make the sum total of human knowledge transmissible to ordinary homes, thus eclipsing libraries, bookshops, newspapers and letter-writing. Paradoxically, the demand for improved functional levels in the language arts has never been greater.

The Bullock Report (1975) concurs that standards of reading and writing need to be raised in order to fulfil the increasingly exacting demands made upon them by modern society. However, it warns that improvements can only be sustained as a result of thoroughly understanding the many complexities of language, and sustained from action on a broad front. Following the 'Great Debate', there were over-publicized histrionics, many heart-searchings by educationists and the evolution of a more realistic view of progress. Lest we forget, *The School Curriculum* (1981) re-emphasizes that: 'The teaching of English is concerned with the essential skills of speech, reading and writing and with literature. Schools will doubtless continue to give them priority.'

Aspects of Secondary Education in England (1979) surveyed the quality of fourth and fifth years' language experience. The report expresses concern for the majority of less-able pupils, especially as general assessments suggest that schools provide less well for those who have more serious problems in language. It also comments that better liaison between remedial and subject departments would help to close the gap.

In his introductory chapter, Colin McCall has already referred to NARE's *Guidelines No. 2* (1979) which outline the developing role of the remedial teacher in a changing world of education.

The language curriculum for children with learning difficulties is discussed in this chapter with these two documents in mind. We shall discuss the formulation of a school policy which covers all aspects of language and takes into consideration the special needs of children with learning difficulties. This is followed by an appraisal of certain key issues of current concern in teaching the four modes of language: literacy, speaking, writing and reading.

Establishing a language policy

National reports have continued to hammer home the Bullock committee's recommendation: 'Whatever the means chosen to implement it, a policy for language across the curriculum should be adopted by every secondary school.'

154

Secondary-school teachers have grown steadily aware of the importance of language across the curriculum since Harold Rosen and the London Association for the Teaching of English published their discussion document more than a decade ago (Barnes *et al.*, 1969). Yet the creation of language policies has proved to be a lengthier and more complicated process than earlier enthusiasts could foretell. HM Inspectorate (1979, *op. cit.*) found that many secondary schools remain daunted by the prospect. In their view, this is partly accounted for by a confusion of the two functions of language, 'the first as a communication of what has to be learned and the second as part of the activity of learning itself'. The survey points out that concentration on the first at the expense of the second may obscure basic stages through which the learner needs to pass. The use of language to explore an experience often reveals what can be discovered in no other way, especially to the pupil who finds the art of abstraction difficult. A change of emphasis from language as evidence of learning achieved to language used in the process of learning is regarded as being a necessary step forward.

General aims of a language policy

A language policy is not simply a document or scheme, but a series of strategies which are employed to help pupils to learn more effectively. It is also intended to promote on-going discussion, enquiry and evaluation within a school concerning its use of language. The National Association for the Teaching of English (1976) underlines the relationship between language and learning and stresses that teachers cannot usefully look at language solely as a set of skills. They must examine the ways in which both children and adults learn through language, including how they learn, what learning is and how it works. A language policy looks for ways of actively involving pupils in learning by using their own language through talking and writing, as well as the language of others in listening and reading. A successful policy produces a coherence in an area of school management, creating a partnership between teachers who agree to use a common approach to language, even though they are teaching different aspects of the curriculum.

Every school has a unique pattern of intake and a distinctive way of organizing its own affairs. It follows, therefore, that a language policy cannot exist outside the school in which it is created, because it relates to specific problems and methods of approach. A minority of schools have taken an independent line in evolving their own policies. Many others have responded to the energetic initiatives taken by LEA advisers. As an example, one local authority in the Midlands has produced discussion papers for both primary and secondary schools. It suggests three general aims:

(a) To enable children to learn and to employ, to the limit of their abilities, the four modes of communication in the language arts — listening, speaking, reading and writing.
(b) To select and present language materials and experiences of all kinds in such a way as to provide interest, pleasure and personal development in addition to progress in the language skills.
(c) To ensure that children are not only competent in the language arts but

are eager to extend these skills throughout their education and into adult life.

The first steps

It is not possible, or desirable, in a short chapter to list specific items to be included in the contents of a language policy. Teachers will find it more helpful to read case studies which describe the developmental process and the progress achieved in schools already tackling the task, and then to relate these to their own situation. Robertson (1980) reports the outcome of investigations, carried out on behalf of the Schools Council, in four secondary schools. A useful series, entitled *Language, Teaching and Learning* (1981) starts from the experience of successful teachers and demonstrates how a language policy can be implemented in the classroom.

Brennan (1979) accepts the wider aims of language across the curriculum as relevant for children with learning difficulties. He stresses that there is much to do in translating the aims of *A Language for Life* into pupil behavioural objectives, and provides an invaluable framework for the language curriculum of those with special educational needs.

The problems likely to be encountered in formulating and implementing such a policy should not be underestimated. Accounts of schools' experiences show that it is a long-term project, far less easy to accomplish than decisions on more pragmatic matters such as a policy for homework. Obviously, the willingness of the headteachers plays a crucial role in the success or failure of any new venture. The trend towards larger secondary schools has resulted in more complex, hierarchical structures in staffing. Besides the goodwill of deputy heads and heads of department, nowadays there are directors of studies, heads of faculty, academic committees and year co-ordinators, all wishing to play their part (or not!) in collective decision-making. Inter-departmental rivalries can cause difficulties. Subject specialists often feel that questions raised about classroom language are irrelevant to the teaching process. Understandably, others feel threatened when the over-zealous suggest radical departures from classroom practice such as recording and analysing lessons. These and other problems are realistically discussed by Nancy Martin (in Marland, 1977).

NARE (1979), calls for specialist remedial teachers to become more closely involved in decision-making at top level within schools. A language policy is intended to encompass the language needs of all pupils, whatever their abilities and attainments. By becoming part of any seminal group concerned with language across the curriculum, remedial staff in secondary schools will help to ensure that the special requirements of children with learning difficulties are better understood by other colleagues.

Once the group is established, it would do well to heed the practical advice of Allen (1975) before it starts work. Reflecting upon the progress made in his own school towards an explicit policy, he recorded the following general points based on his own experiences:

1. Refuse to present a document from the point of view of English. Make sure that any document is the product of collaboration across departments.

156

2. Avoid jargon.
3. Listen.
4. Say what you mean. Manipulation of others by *mock* mildness is the way to get a document produced, but not to get a language policy in operation.
5. Do not present the LATE document (referred to in Barnes, 1969) on a language policy. It is presumptive and closes doors fast.
6. If you must write something, call it 'Some ideas . . .' or 'A discussion paper'.
7. Do not bring in an 'expert'.
8. Think long, slow and small. Do not introduce the issue to a full staff meeting.
9. Each school has its own 'language policy', silent or manifest. The first thing to do is to talk about the existing non-policy.
10. The English department (*and the remedial department, for that matter*) should have talked about language in their own curriculum area and feel they have come to some balanced, unifying description of the different elements.

Modern languages

In this country, modern languages seem to have become the province of brighter children, especially those who are preparing for public examinations. Very often, schools preclude the less-able from modern language teaching by allocating these periods in the timetable to extra work in basic literacy skills.

The School Curriculum (para. 50) poses a number of questions, some of which are relevant to the present discussion:

1. In the development of modern languages, what relative priorities should be given to the length of courses and their extension over the range of ability?
2. How suitable are present courses for pupils up to the age of 13 or 14? What is their educational and practical linguistic value both to themselves and as a preparation for continued study?
3. What should be the 'cultural' element in the course?
4. How far should our membership of the European Communities be taken into account in assessing objectives?

National reports have commented on the narrowness and lack of choice in ·urricula for less-able children. For this reason if no other, planners might wc l reconsider the place of modern languages in the curriculum for children with learning difficulties. Some form of a European studies course could be viable. This could come either in the early years of secondary schooling, or as an option for fourth and fifth-year pupils. Naturally, the success of any course is dependent upon the enthusiasm of the staff concerned, who need to establish a realistic view of the inherent problems before embarking upon such a project. Practical observations show that pupils do respond to the oral work, but find similar difficulties with reading and writing to those that they already experience in English. With younger age-groups in particular, the inclusion of such a course is helpful at a stage in their development when

157

being treated 'the same' as one's more able peers is of vital importance to them.

English as a second language

Equal consideration must be given to children whose first language is not English or Welsh when formulating a language policy.

In areas with ethnic minority communities, there are likely to be small numbers of children who enter secondary education having little or no English. Whether provision is organized by a school itself or by a local education authority's support service, it is vital that a properly structured programme is established under expert guidance. This should be designed to give pupils the basic structures of the English language, reinforced as necessary, helping them to become integrated within the school as soon as possible.

A substantial number of pupils will have already benefited from special support given during their primary education. These go on to achieve success in the British educational system. Nevertheless, teachers working in schools with high-percentage intakes from ethnic minority backgrounds will be aware of intelligent children who are under-functioning, despite the help which they have received. Often this can be attributed to insufficient comprehension of English, which can affect their cognitive development. This is further hampered when little English is spoken in the home, either by choice or of necessity. The present writer is of the view that, even though schools can never fully compensate unaided, they could take greater cognizance of these difficulties by emphasizing listening and speaking in their language policies and by implementing strategies which would lead to greater facility in pupils' use of the English language.

Mother-tongue teaching

The School Curriculum (1981, *op. cit.*) regards the first language of children from ethnic minority groups as a valuable resource, both for them and the nation, which should not be allowed to wither away. It stresses the importance of pupils retaining contacts with their own communities. The question 'How should mother-tongue teaching for such pupils be accommodated within modern-language provision?' implies that the secretaries of state expect schools facing this dilemma to reach a resolution which is beneficial to the children. The development of resources for mother-tongue teaching is one area of concern in Programme 4 of Schools Council's current projects. Using finance from the EEC, a variety of provision is envisaged. In certain areas, part-time classes have been set up under the supervision of LEAs. Schools are giving careful consideration to the use of children's mother-tongue for teaching part of the curriculum.

There will continue to be a minority of children who experience difficulties in both their mother-tongue and English. Departments will need to make early identification of these pupils and to provide for their special educational needs. For the majority, insightful provision of English as a second language and mother-tongue teaching will lead to more effective progress within both the school and the community.

Priorities in the language curriculum

In discussing educational aims, the secretaries of state (1981, *op. cit.*) advise schools to determine curricular priorities in such a way as to offer each pupil a broad, yet balanced and coherent programme. Its content should include topics which are both essential and properly suited to each individual's needs.

Whatever pupils' attainments on entering the secondary school are, it is a fair assumption that teachers will act on a 'buck-stops-here' principle and do their utmost to promote functional levels of competence in language. Nevertheless, thousands of boys and girls leave school each year inadequately prepared to cope with the day-to-day language requirements of adult life. Despite expert teaching, this lack of progress in some cases can be attributed to complex circumstances. In others, functional levels might well have been achieved had schools planned realistic minimum goals in their language curricula, then identified pupils' difficulties at an early stage and implemented corrective measures suited to their individual needs.

The following are suggested as priorities during the compulsory years of secondary schooling:

Oracy (listening and speaking)

1. To ensure that pupils can talk clearly and confidently both at home, at work and when engaged in everyday tasks (such as shopping).
2. To encourage pupils to talk with interest and to have something interesting to say.
3. To be able to understand verbal instructions, also to give simple instructions clearly.
4. To develop the ability to evaluate the words of others before making a judgement.
5. To ensure that they are able to use the telephone with confidence.

Reading

6. To enable pupils to achieve, as a minimum, three aspects of functional literacy:
   (a) Vocabulary — they should know and understand a basic social sight vocabulary in order that they can deal independently with everyday tasks without embarrassment and without endangering themselves or others. (The list might include road signs, warning notices and labels, basic items of diet, and so forth.)
   (b) Problem-solving — to read with sufficient fluency in order to deal with real-life problems such as: the exact dosage on a medicine bottle; the correct amount of bleach to be added to washing, or how to assemble a DIY furniture kit.
   (c) Consulting a reference — the ability to use a telephone directory, an A–Z street guide, a variety of timetables and a simple dictionary.

Writing

7. To ensure that pupils are able to write a letter. This will entail the mastery of:

   (a) a clear, cursive style of handwriting;

159

(b) a working knowledge of simple sentence-construction and punctuation;

(c) the correct spelling of words most commonly used (e.g., those included in the Dolch word-list).

8. To develop a working knowledge of form-filling concerned, for example, with deposits and withdrawals from National Savings Bank accounts, and other post office services.

The framework outlines fundamental applications of everyday language attainable by the vast majority of secondary-school pupils, including those who are the particular concern of this book. It is true that some may need a great deal of encouragement and assistance to attain these goals. The list is not exhaustive and is capable of adaptation by schools to their individual requirements. Nevertheless, such a utilitarian approach should not be over-emphasized to the exclusion of the wider, enriching aspects of the language curriculum.

Identification and assessment

During recent years, increased efforts to strengthen pastoral links between primary and secondary schools has been to the resulting benefit of pupils. Some form of surveillance and appraisal of individual children with special needs is essential as a preparation for their smooth transfer at the age of 11+. NARE (1979, *op. cit.*) regards identification and assessment as a prime function in the specialist remedial teacher's role. Indeed, it is vital for remedial departments to have access to objective test-data and record cards received from primary schools if an early start is to be made in implementing a language programme geared to the needs of children with learning difficulties.

Inevitably, the availability of such information varies from area to area. When insufficient data is available, remedial teachers need to be amongst the vanguard in encouraging close co-operation between schools, especially at classroom level. Blagg (1981) suggests that teachers should ponder the question of when a learning difficulty is regarded as a problem. He points out that, in some schools, even the slightest problem is regarded as being of major significance, whereas others regard more serious learning difficulties as being quite acceptable. Problems are relative to the demands of particular circumstances and the perceptions of teachers concerned.

Thomson and Hinson (1978) outline a system for identifying children's problems, based on the establishment of inter-school relationships and the insightful interpretation of shared data. In localities where such a system is not already in operation, a secondary school might resort to one of two courses of action. It could attempt to formulate an acceptable battery of language (and other) tests with its feeder primary schools, to be given at suitable times prior to pupils' transfer. Alternatively, the school might choose a series of tests to be administered to successive intakes on arrival. This latter choice is best avoided. Even the brightest are unlikely to perform at their best during the period of adjustment to a new régime. Other schools eschew both of these alternatives, admitting their new intake directly into 'mixed-ability' groups. Nevertheless, some form of objective data will inevitably be required.

Particular care should be taken in choosing tests of children's language attainments, adhering to Jackson's axiom (1971): 'If there is one clear principle to fit all situations, it is that a test should be given only when there is a clear need for it, and a prospect of acting upon results.' Group tests which yield standardized scores or norms are of some value in that they enable the teacher to compare an individual's performance with that of other children in his or her age-group. However, these tests are only measuring levels of attainment and, as such, do not offer much help in diagnosing specific difficulties. Standardized scores are useful in determining a cut-off point (say, for example, a reading age of 9.6 years) below which a more detailed investigation of certain pupils should be carried out, using individual and criterion-referenced tests. Detailed appraisals of reading and language tests can be found in Westwood (1975) and Pumphrey (1976 and 1977). Educational psychologists and LEA remedial services are always willing to advise on tests most suited to local needs, in close liaison with the remedial department and senior school personnel.

Tests are technical tools which are servants of the curriculum, and the skilful interpretation of the data which they yield requires both expertise and sensitivity. In-service training, probably organized under the aegis of the local education authority, is a desirable preparation for staff prior to implementing an educational guidance programme in school.

Listening and speaking

During the last two decades, investigations into the different ways in which language is acquired and extended have stressed the fundamental role played by listening and speaking. Marland (1977) succinctly summarizes their importance:

> 'The school's limited use of language may restrict the pupil from deploying his language in learning situations. A language policy is concerned with helping him get *at* the understanding and knowledge on offer and it must also help him to get *into* the understanding and knowledge, since without comprehension, access itself is of little value. The way into ideas, the way of making ideas truly one's own, is to be able to think them through, and the best way to do this for most people is to talk them through. Thus talking is not merely a way of conveying existing ideas to others; it is also a way by which we explore ideas, clarify them and make them our own.'

Encouragingly, *Aspects of Secondary Education in England* (1979, *op. cit.*) reports that in about one fifth of the schools surveyed, the quality of the spoken word was considerable in a range of subjects. In some instances, there was less discussion in class with the more able pupils than with those who had learning difficulties. On matters which they regarded as being relevant and important, or about which they had strong views, the latter showed themselves capable of sustaining lively discussion (para. 6.4.11). Unfortunately, the overall conclusions of HM Inspectorate, reached as a result of observing some 25 000 lessons, were less favourable. It would appear that a majority of teachers are not fully aware of the valuable part that

161

pupils' talk can play in the learning process. Classes usually spend more time in reading and writing than they do in talking and listening. Observers remark, somewhat wryly, that pupils who spend so much of their time listening may need more opportunities than they are given to confirm their understanding and to relate it to other experience.

In an earlier study, Wilkinson (1968) attempted to explain the neglect of spoken language by suggesting three main reasons:

1. Attitudes of society

Society continues to set great store by literacy (he points out that one of its measures of success is an exam system based mainly on reading and writing).

2. Psychological

It is only comparatively recently that the relationship between language and cognitive development has been fully recognized.

3. Practical

The teaching of spoken language skills is more difficult because it involves additional organizational problems in the classroom.

In 1965, Wilkinson coined the term 'oracy' to describe a person's facility in oral expression. Involving both listening and speaking, it is the ability to utter anything and everything. Oracy comes from practice in specific situations, whether these occur naturally, in the classroom, or are created as a specific learning device.

Wilkinson and Stratta (1972) posed the question 'How well do we listen?' Their research suggested that students from primary school to university listened very badly. They quoted Wilt (1950) who demonstrated that even younger children were expected to spend 57·5 per cent of their school day in 'listening'. Wilkinson and Stratta felt that (in 1972) things were not very much different in secondary schools.

Ten years on, despite the entreaties of the Bullock Report (para. 12.2), recent national surveys show that, outside the walls of English (and one hopes remedial) classrooms, insufficient attention is given to the vital role of oracy in the learning process. Subject specialists in particular are reluctant to adopt practices whereby the pupil-teacher dialogue is shared more equally. Formal seating arrangements still tend to predominate in secondary classrooms, resulting in pupils' attention being focused towards the front. In consequence, one person speaking at once becomes the normal requirement and lessons tend to follow the widely used 'lecture-demonstration' format. This type of lesson is not to be totally despised, for, with careful preparation and planning, it remains a valuable way of presenting information. However, since this book is concerned with the effectiveness of the curriculum, it is suggested that a stronger bias should be given in subject lessons towards those aspects of language which are of especial value to children with learning difficulties. To quote the Newsom Report (1965, para. 467): 'Personal and social adequacy depends on being articulate, that is, on having the words and language structures with which to think, to communicate what is thought, and to understand what is heard or read.'

Arguments are still advanced against devoting classroom times to oral work. There remains a widespread feeling that talking in class may lead to a breakdown in discipline, also an anxiety that even purposeful talk might lapse into idle chatter. This is despite considerable evidence of 'mutual consideration and courtesy' on the part of both pupils and teachers in schools where these approaches are working well.

Traditional neglect of spoken language in the classroom is obviously ripe for reappraisal, yet for some teachers there lurks a fear of the unknown, a fear that things might get out of hand. True, it is not easy to get children to talk constructively in class. It is a classroom strategy which needs careful planning and organization. Perhaps this is one instance among many where teachers of children with learning difficulties can not only act as subtle agents for change within a school by setting examples of good practice themselves, but also act in a supportive role to colleagues by advising on ideas and techniques.

'Remedial' pupils can be noisy, and a teacher who is unused to them might be more concerned to quieten their seemingly raucous and idle chatter. Experience shows that success is very much dependent upon our attitudes towards them, also the extent to which we value them for what they are and what they have to offer, rather than moralizing on what we think they ought to be. Children with learning difficulties are often quick to sense, and appreciate, a genuine concern for them as people. Empathy is the foundation of successful talk (read Clements, 1967).

Pupils whose learning difficulties stem from acute social problems are frequently frustrated, because they cannot express themselves adequately. Misunderstandings between teacher and pupil can lead to confrontations where the latter's inarticulate outbursts and aggressive behaviour become unacceptable in the classroom situation. Alternatively, the child's frustrations lead to a state of sullen unco-operativeness. In one special unit to which adolescents experiencing such difficulties are referred, the encouragement of oracy is very much a part of both the curriculum and the educational therapy which is offered. Three simple goals are:

1. encouraging pupils to listen to others carefully and sympathetically, and to respect their views;
2. to consider carefully what has been said in the process of formulating a reply;
3. responding to others in a courteous and coherent manner.

Teachers decided that, within the limited resources available, the improvement of oracy is best achieved through teacher-pupil dialogue, small-group discussions and the creative use of the tape-recorder. At a later stage, one-minute talks or short, verbal reports on any topic are attempted.

Small-group discussion can be very profitable, provided that it is properly organized by the teacher and not allowed to deteriorate into undirected chatter. Group members need to be clear about what they are expected to discuss and the eventual outcome. A short, specified period in which to consider a precise topic is the best approach. The teacher remains in control of the situation, at the same time limiting interruptions and trusting pupils to proceed with the task in hand. Where necessary, discussion will need tactful steering back on positive lines and pupils' findings summarized.

Wilkinson and Stratta (*op. cit.*) outline a general framework which can be used for any spoken communication. David Self (1974) has produced an invaluable guide to oral work in the secondary school, while Adams and Pearce (1974) give practical advice for non-specialist teachers of English. The *Language, Teaching and Learning* series (1981) and Schools Council's *Language in Use* project (Edward Arnold, 1971) are helpful resources in planning work of this nature. Certain of the laboratory-type kits provide a more structured, yet open-ended, form of resource and include both listening and discussion elements. Principal among these are SRA *Listening Labs* and *Language Centres* 2 and 3 (Drake Educational Associates, Cardiff).

Much has been said and written about teachers' use of language in the classroom; indeed the perusal of the many transcripts to be found in the literature can be a salutary experience. In his well-known book, Barnes (1969) discusses the 'language of secondary education'. He sees it as a register which has much in common with publications and documents written in an impersonal style and, since the register is a spoken one, it overlaps with the language of public debates and meetings. Experienced teachers of the less-able will have developed the skill of 'listening to themselves' before they speak to a class. They will also have learned the art of modifying their speech in such a way as to make their utterances comprehensible without patronizing the listeners. Brennan (*op. cit.*) summarizes the situation by suggesting that the teacher should:

> 'Ensure that, in her language, she presents pupils with a model of language relevant to their own but requiring aspiration as they reach towards it; this involves mature statements subsequently rephrased for the pupil but, if possible, involving him in question and explanation about the differences.'

Writing

HM Inspectors (1979, *op. cit.*) gained an immediate impression of the formidable amount of writing undertaken in every one of the schools which they visited. Some of the statistics which they quote are quite astonishing. For example, one able fifth-year pupil had written 200 000 words in six subjects over four terms; a less-able one completed 9000 words in English and 11 000 in a course called 'Planning for Life'. HM Inspectors report that much of the pupils' writing was a re-presentation of teacher or textbook language. Writing is highly regarded by teachers as a permanent means of communication, and observers discovered that much of their teaching was geared to written follow-up. This was frequently at the expense of adequate discussion or definition of the task in hand.

The research team of the Schools Council Project, *The Development of Writing Abilities 11–18*, (Britton *et al.*, 1975) addressed itself to two fundamental questions that all teachers should ask themselves about any writing task which they ask pupils to complete: 'What is writing for ?' and 'Who is it for ?' Following the analysis of 2000 pieces of school writing, the project team developed two dimensions in detail, namely 'sense of audience' (*who* is the writing for) and 'purpose' (*what* is it for). The model which resulted was used in a further development project, *Writing Across the Curriculum*

11–16, which inquired more deeply into the relationships between different kinds of writing.

A sense of audience, or how the writer pictures his or her reader, is crucial in determining how the writing is done. The team point out that differences between pieces of writing occur partly because of who the reader is, also because of the way in which the writer feels about his or her reader. Six categories are suggested:

1. *Child (or adolescent) to self* — This writing does not account for the needs of any other reader, e.g., diaries, rough notes.
2. *Child (or adolescent) to trusted adult* — The writer is able to relate personal experiences or feelings because he or she knows that the reader will respond sympathetically.
3. *Pupil to teacher as partner in dialogue* — This covers writing which is essentially concerned with subject matter. Even so, the writer (pupil) still feels secure in the reader's (teacher's) interest and helpful attitude. Sixty-five per cent of English, 64 per cent of RE, but only 7 per cent of science scripts came into this category.
4. *Pupil to teacher seen as examiner or assessor* — This refers to examinations and all writing produced to satisfy teachers' demands, upon which the writer expects to be judged or assessed. Eighty-seven per cent of science, 81 per cent of geography and 69 per cent of history scripts came within this category.
5. *Child (or adolescent) to his or her peers as co-workers or friends.*
6. *Writer to his or her readers as an unknown or public audience.* Data showed that 51 per cent of first-year writing came within category number 2, but declined to 36 per cent of the total by year 5, whereas category 3 showed a proportional shift from 40 per cent in year 1 to 52 per cent in year 5. Figures suggest that the majority of school-teachers do not see writing as part of the learning process, but as something which happens *after* learning, with an emphasis on maintaining knowledge and performance.

Researchers also distinguished three broad categories of function to which recognizably distinct kinds of writing, typically associated with certain situations, can be allocated. The essential difference between each is the nature of the reader's response which the writer takes for granted:

(a) *Expressive* — The writer takes for granted that he or she is of interest to the reader. Expressive writing is rather like speech written down, or 'thinking aloud' on paper.
(b) *Transactional* — Here, it is taken for granted that the writer means what he or she says. Writing in this category relates to reporting, informing and theorizing and is typical of the impersonal writing most often used in the secondary school.
(c) *Poetic* — The writer takes for granted that the reader will share the experiences and feelings underlying what is presented. Poetic writing shows a heightened awareness of the pattern and imaginative qualities of language. Children's stories and poems are embryonically poetic.

The data shows that most writing is done in the secondary-school subject areas, especially science (92 per cent), history (88 per cent) and geography (88 per cent). Nevertheless, it is through expressive speech that we communicate with each other for most of the time. Because expressive writing is the nearest to speech, it is the form which we use for 'trying out and coming to terms with ideas'. Much effective writing seems to be on a continuum somewhere between either the expressive and transactional mode, or the expressive and poetic.

These findings are of special significance for children with learning difficulties. If they are sufficiently confident to write anything at all, then it is most likely to be similar to 'speech written down'. Colleagues who are subject specialists prefer children to use a transactional mode of writing, yet evidence suggests that this might inhibit learning because it prevents children making links between the new information and what they already know.

A much larger proportion of children are capable of achieving a measure of success in transactional and poetic writing from their achievements and with sympathetic guidance and encouragement. The project team believe expressive writing to be the 'seedbed' of these more specialized forms, also that its use throughout the curriculum would enable pupils to 'think' in writing and to learn through written language in the same way as they use talk.

Mallet and Newsome (1977) suggest that many pupils up to the age of 13+ see writing as a struggle for minimum competence to handle their thoughts at a deliberate level:

'They are probably sufficiently satisfied with making their loaded personal commentary for the teacher. It is only those who battle through the stage of minimum competence who are likely to find in writing a personal satisfaction, without which writing in any of its kinds can be no more than another skill which school demands.'

Helping children with their written work

Utilizing first-hand experience

Mallet and Newsome tell us that very young writers see their experiences from their own perspectives. First-hand experience is a good starting point for writing because the writer certainly knows the context and is aware of what he or she did and felt at the time. This information can be for the benefit of those pupils who have made little progress during their primary schooling and therefore can be regarded as beginning writers. It is suggested that, initially writing should be used to record meaningful situations, possibly as a *natural* outcome of some special occurrence. Children can be helped to overcome their anxiety about the end-product if teachers accept that, in the early stages, these experiences are likely to be presented as a monologue rather than as a coherent statement. Scope should be given for the re-drafting of writing, especially if it is intended as a permanent record, or for display.

Workbooks and worksheets

Evans, Summerfield and D'Arcy (1976) have produced an objective appraisal which is worthy of attention. Elsewhere in this book, Michael Williams discusses the use of worksheets in geography teaching. Assuming that the

166

reprographic quality is good and that the readability levels are commensurate with pupils' reading attainments, the structured format, closed form of instructions and limited range of responses required can be helpful to poor readers in the early stages of learning.

Workbooks and worksheets are useful for implementing individualized learning schedules, especially when designed to teach a specific skill. However, worksheets can be repetitive and boring once the novelty has worn off, the format of lessons becoming stereotyped with little opportunity for linguistic development. Similar criticism can be levelled at workbooks. (Regrettably, certain species of these are used as convenient time-fillers!) Teachers ought to be more discriminating in their use of workbooks and worksheets. Before producing or purchasing such materials, it would be advisable to consider if the learning task could be carried out in some other way.

Free writing

As pupils gain in confidence, they will become enthusiastic to write something of their own. Even though their vocabulary might be limited and sometimes mis-spelt, these opportunities should not be ignored. Colin McCall has already commented on remedial teachers' lost opportunities in capitalizing upon the imaginative thinking of their pupils. Mallet and Newsome (*op. cit.*) found that all children experience a special kind of satisfaction in writing stories and poems for their own pleasure. Early efforts are likely to have an 'expressive' flavour, and later drawing out a fantasy from remembered events and children's feelings about them at the time.

Discussion

In her critical appraisal of the *Writing Across the Curriculum* projects, Williams (1977) comments that many good lessons are destroyed because the interesting demonstration or discussion which she had witnessed was brought to an end with an abrupt 'now write it down'. These projects have made suggestions which are relevant to children with learning difficulties regarding *kinds* of writing, but their teachers need to be vigilant concerning the *quantity* of writing which these pupils undertake. Oral explanations, perhaps recorded on tape, can provide a perfectly satisfactory outcome of learning more often than is supposed. It is also suggested that adequate questioning and discussion should ensue prior to any written task.

Skills of written English

In one local authority, primary and secondary schools have worked together in order to achieve a consensus regarding the skills of written English which children should have attained by the age of secondary transfer. Two general objectives have been established: to see that this standard is reached by children of average attainment; to see that as many children of below average attainment approach this standard as nearly as possible.

'*By the age of transfer the child should be able to*:
  1. Show awareness of the concept of the sentence as a basic unit of meaning; make a consistently correct use of the full stop and accompanying capital letters.

167

2. Show variation in beginning sentences and in sentence length; make correct use of conjunctions (development lies in more subtle use of less common conjunctions).
3. Show some understanding of the use of the comma.
4. Make correct use of the question mark.
5. Make correct use of the exclamation mark.
6. Make correct use of capital letters.
7. Spell correctly most words in very common use — but be unafraid to attempt the more telling but more difficult word when it occurs to him.
8. Make use of certain spelling types or patterns, and certain spelling rules.
9. Use the apostrophe to signify omission (e.g., it's = it is).

(For more able children)
10. Make correct use of inverted commas.

Note: Use of the apostrophe to signify *possession* should not be introduced until the child has demonstrated a firm grasp of the more rudimentary aspects of punctuation named above, and will not normally be a primary-school concern.
Note: It would be useful for the child to have an understanding of certain grammatical terms such as:

vowels and consonants
singular and plural
present, past, future
syllables
stress or emphasis
also, (perhaps) conjunctions, nouns, adjectives, pronouns, verbs, adverbs.

It is, of course, important that children learn the need for *structure* in a piece of written work, i.e., the need for an interesting beginning, a logical development and a recognizable ending. This would represent the early stages of paragraphing, as a basis for further work of this nature in the secondary school.'

The discussion paper also stresses that there is often a clash between two elements of written English, namely that children write freely, creatively and *enjoy* it, also that children write as *correctly* as possible. It stresses the importance of achieving both of these aims, adding the rider that perhaps the best way to do so is to stress only one of them on one occasion of writing.
The schools concerned in the exercise have multi-racial intakes and cope with as wide a range of learning problems as others in any industrial area. This example has been quoted not only to demonstrate the benefits of co-operation between schools, but also to show the attempts which are being made in different parts of the country to identify minimum standards and to ensure continuity between primary and secondary education. This example might well provide encouragement to others. Obviously, some pupils will need to work very hard with a great deal of help and encouragement to achieve these minima by the end of secondary education, whilst others

capable of mastering additional skills should not be prevented from doing so.

Spelling

Poor spelling is the commonest cause of complaints received from colleagues by English and remedial departments concerning pupils' achievements in written expression. Whatever their age and ability, we can improve pupils' confidence and spelling proficiency by ensuring that:

(a) pupils are able to use a basic vocabulary both confidently and correctly. An appropriate word-list underpins any systematically organized spelling programme. Freyburg (1964) found that poor spellers made better progress when taught from spelling lists compiled by their teachers. For example, Bell (1970) gives a word-list used by ESN(M) children for over 70 per cent of their written work, whilst Hinson (1978) demonstrates how basic word-lists can be compiled for use with secondary-school pupils.
(b) they have the ability to find and correct their own careless mistakes by encouraging the proof-reading of their own written work.
(c) children know how they can best learn spellings for themselves. The Look-Cover-Write-Check visuo-motor technique recommended by Peters (1967) and Cripps (1979) has been found to be very effective for those needing remedial spelling.
(d) pupils understand the ways in which they can discover more about words by teaching them the use of a simple dictionary.
(e) as far as possible, teachers mark a child's work in the author's presence. The punitive overtones of spelling corrections can be avoided by discussing the nature of the mistake and how to put it right. Westwood (1975) points out that it is unreasonable to expect pupils to correct those words spelt incorrectly which are beyond their level of reading ability.
(f) Peters has argued convincingly that, for the vast majority, spelling is taught, not caught. There is a strong case for members of remedial, English and other subject departments coming together to gain a consensus on classroom practices that will be consistently applied in order to improve children's spelling achievements.

Handwriting

'If a child is left to develop his handwriting without instruction, he is unlikely to develop a running hand which is simultaneously legible, fast-flowing and individual, and becomes effortless to produce' (*A Language for Life*, 11.51).

Peters (*op. cit.*) has established the close connection between well-ordered and consistent handwriting and good spelling. Children who write letter-patterns with ease and confidence are inevitably good spellers. Handwriting is essentially a tool whose prime function is to serve the needs of all subjects of the curriculum. This being so, poor handwriting can be considered a handicap, whatever the writer's ability. Secondary teachers who, quite rightly, expect a good standard of presentation, need to overcome their reticence in teaching handwriting. It would be particularly helpful if primary and secondary schools could have some measure of agreement on the style to be adopted, as it seems unwise to make children adopt a different one once they have started cursive handwriting. For those who have not started it by secondary transfer, a style should be taught which is as near to script as possible, for example Platignum First Hand. Phillips (1976) and Jarman (1979) give valuable advice, while Bailey (1978) describes a procedure, based on operant conditioning, which is designed to correct severe problems.

There is an increasing number of left-handed children in the school population whose needs should not go unrecognized. Clark (1974) offers valuable advice.

Social writing skills

An introduction to the complexities of form-filling is listed among our priorities in the language curriculum. Form-filling is admirably dealt with in *Real-Life Reading Skills* (Scholastic Publications) and a series of booklets produced by the Home Office Unit for Educational Methods (Macmillan, 1978). MacAuslan (1981) has shown that the form-filling requirements for job applications to different firms vary so much that a locally-based collection would be an advantage for youngsters to inspect prior to applying, in order that they can familiarize themselves with the terminology.

The ability to write a neat letter is not only a social skill, but also embraces several basic elements of social competence: the ability to write one's own name, address and the date correctly; the ability to copy someone else's name and address accurately, and to write simple but coherent sentences in basic English both legibly and correctly spelt. Every opportunity should be taken to develop this skill as part of everyday occurrences and projects arising from school work.

Reading

Reading remains the most researched and opinionated of the language arts. Reading has become the lynch-pin of remedial departments, consequently it is assumed that most teachers of children with learning difficulties are well placed to advise other colleagues concerned about aspects of the reading curriculum.

The Schools Council Project, *The Effective Use of Reading* (Lunzer and Gardner, 1979), has shown that the reading attainments of average and above-average pupils in the 10–15 age-range can be improved. The national secondary survey (1979, *op. cit.*) identifies a fourth category, comprising those pupils whose abilities and attainments are between the 'average' and the 'least able'. Although not considered by schools to merit any particular support, in the fourth and fifth year, they can be carrying a number of examination subjects, yet 'striving with little success to develop some control of the language associated with them' (para. 6.7.12). Many teachers will be aware of localities in which a substantial number of children transfer to the secondary school having reading levels well below their chronological ages. A majority of these are outside the direct responsibility of the remedial department, yet desperately needing help in order to cope with the reading demands of secondary education.

There is a belated but growing awareness that 'something must be done' and the common factor which underpins any improvement is some form of special attention to the reading curriculum, sustained throughout secondary schooling. There are a number of strategies which teachers of children with learning difficulties can initiate, primarily geared to the individual needs of those who are their particular concern, but also providing a resource to colleagues in other departments:

1. From standardized data, they can pinpoint all children requiring additional assessment to be carried out on an individual basis. Besides tests already familiar, it is worth noting the increasing importance of Informal Reading Inventories (see Pumphrey, 1977) and error analysis. The latter technique can be readily adapted to both reading and writing, focusing teachers' attention on the child's performance and encouraging the identification of error patterns which are of diagnostic importance (see also Goodacre, 1972 and Peters, 1975).
2. Using test data, the head of department should then negotiate timetabling arrangements suited to the individual needs of all children requiring special help with their literacy problems.
3. Staff of the remedial department can organize systems geared to the teaching of basic sight vocabulary and phonic skills to pupils with severe reading difficulties. (Phonic resources can be effectively organized using the *Classroom Index of Phonic Resources*, NARE, 1978.)
4. A system for grading supplementary reading material should be implemented, using one of the guides listed at the end of this chapter.
5. Classroom arrangements for hearing children read are not always handled with the sensitivity which they merit. It is suggested that strategies could be explained in detail and demonstrated, perhaps enlisting the help of the LEA support service. It is also essential to discuss and establish an adequate system for recording reading progress.
6. Brennan (1978) concludes that undue stress is often laid on the early, mechanical stages of reading skill at the expense of comprehension, reading speed and the 'higher' functional skills of reading. Fawcett (1979) has shown that 'laboratory'-type kits can have a beneficial effect on children's reading comprehension. They should not, of course, become the sole source of comprehension materials for less-able pupils. Remedial teachers can promote their efficient use over a wider ability range by helping colleagues to familiarize themselves with procedures, organize the materials properly in the classroom and recognize their value and limitations.
7. Walker (1974) and Lunzer and Gardner (*op. cit.*) regard teacher-directed group discussion activities, based on close procedure exercises, as a promising development in the improvement of reading comprehension. Even pupils of low reading ability are able to follow reading discussions and use them as an aid to understanding texts. Other activities which can be organized in this way include group prediction, group SQ3R (an introduction to study skills) and group deletion. They create game-like conditions which children find stimulating, at the same time demanding intensive and careful reading in order to evaluate a particular text.
   The implications of the work of these investigators are far-reaching. Group oral reading procedures can be applied across a wide range of

age and ability and in any subject which makes heavy demands on reading comprehension. Here is a further instance where remedial departments can become agents for change within a school.

8. Teachers of the less-able will be especially conscious of the importance of readability levels in the choosing of reading and textbook materials (see Harrison, 1980). Here is an area in which they can share their knowledge and expertise with other teachers, also giving assistance in the choice of appropriate reading materials, preferably using sets of criteria adapted for the purpose (an example of this is to be found in chapter 8).

9. A working party sponsored by the British Library and Schools Council (1981) has shown that children in secondary schools are not taught how to learn and use the learning resources in their schools. It recommends that a curriculum committee representing all staff should draw up a policy for the whole school about handling information. Every teacher will be interested in the report, because the general principles apply to learning tasks given to pupils of all ages.

10. The Schools Council Project *Children and their Books* (1977) revealed that, by the age of 14+, as many as 36 per cent of children have either failed to establish, or have totally abandoned, the habit of reading books at home. The project acknowledges the importance of class libraries as one way of encouraging positive attitudes towards books. In common with all other children, those with learning difficulties will require frequent opportunities to learn the correct use of a well-stocked school library. Literature and poetry should not be missing from their English lessons, since these children are as capable of as imaginative a response as others, even though they may need more initial encouragement.

Brennan charges us that 'there is something wrong in a democratic society if intelligent members cannot communicate with the less intelligent in situations and about topics which are common to both groups' (*op. cit.*). This chapter has attempted to show that the language curriculum for children with learning difficulties should be considered in the context of the whole school for this to become a reality. Naturally, it will not be easy to persuade some colleagues, blinkered by their own professional immobility, that the time has come to face up to the special needs of these pupils. Substantial evidence from national reports indicates that policy-makers at top level are anxious to see improvements. It has been said that good education demands courage. Once teachers of children with learning difficulties have established effective language curricula within their own departments, they will have the courage of their own convictions to go out and influence colleagues, to the consequent benefit of their pupils.

References and further reading

Adams, A. and Pearce, J., *Every English Teacher*, OUP, 1974.
Allen, D., *Constructing a Language Policy, Pack 8 — Some Issues from the Bullock Report*, Schools Council Project: *Writing Across the Curriculum*, University of London Institute of Education, 1975.

Bailey, T. J. (1978), 'An approach to analysing and improving handwriting' in *Remedial Education*, Vol. 13, No. 2.

Barnes, D., Britton, J. and Rosen, H., *Language, the Learner and the School*, Penguin, 1969.

Bell, P., *Basic Teaching for Slow Learners*, Muller, 1970.

Blagg, N., 'The diagnosis of learning difficulties' in *Ways and Means 2*, Somerset Education Authority/Globe Education, 1981.

Brennan, W. K., *Reading for Slow Learners: a Curriculum Guide*, Schools Council Curriculum Bulletin 7, Evans/Methuen, 1978.

Brennan, W. K., *Curricular Needs of Slow Learners*, Schools Council Working Paper 63, Evans/Methuen, 1979.

Britton, J., Burgess, T. *et al.*, *The Development of Writing Abilities 11–18*, Schools Council Research Study, Macmillan, 1975.

Bullock, Lord (Chairman), *A Language for Life*, HMSO, 1975.

Clark, M. M., *Teaching Left-Handed Children*, Hodder and Stoughton, 1974.

Clements, S., 'Talk in the Secondary School' in Blackburn, T. (ed.), *Handbook for English Teachers 2 — Talking and Writing*, Methuen, 1967.

Cripps, C. C., (1979), 'Spelling: a safe account' in *Remedial Education*, Vol. 14, No. 3.

DES, *Aspects of Secondary Education in England*, HMSO, 1979.

DES/Welsh Office, *The School Curriculum*, HMSO, 1981.

Dolch, E. W., *Psychology and the Teaching of Reading*, Garrard Press, 1951.

Evans, D., Summerfield, A. and D'Arcy, P., 'Do worksheet work?' in *Writing in Science*, Ward Lock Educational, 1975.

Fawcett, R., 'Reading laboratories' in Lunzer, E. and Gardner, K. (eds), *The Effective Use of Reading*, Heinemann, 1979.

Freyburg, P. S (1964), 'A comparison of two approaches to the teaching of spelling, *British Journal of Educational Psychology*, Vol. 34.

Goodacre, E. J., *Hearing Children Read*, Centre for the Teaching of Reading, University of Reading, 1972.

Harrison, C., *Readability in the Classroom*, Cambridge University Press, 1980.

Hinson, M., 'Spelling' in *Encouraging Results*, Macdonald Educational, 1978.

Jackson, S., *A Teacher's Guide to Tests and Testing*, Longman, 1971.

Jarman, C., *The Development of Handwriting Skills*, Blackwell, 1979.

Jeremiah, T. C., *Source Book of Creative Themes*, Blackwell, 1972.

Lunzer, E. and Gardner, K., *The Effective Use of Reading*, Heinemann, 1979.

MacAuslan, A. (1981), 'Fill in this form correctly if you want a job' in *Remedial Education*, Vol. 16, No. 2.

Mallet, M. and Newsome, B., *Talking, Writing and Learning 8–13*, Schools Council working Paper 59, Evans/Methuen, 1977.

Marland, M. (ed.), *Language Across the Curriculum*, Heinemann Educational, 1977.

Martin, N., D'Arcy, P. *et al.*, *Writing and Learning Across the Curriculum 11–16*, Ward Lock Educational, 1976.

Ministry of Education, *Half Our Future*, HMSO, 1965.

National Association for Remedial Education, *The Role of Remedial Teachers, Guidelines* 2, 1979.

National Association for the Teaching of English, *Language Across the Curriculum, Guidelines for Schools*, Ward Lock Educational, 1976.

Peters, M., *Spelling: Caught or Taught?*, Routledge and Kegan Paul, 1963.

Peters, M., *Diagnostic and Remedial Spelling Manual*, Macmillan, 1975.

Phillips, R. C., *The Skills of Handwriting*, R. C. Phillips Ltd, 70 High Street, Oxford, 1976.

Pumphrey, P., *Reading: Tests and Assessment Techniques*, Hodder and Stoughton, 1976.

Pumphrey, P., *Measuring Reading Abilities: Concepts, Sources and Applications*, Hodder and Stoughton, 1977.

Robertson, I., *Language across the Curriculum: Four Case Studies*, Schools Council Working Paper 67, Methuen, 1980.

Schools Council, *Information Skills in the Secondary School*, Schools Council Curriculum Bulletin 9, Methuen Educational, 1981.

Self, D., *Talk: A Practical Guide to Oral Work in the Secondary School*, Ward Lock Educational, 1976.

Thomson, G. and Hinson, M., 'Assessment' in *Encouraging Results*, Macdonald Educational, 1978.

Torbe, M. (ed.), *Language, Teaching and Learning* series, Ward Lock Educational, 1981.

Walker, C., *Reading Development and Extension*, Ward Lock Educational, 1974.

Warwickshire County Council Education Department, *Guidelines on the Use of Reading Tests*, 1981 (available from Milverton Centre, 18 Rugby Road, Leamington Spa, Warwickshire).

Westwood, P., *The Remedial Teacher's Handbook*, Oliver and Boyd, 1975.

Whitehead, F. *et al*, *Children and their Books*, Schools Council Research Study, Macmillan, 1977.

Wilkinson, A. M., *Spoken English*, Educational Review Occasional Publications 2, University of Birmingham, 1965.

Wilkinson, A. M. (1968), 'The implications of oracy' in the *Educational Review*, Vol. 20, No. 2.

Wilkinson, A. and Stratta, L. (1972), 'Listening and the study of spoken language' in the *Educational Review*, Vol. 25, No. 1.

Wilkinson, A. Stratta, L. and Dudley, P., *The Quality of Listening*, Schools Council Research Study, Macmillan, 1974.

Williams, J. T., *Learning to Write, or Writing to Learn*, NFER, 1977.

The following contain lists useful in grading supplementary reading books:

Atkinson, E. J. and Gains, C. W., *The New A–Z List of Reading Books*, National Association for Remedial Education, 1981. (NARE, 2 Lichfield Road, Stafford ST17 4JX).

Sandwell Child Psychology Service, *Evaluation of Reading Books: A Teacher's Guide**, 1982. (SCPS, Child Guidance Centre, 12 Grange Road, West Bromwich, West Midlands B70 8PD)

Segal, S. S. and Pascoe, T. W., *Help in Reading**, National Book League, 1975.

* Contains notes on the use of individual series in the classroom.

12

Mathematics in the secondary school

———————————— TERENCE J. BAILEY ————————————

Introduction

Mathematics is rightly regarded as a key school subject in both the primary and secondary curriculum. It is particularly important for children with learning difficulties, partly because mathematical skills will constantly be demanded for daily living, and partly because a knowledge of mathematics can help them to understand and interpret many aspects of the world in which they live.

If we are to systematically help less-able pupils in the classroom, we need a simple model for teaching mathematics. The model in figure 10, based on Warnock (1978) and Brennan (1979), is presented as one framework for planning and implementing a mathematics curriculum. The model is a cyclical one, in that continuous assessment should lead back to a review of the aims and objectives in the light of experience and knowledge.

Aims

Aims are long-term statements about the general direction of teaching mathematics and will be the same for all pupils, irrespective of their ability level. The fourteen aims defined by HM Inspectorate in *Aspects of Secondary Education* (1979), provide a useful starting point. These statements of intent include the development of appropriate mathematical language; recognition of relationships; understanding of number; appreciation of units of measurement, money and shapes; interpretation of diagrams, and use of mathematical aids.

Objectives

For children with learning difficulties, such broad aims need to be translated into what Brennan (1979) has called 'statements of objectives which are observable, measurable and assessable'. One might add the term 'sequential' to this list, since mathematics is one subject where in many areas there is a definite progression of skills from the simple to the complex. Statements of objectives will indicate what the pupil is expected to be able to do at the end of a learning experience which he could not do previously. They are by no means easy to write. One problem relates to the range of mathematical skills to be covered at the secondary level. Some less-able pupils may still be at the pre-conceptual level, while others will be at the conceptual or abstract thinking stage. It is essential, therefore, that objectives are written to cover the whole range of mathematical functioning.

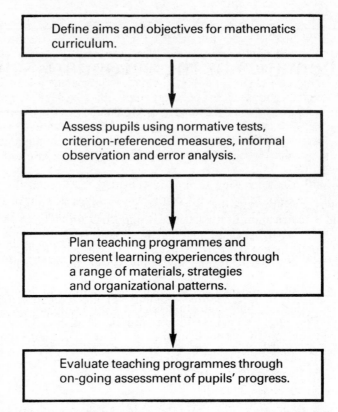

Fig. 10 A model for teaching mathematics to children with learning difficulties.

The major thrust in the field of developing curriculum objectives for mathematics has been within our primary and special schools. Secondary teachers should draw upon and expand this work. Ainscow and Tweddle (1979), in writing about the ESN(M) school, provide valuable advice and give examples of behavioural objectives for developing mathematical objectives which can be applied over a wider ability range.

In the area of basic number and computational skills, two commercial mathematics tests actually provide lists of behavioural objectives which form a useful starting point for developing one's own list. *Yardsticks* (1975) have a list of some 293 objectives, gradually increasing in their level of complexity. The first objective in level 1 merely requires the pupil to count the members of the set up to 10, whereas one later objective at level 5 requires the pupil to identify the highest common factor of a pair of numbers. The *Profile of Mathematical Skills* (1979), has a range of objectives, including the four rules of number — for example, 'multiplication of one- or two-digit numbers by a single digit multiplier: vertical form'.

Checkpoint (1978) lists 110 separate skills in which the individual pupil should be able to demonstrate competence. They cover four major strands of the mathematics curriculum — sets, numbers, measurement and geometry. Each of the checkpoints describes something that the individual child should be able to do — for example: 'Can group any set of objects in hundreds, tens and units, and can use this grouping to say and write the number. Can show the meaning of the digits in any three-digit number.'

Staras (1980) has developed a mathematics curriculum for an ESN(M) school and defined a minimal list of behavioural objectives for measurement, length, area, weight, capacity, volume, time and money. *Assessment in Mathematics* (1981) also provides specific objectives in these areas, as well as fractions, decimals, percentages, angles and scale. Although intended for use largely in the primary years of schooling, they could prove useful for many secondary pupils.

One group of enterprising secondary remedial teachers in the London Borough of Havering (1981), produced a 'Maths Leavers' Course for Less-Able Pupils'. It emphasizes minimal survival skills that pupils need to master and is written in terms of behavioural objectives. For example, the authors see the area of money for school leavers as including shopping, budgeting, savings, credit, bills, leisure and wages. The pupil is required to do the following:

(a) calculate the money earned for a number of hours worked at a flat rate;
(b) calculate overtime money earned for a number of hours worked at a certain overtime rate;
(c) compute gross pay;
(d) total deductions accurately;
(e) subtract deductions from gross pay;
(f) identify codes on a wage slip;
(g) check a wage packet when presented with it.

These examples serve to illustrate the need for secondary teachers dealing with less-able pupils to foster close links with local special schools and primary schools and to come together in study groups to plan and write programmes of objectives for all the fourteen aims referred to previously.

Having defined one's aims and objectives in teaching mathematics, the three fundamental stages which follow are shown in figure 10 to be (1) assessing the child, (2) planning a teaching programme, and (3) evaluating the teaching programme. In other words, we must identify the mathematical difficulties experienced by these pupils, in particular the reasons for their unfavourable attitudes to the subject. After planning and implementing strategies aimed at overcoming these difficulties, we need to assess the effectiveness of our teaching. If we have been successful, we can move on to the next stage in our mathematics programme. However, a reappraisal will be necessary if it is not working. We might decide upon an intensification of certain parts of our teaching, or a drastic change in our strategy. For example, it might be necessary to:

(a) shift from the symbolic (pages of problems) to the pictorial, or to the use of concrete materials more meaningful to the pupil;
(b) change the method of instruction from, say, 'chalk and talk' to taped materials;

177

(c) change the organizational plan from, say, individual work to children working in pairs.

Sometimes, teachers have to accept that certain pupils with severe learning difficulties will continue to have recourse to mathematical 'crutches' throughout their school careers. Children with severe sequential memory problems might always need to consult a table square or to check their work with a calculator. (This is no less realistic than granting a slide rule to an engineer or a computer to a research scientist.)

Initial assessment

Figure 11 presents a more detailed breakdown of the final three stages of the teaching model.

It is sensible to carry out a screening procedure on all pupils at their transfer to the secondary school, bearing in mind that they will have come from a variety of feeder primary schools with differing mathematical standards.

There are a number of standardized group tests of mathematics that are quickly administered and which yield the data necessary for an initial assessment. Some normative tests give standard scores whilst others give mathematical ages. *Profile of Mathematical Skills*, published by Nelson, gives both. The Mathematical Association's publication entitled *Tests* (1979) looks at a variety of both normative and criterion-referenced assessment procedures and provides helpful critiques of each of them.

Standardized test results need to be tempered with judgements based on observation and experience. They should not be used as an excuse for placing a pupil into a particular set for the rest of his school career. Despite its shortcomings at this initial screening stage, I prefer the use of the term 'mathematical age'. This allows the division of pupils into three groupings, based on a Piagetian model of thinking:

Group A — mathematical age below 7 years.
Group B — mathematical age 7–11 years.
Group C — mathematical age 11 years and over.

Such a grouping might appear too simplistic, but it does provide a starting point. In general, each group is likely to have different needs and will exhibit different problems. The second stage of the assessment programme entails a detailed examination of these, mainly through observation of how a particular task is tackled.

Group A

Hopefully, only a small number of pupils will need to be included in Group A. However, following the recommendations of the Warnock Report (1978), there have been moves towards the greater integration of ESN(M) pupils, therefore schools' future intakes might well include a larger number of pupils whose mathematical skills fit this grouping. In Piagetian terms, the pupils are more likely to be functioning at the pre-operational stage, thus necessitating a further assessment of their ability to use mathematical language meaningfully.

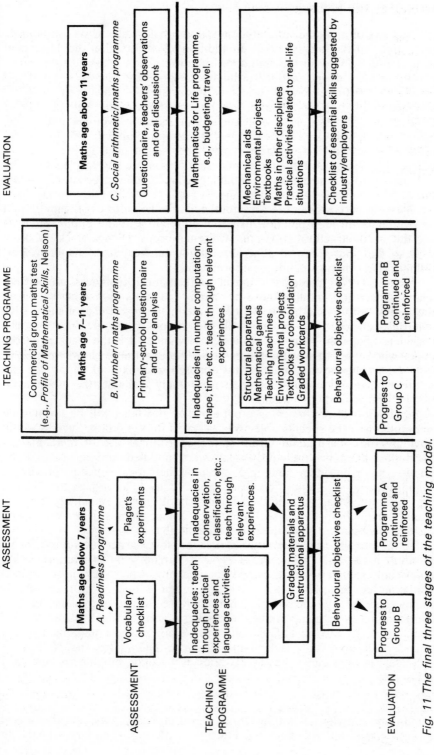

Fig. 11 The final three stages of the teaching model.

179

Any one of a number of mathematical vocabulary checklists can be used (e.g., Bell, 1970; Hughes, 1973). In addition, close attention should be paid to the pupils' ability in the skill areas of conservation, classification, cardination, ordination and cardinal-ordinal correspondence. Nichols (1963) and Fogelman (1970) present a variety of informal tests which can easily be administered by the teacher using a minimum of apparatus. Tanner's (1977) model of disciplinary stages, which she links to Piaget's developmental stages, has particular relevance to teaching mathematics. Pupils in this group are usually at the 'basic disciplinary stage'. They might need to learn how to follow directions; ways of sharing materials, resources and teacher time, be encouraged to ask questions when failing to understand procedures, and so on.

Where weaknesses in the areas outlined are shown to exist, they should be overcome through practical experiences relating to the pupils' interests and the use of structural apparatus (Cuisenaire rods, Dienes blocks, abacus, etc.) so that they learn to generalize about number, size, shape, weight, distance and other visual-motor information.

Nichols (1970) presents a useful mathematical readiness programme where experiences parallel those of reading readiness by making use of all the pupils' sensory pathways. Critics sometimes suggest that manipulative materials can lose their usefulness at the secondary school, since they are considered babyish. (It is not always clear whether it is the teachers or the pupils who object to structural apparatus!) My experience shows that where a school emphasizes the practical (as opposed to a textbook) approach and where a range of structural materials is normally available, the problems of using such apparatus are minimal.

Evaluation of any teaching programme at this level will be through an examination of the specific objectives as stated for the group. Success would obviously be measured in terms of the appropriate use of mathematical vocabulary which was previously unknown or muddled, and the ability of the pupil to show an understanding of those mathematical concepts previously found to be non-existent or confused. Since many children pass through the pre-operational stage during their infant school careers, secondary teachers would benefit from liaison with their local infant schools. They would find the approaches used in mathematics illuminating.

In the process of trying out materials for slow learners eventually incorporated in the *Kent Mathematics Project*, Larcombe (1980) reported that almost all secondary pupils talked about a time when they most enjoyed mathematics. Invariably this was in the infants school. Unfortunately, as pupils move through the school system, they are given clear evidence of their shortcomings in mathematics by the number of crosses which permeate their work. This, as Buxton (1980) points out, leads to the equation of wrong answer = disapproval = lack of moral worth. This makes the problem at secondary level as much one of motivation as it is of developing mathematical skills.

Group B

Pupils who initially fall within Group B will probably constitute the largest group of children with learning difficulties entering secondary schools. In

Piagetian terms, they are likely to have reached the concrete-operational stage. There is a need to check their basic computation in relation to the four rules of number and place value, as well as their ability to work with shape, time, measurement and money. Although there are some published tests such as the *Tameside Numeracy Test* (Schofield and Sims), and the *Mathematics Test* (Oliver and Boyd), which can assist the teacher in looking closer at arithmetical concepts with this group, teachers' observations of pupil errors and subsequent discussions with the students about them can reveal a great deal of information and may show up patterns of mistakes. A simple checklist, similar to *Yardsticks* (1975), would be extremely valuable. Westwood (1975) presents a number of useful questions which teachers can ask about a pupil's performance in the areas outlined. Some questions relate to the child's ability to carry out both simple and more complex addition and subtraction with number, and her understanding of the commutative law in addition, additive composition and the complementary character of addition and subtraction. Other questions seek to ascertain the state of the child's knowledge in relation to place value with hundreds, tens and units, telling the time accurately, measurement with a ruler and the handling of money in practical situations.

No matter what organizational plan is evident in a secondary school, even non-specialist teachers who are called upon to work with less-able pupils in mathematics soon become aware of the abundance and variety of errors exhibited by the pupils. One group of secondary remedial teachers isolated the following possible causes of lack of progress in mathematics, many of which are related to the difficulties of pupils in Group B:

1. Vocabulary concepts are unknown.
2. Reading age of the material is too difficult.
3. Confusion of meanings of arithmetical signs, e.g., + and ×.
4. Poor auditory memory or listening ability.
5. Visual sequencing difficulties.
6. Inability to transfer mechanical computation skills to problems.
7. Difficulties with place value.
8. Notation problems.
9. Inability to think in abstract terms.
10. Pupil is tied to one form of recording.

Obviously, there are other causes of lack of progress in mathematics. Absence from school for any length of time and the unwillingness to try mathematics involving anything other than pages of sums, due to a basic insecurity in the pupil, have been identified as causative factors. To this list, we might add other more severe cognitive disturbances which have been noted by researchers as affecting a pupil's mathematical ability, especially in arithmetic. Kaliski (1967) reported that children with arithmetic disability often confuse spatial relationships such as up-down, top-bottom, and so on. Strauss (1951) noted that some pupils handicapped in number ability exhibited difficulties in seeing objects in sets, in copying numbers correctly and seeing geometric shapes as anything other than unrelated lines. Lerner (1971) points to the difficulties that an inaccurate or imprecise notion of body image can have on an understanding of mathematics. Schrieber (1972) has shown

181

that pupils with poor figure-ground discrimination can have severe difficulties in mathematics.

Kilburn writing in *The Times Educational Supplement* (9.5.1980) in an article entitled 'Maths made difficult' pinpointed faulty teaching as a cause of mathematics difficulty for all ages and abilities of children. He suggests that able mathematics teachers, unless they are sensitive and understanding, may by their skills render children helpless. Their speed of working, their effortless use of difficult words and symbols, and their enjoyment of the subject, which many pupils dislike, can distance them so far that they become threats rather than allies. He goes on to highlight wrong teaching which, while it may lead to right answers immediately, can actually mislead the pupil mathematically. An example is the statement 'When multiplying by 10 add a nought'. Although this works for whole numbers, it obscures the core-concept of place value. When it is applied to 7·3 multipled by 10, a severe feeling of helplessness is likely to be experienced as a trusted and taught method suddenly does not work.

For further discussion of pupils' mathematical difficulties, the reader is referred to Ablewhite (1969), Williams (1970), Arena (1972), Cawley (1972), Otto *et al.* (1973), Miles (1975), Waddon (1975), Sovchik and Heddens (1978), Hopkins (1978), Bailey (1979) and Flinter (1979). (See References.)

Strategies

Armed with the list of possible causes of difficulty in mathematics, the group of teachers previously referred to were presented with a series of problems. They were asked to identify possible major causes of difficulty in each case, and to suggest remedial strategies which might help the pupils to overcome the problem.

Only a sample of the types of difficulties likely to be encountered is given, and readers will be able to extend both the types of problems and the possible remedial strategies.

Example A

On separate occasions, pupils produced the following errors:

$$3 \times 5 = 51$$
$$14 + 9 = 41$$
$$237 \times 9 = 2106$$

Possible major causes of difficulties

1. Visual defect.
2. Visual-sequential memory difficulty (numbers written in wrong order).
3. Spatial difficulties (left-to-right orientation).

Suggested remedial strategies

1. (a) Check eyesight.
   (b) Use the auditory channel by taping basic number activities.
2. (a) Make the distinction between 'wrong' and 'reversed'. Give partial credit if the student indicates the correct answer orally, but makes an error in recording.

(b) Allow the recording of answers on tape.
(c) Allow the use of number tables around the room.
(d) Use mechanical aids as checking devices.
(e) Introduce memory games.
3. Use exercises adapted from a reading programme to develop body awareness and left-to-right sequencing.

Example B

Question:

If a man dies before he has finished paying for his house, his wife can be responsible for the remaining debt. To protect her and his children, a man decided to take out a Mortgage Protection Assurance Policy for a monthly payment of £5.60. This, he was informed, would cover his house valued at £10 000, which he was purchasing over a period of 20 years. How much will he have paid out to the insurance company in 20 years?

Answer: Left blank.

Possible difficulties

1. Reading level of text is too high for the pupil (many polysyllabic words and sentences that are too long).
2. Level of abstraction is too high, leading to inability to discard irrelevant elements.
3. Visual memory is probably poor; by the end of the question, the pupil would have forgotten previous information.

Suggested strategies

1. Teach difficult vocabulary beforehand through discussion.
2. Improve reading skills, e.g., show how to break words into syllables.
3. Put the problem on tape or present it orally.
4. Rewrite the problem using simpler language and reduce sentence length to eliminate redundant information.
5. Make the question more relevant and interesting.
6. Use textbooks with lower readability levels.

Example C

Question: What is the difference between 719 and 56?
Answer: 719 is bigger.

Question: Look carefully at the triangle. Is it a right-angled, isosceles or equilateral triangle?

Answer: Left blank

On separate occasions, this pupil produced the following responses:

Task	Answer
Take away 56 from 719	663
719 subtract 56	663
719 minus 56	Left blank

Difficulties

There are vocabulary difficulties, causing the pupil to misunderstand the question or not understand at all.

Suggested strategies

1. Teach vocabulary needed for the question through meaningful experiences and discussion.
2. Ask questions to verify that the pupil understands verbal information or instructions before beginning the task.
3. To avoid the pupil becoming lost during verbal instructions, say only what is necessary.
4. Select and simplify words in describing a concept or skill.
5. Establish the understanding of one term thoroughly before teaching other terms.
6. Ensure all terms used by teacher and textbook or worksheet are taught and overlearned.
7. Use vocabulary wallcharts and, if possible, picture cues.

Example D

On different occasions, a pupil produced the following responses:

(i)
$$26$$
$$657$$
$$+295$$
$$978$$

(ii) $$657 + 295 + 26 = 101,618$$

Difficulties

The pupil is tied to one form of recording.

Strategies

Ensure opportunities for all forms of recording, initially with smaller numbers.

Example E

On separate occasions, a pupil produced these answers:

(i) $$385 - 127 = 258$$

(ii) *Question*: There are 385 pages in Donald's book. He has read 127 of them. How many pages has he still to read?
Answer: Left blank.

Difficulties

1. The pupil can work with numbers, but has difficulty transferring the process to problem situations, due to lack of experience or difficulties in abstract thinking.
2. The language structure on the workcard is not related to pupil's language experiences, e.g., 'has he still to read'.

Strategies

1. Encourage the pupil to draw pictures, graphs or diagrams to help him think in concrete terms.
2. Physically act out problems, e.g., turn pages in a book.
3. Give some calculation in numerical and problem form.
4. Relate the problem to real-life experiences.
5. Underline important points, e.g., 385 and 127.
6. Simplify the language structure of the question.

Example F

(i) A pupil recited the six-times table correctly up to $5 \times 6 = 30$, but then jumped to $8 \times 6 = 34$ and got completely lost.
(ii) When asked to recite months of year, the same pupil gave: January, February, May, August, July, etc.

Difficulties

1. Poor visual memory and/or visual sequencing.
2. Distractability or poor listening skills.

Strategies

1. Tape tables and use them daily (overlearning).
2. Allow a shortened form of the answer for recitation, e.g., instead of $1 \times 6 = 6$, etc., accept 6, 12, 18, etc.
3. Encourage forms $6 \times 1 = \quad$, $6 \times 2 = \quad$, as opposed to $1 \times 6 = \quad$, etc., to help relieve the memory load.
4. Allow the use of a table square, months-of-year chart or machines for computation.
5. Provide memory games.
6. Use activities to improve listening skills.

Example G

(i)
$$\begin{array}{r} 84 \\ -36 \\ \hline 52 \\ \hline \end{array}$$

(ii)
$$7\overline{\smash{)}704} \quad \text{10 remainder 4}$$

(iii) *Question*: In this number (33), how many times bigger is the first 3 than the second 3?
Answer: 3

185

(iv) *Question*: What is 2 worth in this number: 3825?
   Answer: 2

Difficulties

The pupil has difficulties in place value and borrowing.

Strategies

1. Use an abacus and other structural apparatus, e.g., Stern's dual board.
2. Put place value charts in the classroom.
3. Use a mileometer or click counters.
4. Return to smaller, meaningful numbers.

Example H

(i)
$$627 \times 13 = 640$$
$$582 \div 6 = 576$$

(ii) *Question*: Which of these, $+ - \times \div$, do we use in division?
   Answer: $\times$

Difficulties

The pupil confuses arithmetical signs.

Strategies

1. Highlight signs in different colours.
2. Give examples of differences on a chart.

Example I

Question: Add these amounts together:
                   5p, £1.27 and 76p
Answer: $\cdot$5
                   1$\cdot$27
                    $\cdot$76
                   ———
                   £2$\cdot$53
                   ———

Question: Add these amounts together:
                   $3\cdot5 + 8\cdot64 + 9\cdot352$
Answer: 102$\cdot$51

Difficulties

1. Difficulty with written expression of small sum of money as part of pound.
2. Difficulty with place value.

Strategies

1. Give more real-life experience using money.
2. Give more experience in the written form of money, following practical work.
3. Use examples such as shopping bills from a supermarket.

186

Example J

(i) A pupil is shown that $19 + 7 = 26$, and is then asked to say what is $7 + 19 = \quad$. She cannot answer immediately, but works the sum out again.
(ii) A pupil is shown that $35 + 17 = 52$, and is then asked to say what is $52 - 35 = \quad$. He cannot see the answer immediately.

Difficulties

There are concept formation difficulties. In (i), there is a lack of understanding of the commutative law of addition ($a + b = b + a$); in (ii) there are difficulties with the reverse law of addition and subtraction (if $a + b = c$, $c - a = b$, etc.).

Strategies

Use structural apparatus and everyday objects. Work on the partitioning of sets.

Example K

A teacher gave a pupil the following questions orally:
(i) *Question*: Write down the number two hundred and three.
   Answer: 2003.
(ii) *Question*: Write down the next number after twenty nine.
   Answer: (2010) twenty ten.

Difficulties

1. Lack of understanding of notation, i.e., of the representation of numbers and quantities of symbols.

Strategies

1. Introduce experiences in counting and grouping objects using everyday materials; a trundle wheel, the pupil's own strides, mathematical games.
2. Use a '100' wallchart for daily counting.

Example L

A pupil completed the following sums:
$$36 - 9 = 28$$
$$25 + 17 = 41$$

Difficulties

1. Counting back incorrectly.

Strategies

1. Demonstrate the correct process with structural apparatus, e.g., number ladders.
2. Allow the pupil self-help aids, such as objects, counting on fingers, tally marks.
3. From the stage of counting using objects, take the pupil forward gradually

and systematically so that counting is condensed into spoken words, and is then internalized (mental arithmetic or counting in the mind).

Example M

A pupil was asked to complete the following:

Tasks	Answers
$4^2 = ?$	8
$3y = 9$	
$y = ?$	27

Difficulties

1. Inability to think in abstract terms.
2. The above type of problems are too complex for less-able pupils.

Strategies

1. Present the problem in practical, concrete terms, e.g., if 3 apples are worth 9 bananas, what is 1 apple worth?
2. Use a calculating machine.

The analysis of pupils' errors and the identification of possible causative factors are those stages of assessment and diagnosis which must precede the implementation of appropriate strategies. They will form the basis of a remedial programme which is continually evaluated.

For more detailed teaching programmes for pupils in group B, suggestions can be found in Tansley and Gulliford (1960), Bell (1970), Williams (1970), Irving (1972), Hughes (1973), Duncan (1978) and Westwood (1975). Most of these authorities suggest that for less-able pupils there is a certain minimal core of essential knowledge which should be taught at the secondary stage. Such a programme should utilize a variety of approaches including: structural material; pictorial material; teaching machines (calculator, digitor, Audiopage, Dataman, and Speak and Maths); projects and topics; mathematical games, particularly where throwing of a dice is involved and, for consolidation, workbooks, workcards or worksheets. Mathematical games, both commercial and home-made, can emphasize memory, logical deduction and mental arithmetic. Audio-visual aids have a high potential for motivation, e.g. tape-recorders for teaching tables.

Teachers will frequently talk about pupils having a short attention span, being distractable and being uninterested in mathematics. These symptoms of failure are often the result of boredom with the teaching programme. Highly distractable children can spend hours playing with a pin-ball machine, cards, dice, darts and space-invader games, and not infrequently show adequate mathematical skills. As Lister (*TES* 24.4.1981) points out, these pupils may appear to calculate nothing in the classroom, but will calculate any combination of doubles on a dart-board, the number of points for clearing all the colours on a snooker table, and the return on an 'each-way yankee' in a betting shop. Worksheets are a useful way of organizing individual or paired work for many students, but in planning them, teachers should heed the advice of the Association of Teachers of Mathematics (1977), and Larcombe (1978):

1. Worksheets should use as few words as possible. The vocabulary should be within the pupils' understanding.
2. Do not put too many questions on a sheet. This allows pupils the satisfaction of finishing a piece of work fairly often.
3. Ensure the layout is clear and visually stimulating and that not too much information is crammed on a page.
4. Use pictures where possible. Make them interesting.
5. Use typing or printing whenever possible.

No one set of materials can solve all the problems manifested by pupils with mathematical difficulties. However, the following five structured materials might prove valuable:

1. *The Kent Maths Project* — L Pack, Ward Lock Educational.
2. *Smile — Secondary Maths Independent Learning Experiment*, ILEA.
3. *Distar Maths*, SRA.
4. *Schools Maths Project* — 7–13 years, Cambridge University Press.
5. *Checkpoint*, ILEA.

For interested readers, the rationale behind the *Kent Maths Project* is given by Larcombe (1979). The *Smile* materials are discussed in *Struggle* (Vol. 3, Autumn 1980), an evaluation of *Distar Maths* is given in *Distar News* (No. 5, 1978), and a discussion of *Checkpoint* by Mc.Erlain can be found in 'Struggle' (Vol. 3, Summer 1980).

Lumb (1980), in an article entitled Mathematics and the Less Gifted in the Middle School Years, published in *Mathematics in School*, carried out a '*Which?*'-type survey on commercial materials available for Group B children that considers both language and interest levels. This is supplemented by another important booklet, *The Topic Index of Mathematical Books for Less-Gifted Children* by Lumb and Brown (1980).

There is no one right way to teach a mathematical concept to a pupil. If one technique does not work, another must be tried. However, any formal skills programme should contain the following components:

(a) Explanation and demonstration by the teachers several times over in various ways.
(b) Attempted mastery by the pupil. It is essential to ensure that the pupil knows what he or she is looking for in carrying out tasks. In addition, teachers must provide sufficient concrete experiences with an adequate range of materials and situations to allow generalization to occur and principles to become firmly established.
(c) Teachers should emphasize talk and verbal explanation of a task by the pupil. In other words, pupils should be encouraged to say what they are doing or what they plan to do.

Otto *et al.* (1973) suggest a useful remedial technique which is especially applicable to pupils in Group B working on computational skills. It consists of taking the pupil through each step of an operation by having him work the problem aloud and answering pertinent questions. Questions which require a pupil to calculate the answer initially and decide whether his solution

189

appears reasonable will reveal whether he has an understanding of what he is doing or whether he is working by rote.

In terms of Tanner's (1977) model in this 'constructive stage', pupils should be able to work with others to achieve mutually agreed goals. Where the subject matter lends itself, co-operative ventures should therefore be encouraged.

Evaluation of the mathematics programme with Group B pupils would again be in terms of the behavioural checklist of objectives devised for the course.

Group C

Following screening at secondary transfer, one would expect that, in general, Group C pupils with mathematical ages at least commensurate with their chronological ages would come from the average or above average ability bands. These pupils would follow a normal secondary mathematics syllabus. Pupils of lower ability who do reach a mathematical age of 11+ years and who begin to think abstractly in Piagetian terms, are most likely to attain this stage of cognition during their fourth and fifth years in the secondary school. Therefore, Group C really presents an outward-looking programme for fourth- and fifth-year less-able pupils, the objectives of which are to prepare them for adult living in a technologically orientated society. Unfortunately, as the HMI's report (1979) pointed out, 60 per cent of secondary schools need new courses for less-able pupils in mathematics in their fourth and fifth years at school. The type of syllabus relevant to the needs of these pupils can be gleaned from Moore (1968), Dobinson (1976), Hanson (1976), Cawley (1976), Moore and Williams (1977), Lumb (1978), Edwards (1978), and the Remedial Resources Centre, London Borough of Havering (1981).

Civic and commercial mathematics will play a major part in any such curriculum. The following are just samples of the major topic areas that might be covered:

(a) Form-filling, shopping, profit-loss, budgeting, hire purchase, credit cards, interest, VAT, value.
(b) Home finance, family budgets, bills, insurance, taxes, rates.
(c) Reading meters — gas, electricity, telephone bills, methods of payment.
(d) Running a car, motor-cycle, moped.
(e) Banks, building societies, cheques, overdrafts, loans, mortgages.
(f) Wages, wage slips, income tax, PAYE, overtime, piece-work, rates of pay, National Insurance.
(g) House decorating.
(h) Social Security, unemployment benefits.
(i) Holidays, timetables, journeys (distance, time, cost, etc.).
(j) Travel brochures.
(k) Leisure activities.

Tanner's (1977) model suggests that the most striking feature about pupils in this 'generative' stage is that they are self-directing. The pupil is orientated towards conceptualizing problems and generating and testing solutions. Teachers need to provide opportunities for pupils to solve relevant mathematical problems by developing plans of action.

190

The topics mentioned above need to use a limited number of mathematical skills, which should be reinforced through a wide variety of social situations. The project approach, if skillfully carried out, is the most productive, provided that it is linked to real-life problem situations. One way of finding out what are real-life problem situations for the pupils is to ask them. Burton and Stacey (1981), using this method, found a variety of suggestions to work on, including how to balance homework and leisure, how to manage pocket-money, how to re-decorate a bedroom on a fixed income, and the purchase of a motor-cycle on hire purchase. This approach allows pupils to see the value of what they are doing. Edwards (1978) illustrates well the process of consultation prior to the development of an environmental project and the subsequent enthusiasm for the task.

It is essential that where possible real money, real clocks, actual time-tables and realistic shopping expeditions are made. Again, practical mathematics should be reinforced through its use in other subject areas and curriculum topics. Link courses, work experience and the simulation of work conditions within the school, e.g., clocking in, provide the opportunities for the practical application of mathematical skills, while textbooks and work-sheets can reinforce and extend these experiences. For some pupils who still find computation difficult, mechanical aids become even more essential. Occasionally, machines can provide motivation to those who have always failed at mathematics. We are moving into the computer age, and some teachers have begun to write mathematics programmes for desk-top computers. This is likely to be a growth area in the next few years. Not only can these machines provide positive reinforcement when the correct answer is achieved, but it is possible to gain in computational skills by using a machine, since the fear of failure is removed and a structure is provided through which complicated processes can be more easily understood.

One useful technique to help pupils in Group C is the flow-chart idea suggested by Younie (1974). An analysis of the task is made, and all the steps involved in a particular process are written down. To direct a pupil's thinking at certain points, relevant questions are asked. Figures 12 and 13 give examples of flow-charts concerned with the use of a train timetable and measurement. Such a flow-chart allows pupils to see their thinking in a concrete form and, as there is more than one way of making a flow-chart, there is frequently a reduction in the feeling of failure that arises when they compare their work with the more-able pupils. Provided the flow-chart is based on problems having high intrinsic interest and is not made the primary teaching method, it can indicate how a pupil is thinking and how much content has been mastered.

Close links with industry are essential if the less-able pupil is to have any chance of employment in the present precarious job market. Employers are now indicating more clearly what they want in terms of basic numeracy and other skills. It is interesting to compare their demands with the objectives put forward by mathematics advisers such as Lumb (1978), and by teachers' working parties in various local authorities. Bird and Hiscox (1981) report on a range of these basic core syllabuses, including the Mathematical Association's tripartite model with a so-called *kernel* that everyone *must* know, a *core* that they *should* know and an outer *flesh* of what they *could* know.

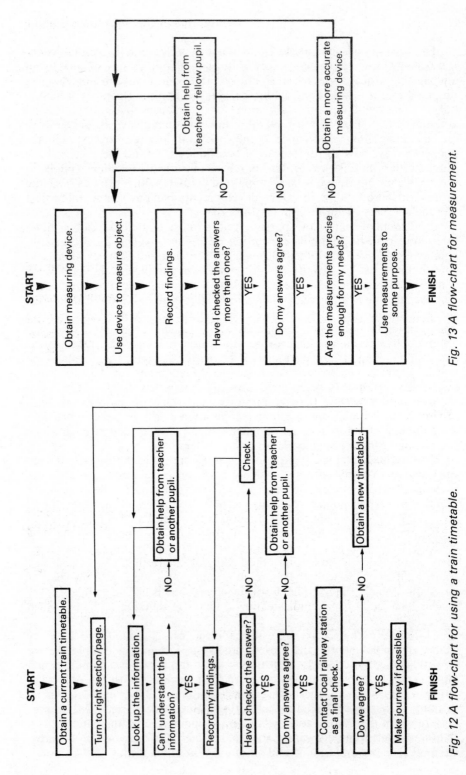

192

START

Obtain measuring device.

Use device to measure object.

Record findings.

Have I checked the answers more than once? — NO — Obtain help from teacher or fellow pupil.

YES

Do my answers agree? — NO — Obtain help from teacher or fellow pupil.

YES

Are the measurements precise enough for my needs? — NO — Obtain a more accurate measuring device.

YES

Use measurements to some purpose.

FINISH

Fig. 13 A flow-chart for measurement.

START

Obtain a current train timetable.

Turn to right section/page.

Look up the information.

Can I understand the information? — NO — Obtain help from teacher or another pupil.

YES

Record my findings.

Have I checked the answer? — NO — Check.

YES

Do my answers agree? — NO — Obtain help from teacher or another pupil.

YES

Contact local railway station as a final check.

Do we agree? — NO — Obtain a new timetable.

YES

Make journey if possible.

FINISH

Fig. 12 A flow-chart for using a train timetable.

In 1976 the Institute of Mathematics and its Applications, whose members are mostly employed in industry, government service or in universities, advocated an end-of-school test concerned with the minimum mathematical skills that most people need in life. They listed ten such skills:

1. Addition and subtraction of whole numbers and decimals of up to two decimal digits.
2. Multiplication and division of whole numbers of less than 100.
3. Multiplication and division of decimals by whole numbers less than 10.
4. Ratios of whole numbers less than 10 and their conversion to percentages and decimals.
5. Understanding the size of numbers.
6. Use of approximations.
7. Averages and the idea of statistical spread.
8. Common units of measurement and money.
9. Areas of circles, squares and rectangles and volumes of cubes and rectangular blocks.
10. Statistical presentation and interpretation of simple graphs and diagrams.

Bearing in mind that these items refer to work and not to home or leisure, we find a fair measure of agreement between employers and educationalists, such as Lumb (1978), who presents the following basic topics for what he calls the 'mathematically less gifted in the 14–16 year age range'.

1. Number computation.
2. Civic and commercial mathematics.
3. Measurement.
4. Representation.
5. Simple statistical notions.
6. Deduction.
7. Basic ideas of chance.
8. Algorithms.

The 'kernel' presented by the Mathematical Association in Bird and Hiscox (1981) contains similar priorities to those presented by Lumb and the Institute of Mathematics.

The resources in terms of books, kit, worksheets, etc., that are available for use with Group C pupils have been well reviewed by Lumb (1978), who assesses them under headings of difficulty, interest, suitability and mode of working, and Rothery (1981). Materials need to be sophisticated enough to reflect the pupils' interests. The following materials have been shown to be of value for this particular group of pupils:

1. *Maths for the Majority*, Schofield and Sims.
2. *Assignment Maths*, Brodie.
3. *Countdown* TV Series, BBC.
4. *Mathematics Minipacks*, Addison Wesley.
5. *Mathematics for General Education*, Macmillan.
6. *Maths for Life Series*, B and C, Oxford.
7. *Maths Sheets*, John Murray.
8. *Maths You Need*, Nelson.

9. *Maths Matters*, Addison Wesley.

Any new resources that come on the market can be evaluated by asking the types of pertinent questions posed by Cawley (1980) and Larcombe (1978). Larcombe offers the following checklist for assessment:

1. Is there as little verbal expression as possible and where used is it:
   (a) Clearly arranged in small areas of writing?
   (b) Supported by teaching diagrams (if appropriate)?
   (c) In short-sentence form using familiar, readable words and language likely to convey accurately the meaning to the pupil?
2. Are clear diagrams and illustrations used wherever possible, and do they always aid the teaching rather than make the work look attractive?
3. Are instructions direct and specific, giving an opportunity for the pupil to respond immediately?
4. Does learning arise from activity or does the reverse occur: a principle being learned and followed by activity, as in orthodox worked examples followed by straight practice?
5. Are the conceptual steps sufficiently small?
6. Does each new task have only two or three new teaching points?
7. Where real-life examples are used, are they appropriate to the pupil's real life?
8. Where open-ended questions or problem-solving are used, are they really within the range of the pupil; does he/she have (a) the confidence to tackle them, (b) the mathematical expertise to make a worthwhile attempt?

Evaluation will be in terms of a checklist of essential skills suggested by industry and employers.

It is suggested that several different types of records should be kept on the pupils. We have already made mention of the checklists of specific objectives. These should form an on-going assessment and guide to future work. The method of recording need not be elaborate. All one needs is the list of objectives and two columns: the first to indicate by a tick or a cross, or perhaps a raw score and the date, whether the objective was achieved or not achieved, and the second to indicate the results of some future re-test date. An example of such checklist is given in figure 14.

1. Objectives not tested can be left blank.
2. Objectives tested and achieved can be dated and ticked.
3. Objectives tested and not achieved can be dated, crossed, and notes made.

In addition to the checklists, it is helpful to have samples of pupils' work with relevant comments. This allows both teacher and pupil to observe progression and analyse errors and particular needs. Finally, statements should be made regarding the pupils' confidence, their reaction to failure or difficulty, their likes and dislikes, their special interests, the avoidance techniques used, and so on.

In summary, we can do no better than consider the comments made, firstly by Brennan in the Schools Council Working Paper 63 — *Curricular*

Objective	Assessment 1 plus comments	Assessment 2 plus comments
1	✓ $\frac{11}{81}$	
2	✓ $\frac{11}{81}$	
3	✗ $\frac{12}{81}$	✓ $\frac{2}{82}$
4		

Fig. 14 A checklist of specific objectives.

Needs of Slow Learners (1979), secondly those of the Schools Council Project *Low Attainment in Mathematics* (1981), and finally the Schools Council's evidence to the Cockcroft Committee (1980). In the case of the first report, the comments concerning remedial teaching and mathematics at the secondary level can be summarized as follows:

It is essential to:
1. understand the developmental factors relating to mathematics. Some mature pupils are still at the stage of concrete operations in their thinking, and a few still possibly at the intuitive stage;
2. make a careful assessment and develop descriptive programmes to meet the needs of individual pupils;
3. ensure that a range of curriculum activities is presented and there is not just an over-reliance on textbooks or teacher-produced assignment cards;
4. ensure that over-learning takes place through repetition in as many different guises as possible.

The second report, *Low Attainment in Mathematics, 5–16 Years* is to be published in 1982. It focuses attention on the 20 per cent of children who have the lowest attainment in mathematics. The project team collected suggestions during its visits to schools which were regarded as being examples of good practice. The report will provide information about the ways in which different schools are tackling the needs of pupils who have mathematical difficulties. Not unnaturally, they discovered that there was considerable variation in the approaches, organizational patterns, materials used and assessment procedures carried out. Not surprisingly, the ability, personality and commitment of the teacher were found to be the most significant factors in the successful teaching of children with a low attainment in mathematics. The team identified 13 aspects which they felt influenced the success of the work with such pupils:

1. A planned curriculum which is related to pupils' immediate and future needs. It should include aesthetic appreciation.
2. Pupils should start at their own level of achievement rather than from a common point of failure. This implies some form of individual assessment.
3. Work should be well matched to the pupil and presented in a way that facilitates successful learning.
4. Variety in the presentation, communication and discussion of arithmetical ideas, approximation and estimation should be emphasized in the preparation of work materials.
5. Teaching should be essentially material-based and realistic applications should be used, where appropriate.
6. Teaching should include the sensible use of electronic calculators which are easily accessible to pupils.
7. When appropriate, transfer back to the mainstream should be encouraged in schools where remedial work is organized on a withdrawal basis or in special groups.
8. The programme of work should be flexible enough to take into account pupils' interests.
9. Pupils ought to be encouraged to understand what they are doing and why. They should enjoy working.
10. There should be a wide variety of approaches and stimuli.
11. The curriculum should be wide and not restricted to computation.
12. Pupils should be encouraged to organize their own work and to become self-reliant.
13. Mathematics across the curriculum should be developed, whenever possible.

Finally, the evidence from the Schools Council to the Committee of Inquiry into the teaching of Mathematics in Schools listed fourteen recommendations which related to low attainers, some of which are appropriate to the needs of pupils in secondary schools.

1. There is a need to develop diagnostic activities to pinpoint the difficulties of individual pupils found to be 'at risk' in mathematics.
2. Secondary-school departments should be realistic in their expectations of what pupils can do. They should accept that a few pupils will not meet all of the standard requirements.
3. School and class organization must be sufficiently flexible to allow for some individual attention to pupils.
4. Teachers should analyse their objectives in teaching low attainers and test to see whether their teaching of these objectives has been effective.
5. Teachers need a variety of techniques to help the low attainers learn.
6. Attention must be paid to the language level of class discussion and to the reading age of printed material.
7. The curriculum of the low attainers in mathematics must be planned so that it covers a variety of experiences to establish particular concepts, is not confined to computation, but includes other branches of mathematics, relates to the current interests of the pupils and uses work which is at their level of understanding.

8. Work needs to be undertaken to develop pupil material that stresses the applicability of mathematics in contexts that engage the interests of low attainers.

In summary, the planning of a curriculum for pupils who are 'at risk' mathematically must involve the translation of the broad aims of teaching mathematics, which are the same for all pupils, into clear statements of objectives for analysing and sequencing the mathematical skills that are to be taught. An essential precursor to any teaching programme must be the identification of each individual pupil's present level of development in the mathematical areas which make up the curriculum. Assessment should then be followed by a whole range of teaching strategies, materials, and organizational plans designed to move pupils along a skills continuum, in small stages. Re-assessment at regular intervals will help teachers to focus on the efficacy of analysing a task sufficiently for teaching purposes and presenting appropriate learning experiences, rather than of retreating to the shaky premise that intellectual and environmental factors prevent the pupil from making progress.

References and further reading

Ablewhite, R., *Mathematics and the Less Able*, Heinemann, 1969.

Ainscow, M. and Tweddle, D., *Preventing Classroom Failure*, John Wiley, 1979.

Arena, J. (ed.), *Building Number Skills in Dyslexic Children*, Academic Therapy Publications, 1972.

Association of Teachers of Mathematics, *Ideas for Slow Learners*, 1 and 2, 1977.

Bailey, T. J. (1979), 'Arithmetical difficulties of less able pupils in the secondary school — some thoughts on assessment and remediation' in *Remedial Education*, Vol. 14, No. 4.

Bell, P., *Basic Teaching for Slow Learners*, Muller, 1970.

Bird, D. and Hiscox, M., *Mathematics in School and Employment — A Study of Liaison Activities*, Methuen, 1981.

Brennan, W. K., *Curricular Needs of Slow Learners*, Schools Council Working Paper 63, Evans/Methuen, 1979.

Burton, L. and Stacey, K. (1981), 'Solving problems' in *Struggle: Mathematics for Low Attainers*, Vol. 4, ILEA.

Buxton, L. (1980), 'Mathematics and anxiety' in *Struggle: Mathematics for Low Attainers*, Vol. 3, ILEA.

Cawley, N. (1972), 'Diagnosing difficulties in number' in *Remedial Education*, Vol. 7, No. 3.

Cawley, N. (1976), 'Social mathematics — remediation or stimulation?' in *Remedial Education*, Vol. 11, No. 2.

Cawley, N. (1980), 'Worth considering? Looking more analytically at new schemes and books' in *Struggle: Mathematics for Low Attainers*, Vol. 2, ILEA.

Checkpoint, ILEA, 1978.

DES, *Aspects of Secondary Education in England*, HMSO, 1979.

Dobinson, H. M., *Basic Skills you Need*, Nelson, 1976.

Designing a Leaver's Course for the Less Able with Special Reference to Mathematics, London Borough of Havering, Remedial Resources Centre, 1981.

Duncan, A., *Teaching Mathematics to Slow Learners*, Ward Lock, 1978.

Edwards, R., 'Mathematics 14–16' in (ed.) Hinson, M., *Encouraging Results*, Macdonald Educational, 1978.

Flinter, P. (1979), 'Educational implications of dyscalculia' in the *Arithmetic Teacher*, Vol. 26, No. 7, pp. 42–46.

Fogelman, K. R., *Piagetian Tests for Teachers*, NFER, 1970.

France, N., *Profile of Mathematical Skills*, Nelson, 1979.

Hanson, A., *Ready to Leave*, Collins, 1976.

Hopkins, M. (1978), 'Diagnosis of learning styles and mathematics' in the *Arithmetic Teacher*, Vol. 25, No. 7.

Hughes, J. M., *The Slow Learner in your Class*, Nelson, 1973.

Institute of Mathematics and its Applications checklist in B. Doe, 'Mathematicians join in chorus for basic skills and national testing' in *The Times Educational Supplement*, 29.10.1976.

Irving, J., 'Mathematics for the slow learner' in Crouch, B. (ed.) *Overcoming Learning Difficulties*, Benn, 1972.

Kilburn, J., 'Maths made difficult' in *The Times Educational Supplement*, 9.5.1980.

Kaliski, L., 'Arithmetic and the brain-injured child' in Frierson, E. and Barbe, W. (eds), *Educating Children with Learning Difficulties*, Appleton Century-Crofts, USA, 1967.

Larcombe, T., 'Mathematics 11–14' in Hinson, M. (ed.), *Encouraging Results*, Macdonald Educational, 1978.

Larcombe, T., 'An experience of success' in *The Times Educational Supplement*, 9.5.1980.

Lerner, J., *Children with Learning Disabilities*, Houghton Mifflin, 1971.

Lister, D., 'Games give maths a good hand' in *The Times Educational Supplement*, 24.4.1981.

Lumb, D. (1978), 'Mathematics for the less gifted' in *Mathematics in School*, Vol. 7, No. 2.

Lumb, D. (1980), 'Mathematics and the less gifted in the middle years' in *Mathematics in School*, Vol. 9, No. 3.

Lumb, D. and Brown, M., *Topic Index of Mathematics Books for Less Gifted Children*, Newcastle-upon-Tyne Education Department, 1980.

Tests, Mathematical Association, 1979.

McErlain, P. (1980), '*Checkpoint* assessment cards' in *Struggle: Mathematics for Low Attainers*, Vol. 3, pp. 23–23, ILEA.

Miles, T., *More Help for the Dyslexic Child*, Methuen, 1975.

Moore, N. (1968), 'Teaching social arithmetic to slow learning children' in *Remedial Education*, Vol. 3, No. 1.

Moore, N. and Williams, A., *Mathematics for Life*, OUP, 1977.

Morrison, C., *Skills for Living*, Macdonald Educational, 1982.

Nichols, R. H. (1963), 'Programming Piaget in practice' in *Teaching Arithmetic* Vol. 1, No. 3.

Nichols, R. H., 'Number and the handicapped child' in Petrie, (ed.), *Han-*

dicapped Children: Their Potential and Fulfilment, Joint Council for the Education of Handicapped Children, 1970.

Otto, W. McMenemy, R. and Smith, J., Corrective and Remedial Teaching, Houghton Mifflin, USA, 1973.

Rothery, A., 'Competence and confidence' in The Times Educational Supplement, 13.2.1981.

Schools Council, Mathematics Teaching in Schools, (pamphlet 17), 1980.

Schrieber, A., 'An empirical approach at the secondary level' in Arena, J. (ed.), Building Number Skills, Academic Therapy Publications, 1972.

Sovchik, R. and Heddens, J. (1978), 'Classroom diagnosis and remediation' in the Arithmetic Teacher, Vol. 24, No. 4.

Scientific Research Associates (1978), 'The Distar Arithmetic Programme', Distar News No. 5.

Staras, A. (1980), 'Mathematics Curriculum' Pinewood ESN(M) School, Ware (unpublished).

Stolz, C., 'Low Attainers in Mathematics 5–16, the Schools Council Project' in The Times Educational Supplement, 27.3.1981.

Strauss, A. (1951), 'The education of the brain-injured child' in the American Journal of Mental Deficiency, Vol. 56.

Tanner, L., Classroom Discipline, Holt, Rinehart and Winston, 1977.

Tansley, A. and Gulliford, R., The Education of Slow-Learning Children, Routledge and Kegan Paul, 1960.

Turnbull, J., Maths Links, NARE, 1982.

Waddon, A., 'Problems of numeracy in dyslexia' in the Dyslexia Review, No. 14.

Warnock, M. (Chairman), Special Educational Needs, HMSO, 1978.

Westwood, P., The Remedial Teacher's Handbook, Oliver and Boyd, 1975.

Williams, A., Basic Subjects for the Slow Learner, Methuen, 1970.

Younie, W., Instructional Approaches to Slow Learning, Teachers' College Press, 1974.

The following give details of various assessment procedures:

Assessment in Mathematics, Globe Education, Macmillan, 1981.

O and B Mathematics Tests, Oliver and Boyd, 1976.

Tameside Numeracy Test, Schofield and Sims, 1981.

Yardsticks, Criterion-Referenced Tests in Mathematics, Nelson, 1975.

13

Life skills programmes

JIM McNICHOLAS

We have witnessed a proliferation of programmes commonly known as 'life skills' in both our secondary schools and in post-16 education. A survey involving some 200 remedial departments in secondary schools (NARE, 1981) reveals that approximately 40 per cent of remedial teachers are concerned with life-skills teaching. In many schools, careers teachers and other subject specialists are also involved.

What are life skills courses?

The Further Education Unit (1980) has provided one acceptable definition: '. . . curricula whose objectives have been primarily derived from real or imagined analysis of the social demands made on people at work and in the everyday requirements of life in the community.'

Concern with life skills courses has not been confined to this country. Over the last decade, considerable interest has been shown in the United States, whilst in Europe the Council for Cultural Co-operation's project, *Preparation for Life* (Befring, 1980) indicates the increasing prominence being given to this area of study. A definition of life skills to be found in the project's papers reveals similar thinking to that of the FEU: '. . . the preparation necessary in order to live a constructive life as an individual and in the community.'

Why are such programmes important?

What has brought about their increasing prominence? The efficacy of the present curriculum for many school-leavers has been questioned by employers and by those responsible for Youth Opportunity Programmes and work experience programmes. An accumulation of evidence has shown the ill-preparedness of many youngsters for life after school. Additional weight has been added to this criticism by the Warnock Report (1978) and *Aspects of Secondary Education in England* (1979). Both reports urge that increased attention should be paid to the needs of school-leavers. In the latter, HM Inspectorate draw attention to the curricular needs of fourth and fifth-year non-examination students.

Added poignancy is provided by the current increase in unemployment, especially among the young. In 1978, one third of school-leavers were unable to obtain jobs. The Manpower Services Commission has estimated that, by 1984, 80 per cent of teenagers will be on YOP courses.

Currently, there is a growing demand for a relevant curriculum, capable of preparing students for life in an electronic age and enabling them to cope with all the changes in life-style which this heralds. Frequently, the demands made on schools by the examination system have relegated such ideals into the educational 'second division'. As far back as 1963, when the Newsom Report encouraged the setting-up of ROSLA courses, teachers were having to justify their inclusion alongside academic curricula. Courses of this nature have helped to breed the assumption that 'life skills' are only suitable for non-academic pupils. Attention has mainly focused on logistic problems such as timetables, additional resources and extra teachers. The principal issues raised have been pragmatic: 'What shall we teach? 'Where shall we teach?' and 'Whom shall we teach?'

Rationale for the life skills curriculum

We clearly require an operational philosophy for the life skills curriculum. This needs to be accompanied by a disciplined model which contains four essential elements: objectives, content, methods and evaluation. Dewey's (1938) philosophies have long since been absorbed by our child-centred primary schools, but have been largely ignored (and at what deep loss?) by secondary schools. Dewey reminds us that 'Collateral learning, in the way of formation of enduring attitudes, of likes and dislikes, may be and often is much more important than the spelling lesson or lesson in geography or history that is learned.'

The development of a curriculum theory also enables a more rigorous analysis of courses. Over-emphasizing the cognitive aspects of the curriculum might have a deleterious effect on the personal growth of students. The affective side of their development must also be considered in order to obtain a balance, (see Krathwohl, 1964). We should attempt to promote a confluent theory of teaching, that is, a conjunction of the cognitive and affective domains. George Kelly's theory of personal constructs emphasizes the uniqueness of the individual. A basic element of his theory is that 'a person's processes are psychologically channellized by the ways in which he anticipates events' (Bannister and Fransella, 1971). The lessons to be learned here are that we must treat each individual student as a whole person, remembering that his or her perspective of a problem may differ from ours and that this is deserving of respect.

The degree of attention now being given to life skills and work experience courses is exemplified in this and the next three chapters. We begin with a description of a course recently introduced for fourth and fifth-years students in a Cheshire comprehensive school (previously reported in *Remedial Education*, Vol. 14, No. 3).

Prior considerations

1. Non-academic students are weak in writing and reading skills. However, they are not necessarily weak in every subject and may be capable of working with interest and success alongside more academically motivated students in some subjects.
2. Less successful students are a varied group. We must not equate low attainment with low potential — it does not follow that these students are limited in ability or that their attainments will remain low. With remedial

help and the stimulation of a wider curriculum, both ability and attainment may improve.

3. We have to be aware of the danger, when separating less successful students into a special group, that we do not reinforce feelings of failure or foster a lowering of student and teacher expectation.

Philosophy

Courses for the least academically successful should not close doors to educational opportunities prematurely. Nevertheless, pupils' personal and social needs indicated a requirement for courses with a greater emphasis on social and functional topics.

Of prime importance was the need for less academic students to acquire and improve their basic skills in communication. Learning and activity in areas of interest across the curriculum can create the need and desire to improve basic skills and provide the motivation necessary to practise.

Secondly, the course was seen as a means of compensating students for certain inadequacies and deprivations in their prior development and experience. A varied and stimulating curriculum could be a means of improving thinking and language skills, where the content learned was less important than the ability to think, to discuss, to make and create.

Aims and objectives of the course

1. 'We have to ensure that the curriculum does everything possible to help pupils develop as individuals, to begin to find their way in a complicated society, and to face with some security the world they encounter after the age of 16' (*Curriculum 11–16*, 1977). This statement of aims could be taken further: our students should develop questioning minds, challenging things in society which need to be changed. Students should develop the knowledge, skills and attitudes necessary to create a better society.

2. The main emphasis should be on personal development. Less academic students often evince some of these characteristics: emotional immaturity, poor adjustment, delinquency, difficulties in relationships and social behaviour. (Are these characteristics the cause or effect of low achievement?) Our curriculum can contribute to the amelioration of these problems, albeit indirectly, by providing activities which promote interest, success, confidence and enjoyment. In addition, there is a need to develop directly thought and awareness of moral and social issues.

3. Care was taken to avoid patronizing the students. Difficulties with reading and writing do not necessarily impair their ability to produce good thinking. The course we provided was in no way be regarded as a 'poor relation' — it presented challenges as real as in other elements of the curriculum.

4. Our goal should be, as in all education, to prepare students intellectually, aesthetically, emotionally, socially and morally for mature, responsible adulthood. In particular, the course emphasized personal and social competence, skills in house management, allied crafts and hobbies, the development of correct attitudes in family relationships and mature attitudes to work and society. Many of the attributes we wish to develop will be engendered in the process of teaching; all cannot be planned in detail.

Other objectives can be designated under the following three headings which individual teachers involved with the course were able to expand: knowledge, skills, qualities.

The objectives detailed in figure 15 are guidelines. The course was taught by taking students through these activities using the strong interests of both teachers and taught.

Organization and methods

The syllabus was organized into topics which were of a week's duration. This was a flexible arrangement, so that some topics which were progressing well and needed more time could spill over into part of, or even the whole of, the next week. These short periods made for variety and interest; they also helped the student who missed school for a week or two to feel secure in the knowledge of starting afresh on a new topic.

Throughout, the emphasis was on direct experience: gathering it, thinking about it, discussing and recording. Teachers proceeded from concrete situations, if possible in real, practical areas, to the more abstract. Great use was made of visits, films, tape-recordings and visual aids.

A review of early progress

We learned from experience that advance planning was vital in order to ensure that sufficient interested teachers with the correct attitude towards non-academic children were available and could be released from other teaching commitments. Initially, the constraints of timetabling did not allow for this. We learned that preparations needed to be made at least six months in advance so that these difficulties could be resolved and staff could prepare adequately.

It should be stated at the outset that teaching a course of this kind was not easy. This was not a traditional curriculum subject; we were unable to follow a set book. The main resource was the skill of the teachers in assessing and using students' and their own interests to stimulate thought, discussion and the recording of experiences.

One of the problems we encountered might have been of our own creation. Fourth-year students chose their option courses towards the end of the third year, but in life skills we gave no option. Feedback from students informed us that in some cases resentment arose because there was no option for this course, only selection by staff. We had the added resentment from some students, who had never been to remedial lessons, of identification with the remedial department, its classrooms and its teachers. It was difficult, initially, to motivate such students.

To offset the problem in later years, life skills was offered as an option along with the other subjects. With guidance, most of the third-year children we thought should be on the course opted for it. A detailed account of the aims, objectives and strategies also appeared in the option brochure which each parent received.

Most children were won over by interest, by the lack of academic pressure, by the use of visits and the good work of the staff involved. It is difficult to report on the successes of the course in any objective sense.

Course objectives

1. Home management

Knowledge	Skills	Qualities
Know the mechanics of housekeeping: how to run, maintain and repair the home. A knowledge of rates, mortgages, insurance, careful shopping.	Be able to cope with shopping; work out HP agreements. Be able to mend fuses, wire a plug, read meters, fix tap washers and ball cocks; wallpaper.	Learn to make decisions on the need for wise spending – homes, clothes, furnishings, holidays. Aesthetic: taste in home decorating. Discrimination regarding advertising. Hygiene.

2. World of work

Knowledge	Skills	Qualities
Knowledge of work involved in factories, offices and the welfare services; related money matters. An understanding of the correct procedures in form-filling, making applications, presentation for interview. Knowledge of further training facilities.	Be able to keep accounts, work out pay packets, fill in forms, tax, etc. Address letters, make applications. Answer phone. Take messages sensibly.	Develop a responsible attitude to work. Develop feelings of loyalty, efficiency, conscientiousness.

3. Personal/emotional/social

Knowledge	Skills	Qualities
Knowledge of one's own and other's drives, feelings and emotions. Know the moral values relating to dealing with people and property. How to look after and fit in with others at home and work. Knowledge of social customs, manners, conventions. Child care.	Be able to discuss sensibly social, moral issues. Develop ability to mix in society. Behave with consideration, courtesy and propriety. Develop independence. Be able to cope with and look after young children.	Develop a set of moral values – tolerance, respect of others, and their property. Realization of the part an individual can play in changing his or her environment.

4. Recreational

Knowledge	Skills	Qualities
A knowledge of recreative activities for aesthetic, intellectual reasons and for enjoyment. Rug-making, photography, film-making, toy-making, outdoor pursuits.	Be able to use leisure time in a creative, enjoyable fashion. Be able to develop skills in the areas taught.	Find use and enjoyment in purposeful leisure activities.

Fig. 15

204

There was obvious enthusiasm for the visits to local factories, shopping centres, foundries, glassworks, and so forth. The questions that students asked were evidence of their interest and proof enough that they were as capable as others of asking the important 'how' and 'why' questions. After one visit to a local church where the stonemasons were erecting a new marble altar and a wall mosaic, some boys were keen enough to go back a week later on their own to get some polish for pieces of marble they had been given to buff up at home.

One stimulating lesson was provided by a boy never known to show any animation in class before. He became very voluble and interested when showing off his pet ferret, answering explicit questions concerning its diet, its habits, and so on. Later, a worksheet and crossword were compiled using his expertise and the *Encyclopaedia Britannica*.

Once a month, each group had a coffee session. Fifteen minutes from the end of a double lesson, the students sat down to a cup of coffee in the child-care room, chatting in comfortably carpeted and furnished surroundings. We did this to instil a sense of togetherness, to improve relationships, encourage the social graces and to learn to relax with each other and with teachers.

Perspectives from the course

1. An inspector visiting the school commented on the worthwhileness of the course. He asked, 'Why don't the academic pupils get some of this? Why do the non-academics get the goodies?' Havighurst (1951) and Maslow (1968) have produced elegant theories which suggest that personal development is a goal which students feel the need to achieve before, or at least alongside, academic development. At least some elements of life skills programmes should be available to all students. Official backing for these ideas has recently come from the DES (1981).
2. Prior to 1979, the paucity of literature on this theme was indicative of the lack of rigorous thinking and the shortage of positive help for teachers. Since then, publications by the FEU (1980), MSC (1980), Hopson and Scally (1981) and Priestley and McGuire (1981) have enabled us to refine our thinking concerning the initiation, teaching and evaluation of life skills courses. Resource books for teachers and students have recently been published by Hopson and Scally (1981), McNicholas (1981) and Ashbee (1981).
3. One urgent need yet remains to be fulfilled. To date, there are relatively few in-service opportunities in this field, specially designed to prepare for running life skills courses.
4. Life skills programmes are a means of securing the co-operation of teachers across the curriculum. A fully effective course requires the expertise and involvement of many members of staff. It is essential to have a co-ordinator who can oversee the general pattern of student activities, ensuring that there are no overlaps or serious omissions in the planned curriculum.

These are the four most important factors which need careful consideration in the development of effective live skills courses.

In the chapters which follow, Peter Jones describes a successful course operating in a West Midlands comprehensive school, Avril Lofthouse outlines a work preparation programme operating under the auspices of the Manpower Services Commission and Mike Cahill reports on his work as National Co-ordinator of the Schools Council's *Skills for Employment* project.

References

Ashbee, C., *Real-Life Maths Skills*, Scholastic Publications, 1981.

Bannister, D. and Fransella, F., *Inquiring Man: The Theory of Personal Constructs*, Penguin, 1971.

Befring, E., *Project No. 1: Preparation for Life*, Council for Cultural Co-operation, 1980.

DES, *Aspects of Secondary Education in England*, HMSO, 1979.

DES, *Curriculum 11–16*, HMSO, 1977.

DES, *Curriculum 11–16: A Review of Progress*, HMSO, 1981.

Dewey, J., *Experience and Education*, Collier-Macmillan, 1938.

Further Education Unit, *Developing Social and Life Skills*, FECRDU, Elizabeth House, London, 1980.

Havighurst, R. J., *Developmental Tasks and Education*, 1951.

Hopson, B. and Scally, M., *Life Skills Teaching*, McGraw Hill, 1981.

Kelly, G. A., *A Theory of Personality*, Norton, New York, 1963.

Krathwohl, D. R. *et al.*, *Taxonomy of Educational Objectives*, Book 2 — *The Affective Domain*. David McKay, USA, 1964.

McGuire, J. and Priestley, P., *Life After School*, Pergamon, 1981.

McNicholas, J., *Real-Life Reading Skills*, Scholastic Publications, 1981.

Manpower Services Commission, *Instructional Guide to Social and Life Skills*, 1980.

Maslow, A. H., *Towards a Psychology of Being*, Van Nostrand Reinhold, 1968.

Ministry of Education, *Half Our Future*, HMSO, 1963.

Warnock, M. (Chairman), *Special Educational Needs*, HMSO, 1978.

14

Education for life skills

PETER JONES

Introduction

Design for Living, or Life Education, at Aston Manor Comprehensive School is a core curriculum course for all fourth and fifth-year pupils. The school's population is rising towards the 1000 mark, and the approximate ethnic composition is 10 per cent white, 10 per cent Asian and 80 per cent West Indian.

In the early 1970s, it became obvious that this inner-ring school was not meeting all the needs of its pupils. The school was not adequately preparing the pupils for the 'world outside', as successfully as other schools in different areas of the city. The examination passes the pupils achieved were proving to be of little use, because they could not cope with the final job interview. Examination passes were not necessarily making the pupils worldly, and the gap that existed between the outside world and a restricted home background was too great. The old theory of 'all the examination passes in the world do not make a person' were ringing true. Something was needed to bolster them.

The question that had to be answered was 'What are we trying to do in the school?' The answers arrived at would fit most schools:

1. We are trying to prepare our pupils for the 'life outside', so that they can stand on their own two feet and compete on more equal basis with other people, and
2. We are trying to improve or increase their life opportunities in terms of jobs, leisure, personal lives, etc.

All this so that they may lead as fulfilling a life as possible.

This rather simplistic, but honest, philosophy was the background to the Design for Living course. The course has steadily matured since its early beginnings and has learned from its early mistakes. It has become more of an approach to education rather than just another subject on the timetable.

General aims of the course

There is certainly nothing new about the general aims of the Design for Living or Life Education course. These are:

1. To develop self-awareness

This is, of course, important for any child, but perhaps even more so for those from a different ethnic background or for those classified as being children with learning difficulties. Many of our pupils lose any identity they have built up over their years at school as soon as they leave. The school and home environments often give children a false sense of security. As soon as they leave these somewhat protected areas, and have to face the responsibility of conducting their own lives, they can find that they were not as 'solid' as they at first thought. I suppose it is the 'big fish in a small sea' to the 'small fish in a big sea' idea.

Self-confidence and self-esteem are so important to individuals, but are often desperately lacking in many of our pupils. The child with learning difficulties who has endured years of ridicule from his or her peers (or even teachers) cannot possibly have any self-confidence or self-esteem. Somehow, the school has got to provide the means for *all* its pupils, not just the 'bright kids', to develop a personal awareness which can help the child to understand his or her limitations realistically. Having reached this awareness, the child must still have the confidence to compete with others, and not just give up, accepting failure as a normal part of life. Why should a child have to go through life believing, 'I'm not very clever, therefore there is not much I can do because I haven't got the right examinations', or 'It is no good trying because people won't accept me as I'm black'? All children have the right to feel that they are in some way as valuable as the next person, in spite of their own limitations.

2. To develop decision-making skills

One day, parents or teachers will no longer be around to 'lean on'. Decisions will have to be made, and the consequences of those decisions faced by the individual alone. All the way through school, children are very rarely allowed to make any important decisions. Apart from turning up to lessons with a pen, pencil and ruler — routine decisions — there is perhaps very little else to bother about. Teachers or parents do everything else. Industrialists are very quick to criticize the young of today, since they see pupils as being unable to think a problem through logically from start to finish. Children need to be taught logical thinking and then be given the opportunity to practise making decisions. How much practice at planning and real decision-making is a child given in the course of a normal day?

3. To develop a sense of personal and social responsibility

Again, how often do schools put pupils in a position to feel totally responsible for their own decisions? Teachers and parents are naturally there to stop the children in their care from making mistakes. In this way a child may develop a sense that if something goes wrong it doesn't matter because the teacher or parent will be there to cover up or tidy up afterwards. Is this a proper grounding for responsible citizenship? Is this not encouraging 'passing the buck'? Somehow, pupils should be made to realize that what they do will also have an effect on other people, and that there will not always be someone to 'sweep up' after them.

It is, of course, very difficult to engender a sense of social responsibility amongst children who see society as being very hard on them. Many of our pupils have had problematic upbringings and are going to be shunted into a world which many of them see as having very little to offer in the way of jobs or security. Teachers, and the rest of society, can no longer fall back on the old 'arm-twister' that those who work hard and get the examination results will be rewarded with a 'steady job'. What jobs? Many of today's younger generation may never actually be employed. It is, therefore, easy to understand the frustrated attitudes of pupils which are now creeping in! 'Why should I bother . . . there's nothing at the end of my school days.' 'Why should I be nice to society if society is not nice to me?' Somehow these frustrations have got to be rationalized, or bitter disillusionment will result.

4. To develop a greater understanding of the adult world of employment and leisure

In an ever-changing and increasingly complex world, it is becoming more and more difficult for a young person to understand the outside world from behind a desk. How can pupils be adequately prepared for the real world of employment, leisure and relationships without actually seeing much of it for themselves? Why should there be this ominous gap between school and the real world? It is all very well telling them about 'real life', but surely it is more meaningful for them to experience it in some way. The onus here, therefore, is on the school to provide as much opportunity as possible for pupils to be out amongst the world 'outside', in order to close the gap that exists.

The school's attitude towards the world of employment and unemployment needs to be looked at carefully. Society is still very much geared towards employment. Employment can provide money, aims, ambition, an interest; too often employment is seen as the only means to a 'successful' life. Leisure is only satisfying when seen as an enjoyable alternative to work. What will happen to the skilled or unskilled people whose jobs are now being performed by robots or computers, and who are therefore left with very few options? Do they have to face 168 hours of nothing every week? Obviously, a new philosophy will have to be developed, and schools will have to play a big part in providing courses which prepare its school-leavers for this. Perhaps it will be the idea of having work to do, even though one is unemployed. Are there going to be opportunities for a young person to grasp even though he or she is unemployed?

Course structure and content

The problems are enormous and the aims may seem somewhat impossible to reach — but, somehow, educationalists have got to set about achieving them. This is how we go about achieving these aims at Aston Manor School. The structure and content of the Life Education course can best be illustrated in a diagram (figure 16).

The careers, health and sex education, and leisure education sections of the course are fairly structured. The important thing to note is that they are taught under the same 'wing'. Matters that arise in the health programme may have a direct bearing on the careers or leisure side of life. Such topics cannot be taught in isolation as they are totally inter-related.

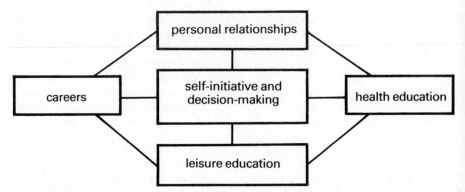

Fig. 16 The structure and content of the life-skills course at Aston Manor Comprehensive.

The self-initiative and decision-making section

Perhaps the most exciting—and most controversial—part of the course is the self-initiative and decision-making section. It is here that the real-life situations that have been discussed hypothetically in the other sections (careers, health and leisure) are, if you like, put into practice. It is here that pupils are either sent out of school to face the real world or the real world is brought into school. This means that we allow pupils out of school — unsupervised by teachers — to find things out for themselves. Parents are informed that their children will be out of school, often unsupervised, and their permission is sought by way of a returned consent form.

Because of the way that pupils are introduced to this new freedom, problems rarely, if ever, arise. Pupils are given the opportunity to plan this part of the course completely for themselves, usually for an initial period of five to six weeks. Traditionally, when children are given a 'project' to do, they can tend to be a little unimaginative in their choices. Football, cars or fashion are old favourites and if left to it, they will happily produce marvellous, neat charts of the FA Cup winners for the last 50 years, beautiful drawings of fashion through the ages, or pictures of the last ten Rolls-Royce editions. All this is very nice and workmanlike, but little use to a young adult who is moving into the outside world.

If a pupil chooses a project on cars because that is what interests him, surely questions such as: How much does a car cost new or second-hand? What will the insurance be? What is an MOT test? How do you take a driving test? How much are the driving lessons? Where's the cheapest driving school? How do you tax the car? Where do you get a driving licence? are more relevant? Having formulated these questions, the pupil is then encouraged to go out and find the answers. He or she has to actually go and visit the insurance broker, go and talk to the car sales staff, go to the post office for the necessary forms — and then have a go at filling them in. Surely there is far more learning potential for the pupils, than simply being told the answers from behind a desk. They are actually facing the adults 'outside', and having practice at asking the right questions to gain the information needed.

210

Pupils are also encouraged to write to local firms in order to organize visits. The difference from most schools is that the teacher does not go with them. The pupils go on their own, having to meet the people at the other end, ask the questions themselves, and thank the people concerned at the end of the visit, all without being prompted or pushed by teacher!

Pupils are allowed to use telephones — a skill so often neglected or taken for granted by teachers. The important ingredient in this work is that pupils are doing it because they want to. They are told that if they find the next five or six weeks boring, they only have themselves to blame!

Naturally, the teaching staff monitor all that the pupils do. Often phone calls are made, without the pupil's knowledge, to people about to receive visits to prepare them for what is to come. They can sometimes be wary of having unsupervised children because of past experience with *supervised* groups. Happily, we have never had a complaint from anywhere concerning our pupils' behaviour on unsupervised visits. In fact, people are generally very complimentary.

Children with learning difficulties may be slow readers and writers, but they are so often perfectly capable of conducting their own affairs. This sort of opportunity can only serve to bolster their confidence. To give an example: a group of four remedial boys in the fifth year made contact with a local nursery school, which agreed to allow a visit. The lads went along with their questionnaires, and enjoyed that visit so much that they arranged a weekly visit to the nursery in order to go and 'help out'. This involved them reading stories (although the stories they 'read' did not always resemble the actual text) and generally helping the children with their work. They eventually, with help, prepared actual lessons or play sessions for a regular group of nursery children. The ultimate success for these lads was the planning and execution of a visit for a party of 12 nursery children to a local nature reserve. This involved the lads making phone calls, preliminary visits, talking to the wardens about the visit, checking bus timetables, preparing work sheets, costing — the list is a long one. They managed the visit, and the immense feeling of pride and success for those lads far outshone any adverse experiences of failure they had experienced within the school. They had achieved something substantial on their own, and the new-found self-confidence and self-esteem meant that they could hold their heads high amongst their 'brighter' peers.

The role of the teacher

In this way, pupils can be made to feel responsible for their work. The teacher merely acts as a reference or resource centre, perhaps producing ideas of ways to stretch the pupils' aims. This approach is, of course, far more child-centred than many, and this calls on a different expertise than is normally expected from classroom-based teachers.

In our school, if a particular year group wants a 'disco', they will approach someone for permission. Then, instead of the teacher going away and organizing it for them, he will turn to the pupils and say, 'Right, off you go and organize it. After all, its *your* disco, so why should I organize it!?' Any teacher with management skills can organize a disco in a nominal amount of time. He will get his regular band of helpers and tell them how to clear the room, how to set up the sound system, tell them how to sell the tickets . . . In fact, all his helpers are doing is to obey his instructions. Where is the pupil's responsibility? At Aston Manor, discos are planned and carried out by the pupils themselves with the teacher as an overseer, not the central co-ordinator. The teacher remains in the background, but casting a careful eye!

Here, for example, are some of the jobs that are needed to be done by the pupils themselves. Permission is gained from staff; letters are prepared and sent to parents; tickets are made; posters are made; the caretaker is informed; tickets are numbered and sold; refreshments are arranged; the actual disco equipment is arranged; the room is prepared; the records are collected . . . Obviously, the list is longer. However, one can already see the range of social and practical skills that the pupils have needed. They have, for example, needed to liaise with tutorial staff and the caretaker (permission), art department staff (materials to make tickets and posters), secretarial staff (stencils to type and duplicate the letter to parents), audio-visual department (for disco equipment), PE staff (for changing rooms) . . . the list goes on.

Making the most of mistakes

Often the earlier attempts by the organizing pupils are chaotic, and, therefore, unsuccessful in their own eyes. Good! Excellent! This is where they are beginning to learn through harsh experience, which is how they will often learn in the hard world outside. I can remember one totally disorganized fourth-year group who eventually managed to scramble some sort of disco together one lunchtime. Tickets had been sold, and the crowd was awaiting the first record. Unfortunately, the final straw was that the needle had disappeared. I shall never forget the embarrassed faces of the organizers as they had to return the money, tempers fraying as they had to admit that the 'disco' had been a disaster from first to last, because of their bad organization.

At this stage, we sat down and discussed how they could have managed things better. Where did they go wrong? Why did they argue so much amongst themselves? At least they felt responsible for the flop! Their next disco was a great success, as their organization was excellent and they knew that they had achieved an outstanding disco, instead of a badly-organized, mediocre one (I still have not admitted to them that it was I who 'stole' the needle!).

This again raises the question of mistakes. I have already touched upon the point that teachers are afraid to allow pupils in their charge to make mistakes. It naturally runs against the grain of everything we have been trained to do as teachers. Teachers generally tend to feel that if a pupil of theirs is seen to make a mistake, then it reflects badly on them as professional people. However, we at Aston Manor are at times openly encouraging pupils to make mistakes so that they will learn and gain more from a situation. In the hands of a sensitive and skilful teacher, out of the chaos will come greater learning.

I hope the reader does not get the impression that schooling at Aston Manor is centred around one disco after another! The self-initiative section of the course has provided a great many excellent real-life learning situations, both within the school and outside the school. Most of the social functions are organized by the pupils, as are many fund-raising events. It involves the pupils using and organizing the staff, instead of the other way round. The greater emphasis is placed on the means to the end, rather than on the end itself.

Using a residential centre

Another integral part of the course is the residential component. Here, pupils are given the opportunity to plan and design a whole week's course at one of the residential centres at our disposal. Emphasis is placed on leisure pursuits, social events (concerts, entertaining guests, etc.) and educational aspects (guest speakers, visits, films, etc.). The benefit of such a course is immense.

It is intended that our Life Education course should help with the attitudes and the behaviour of the pupils throughout the school, in preparation for later life. The approaches described are now in operation in the third year, and even the first-year pupils are allowed some freedom in planning their own residential courses.

A question of attitudes

The emphasis is on personal relationships as it is this area that is the very fabric of life outside. Getting on with people is really what it is all about. It is, therefore, crucial that the staff involved in such a course should be pastorally-minded, and prepared to be greatly involved in extra-curricular pursuits. They must be fully aware of the importance of the hidden curriculum. Much of the work is done outside the classroom as pupils seek advice on their work. The course improves the pupils' ability to discuss problems openly, as it gives them the platform to do this.

A recent television documentary about the attitudes of teachers to ethnic minorities was questioning a home economics teacher about her approach to teaching a class which was largely made up of Asian and West Indian girls. The afternoon's lesson had been concerned with making traditional English dishes. The interviewer naturally asked why her syllabus had little, if any, evidence of Asian or West Indian cooking. Her answer was that she knew nothing of such cooking and that the pupils doubtlessly knew more than she did about it. What an ideal opportunity this was for that teacher to come down off her 'teacher knows best' pedestal, and hand over to her pupils. Why could they not run the sessions where foods from different cultures could be prepared and exchanged by the pupils? Let the pupil be more responsible!

Conclusion

I recently attended a lecture given by an industrialist. He was critical of schools for three reasons:

1. They do not allow pupils to develop responsible and co-operative relationships with a wide range of adults.
2. They do not allow pupil involvement in, and a responsibility for, what they learn.

213

3. There is not enough adequate formal preparation for some of the adult roles that pupils will take.

I would like to think that our course at Aston Manor, though by no means anywhere near perfect, is at least trying to tackle these problems and is nearer to achieving the aims we set out with.

15

Skills for adult and working life

———————— MICHAEL J. CAHILL ————————

Introduction

By way of introduction, I should like to make it clear that I look at my pupils as individuals who have a great many needs in common with each other. These pupils vary in size, health, enthusiasm, motivation, determination. sense of humour and in the range and quality of experiences they have had and in their responses to those experiences. It follows that they will need individual help if they are to develop and achieve.

Let me now try to get out of the way any misunderstandings about the nature and scope of the project which may arise from its original title 'Skills for Employment'.

First of all, *skills* does not merely refer to what have been called the basic skills — literacy and numeracy, or being able to spell and add fractions. These are part of the concerns of the project, but so is the range of personal and social or life skills which may have a better claim to be regarded as 'basic'.

Secondly, *employment* was never intended to refer solely to paid employment, but includes a variety of activities which could properly be called 'work' — including voluntary and community activities, participation in which should allow people to feel that they are valued, contributing members of society.

Background to the project

For as long as I can remember there have been criticisms, voiced by employers in particular, about the inadequacies of school-leavers. Often these have taken the form of sweeping generalizations about the letter-writing or arithmetical competence of apprentices or other young workers. Frequently, such criticisms have been answered by declarations from teachers of their role as educators rather than (narrow) vocational trainers.

Clearly, there has to be some middle ground between these two positions and it is on that that I wish to focus.

Employers do not in fact expect schools to undertake vocational preparation for specific jobs, and teachers do not want their pupils to go into the market place lacking in the skills needed to be autonomous young adults. However, there does seem to be a mismatch between what is being done in school and what is needed in adult life, and this merits closer examination.

The project, originally called 'The Identification and Achievement of Skills for Employment', known from now on as Skills, was set up by Schools

Council in co-operation with the Department of Education and Science (DES), Department of Industry (DoI), Manpower Services Commission (MSC), Confederation of British Industries (CBI) and the Trades Union Congress (TUC).

Aims of the project

Within the overall aim of strengthening the relationship between education and preparation for adult and working life, Skills was to encourage and support the following activities:

(a) identifying skills which are common to a wide range of occupations and to adult life in general;
(b) considering which of these skills can and should be acquired by pupils before leaving school at 16+;
(c) examining the relationship between skills, attitudes and knowledge within the context of education in schools and the context of work and employment;
(d) developing structured learning situations in which pupils can be helped to acquire social and life skills, as well as specific skills needed in working life, and to see the relevance and use of such skills in a variety of contexts and situations.

Working in the project

Phase one

The first project activity was a review of research into the skills needed by entrants to employment. A wide variety of research was drawn together, and a summary produced for use in the development of work in schools. Two particularly influential items referred to were the *A–Z Study* about which I shall say more later, and the following statement on behalf of the Manpower Services Commission, which indicates the range of abilities, knowledge and attitudes employers consider to be basic requirements for a 'good worker':

> to read, write and do arithmetic;
> to have some understanding of the need to produce materials, manufacture goods and distribute and sell them at a price people can afford;
> to appreciate the need to work consistently, quickly and accurately and to recognize the need for punctuality;
> to understand the different types of jobs and industries;
> to be able to communicate, take part in group discussion and use the telephone;
> to produce practical solutions to everyday problems;
> to learn without being formally instructed, i.e., from experience and from situations arising at work;
> to get on with a range of people at work and to recognize the need to share knowledge and skills in achieving results.

This is a long way from 'employers are only interested in pieces of paper'.

The *A–Z Study*, conducted by the Industrial Training Research Unit, looked at the qualities and characteristics of young people from the lower ability range in their first job.

Some boys and girls who do poorly at school make a good start at work and improve as time goes on (the As), and the researchers attempted to find out what distinguished them from those who fail to progress or to please (the Zs). Information was obtained from the immediate supervisors of the young employees, as being the only people with direct experience of observing their day-to-day behaviour and responses to various situations. Certain categories of behaviour were mentioned frequently, and two aspects of each behaviour factor emerged, namely the priority and frequency of mention.

The diagram shown in figure 17 is based on multiplying the number of times each of the thirteen factors was mentioned by a 'weighting' ($\times$ 13 for first priority down to $\times$ 1 for thirteenth priority) and totalling the resulting points for each factor.

My reason for describing this study is that it shows where the main improvement areas lie for young people in the bottom 40 per cent of the ability range. More than that, it is being followed up in schools and by the Basic Skills Unit which is producing curriculum material based on it.

Phase two

The second phase of the project which started in September 1980 directly involves sixteen schools drawn from five local education authorities — Derbyshire, Hampshire, Leeds, Norfolk and Sunderland.

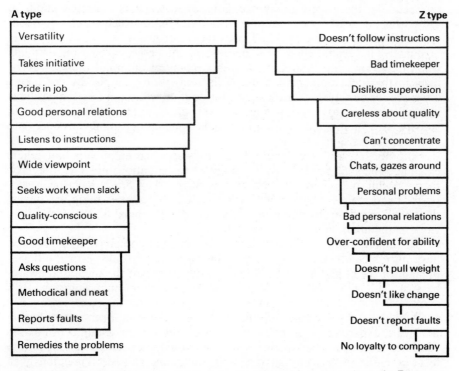

Fig. 17 Weighted importance of factors mentioned by supervisors in East Anglia.

217

School-based working groups have been formed and consist of teachers and other adults from the local business community, including, for example, senior industrialists, training officers, a works convenor, a hairdresser and members of the careers service. The groups have started work in ways reflecting their own priorities but all within the aims of the project as described earlier.

A number of groups have involved all the teachers in the school in considering what contribution they make through their subject teaching to their pupils' acquisition of skills. For example, in one school, teachers were given an extensive list of skills and invited to say which of them they

(a) taught almost continually;
(b) required pupils to use;
(c) were not applicable in their lessons.

Teachers report that this was a useful activity and helped them to focus on their objectives in terms of skills. It has also led to considerable discussion in the staffroom, because several important results emerged when the responses of all the staff were compared.

First of all, it became obvious that many teachers were teaching the same skill or aspects of the same skill without co-operating on the timing and type of learning experience offered.

Secondly, there were many occasions when teachers expected pupils to use particular skills — for example in note-taking or calculation — without considering whether the skill had been taught or not.

Finally, it became clear that, because of the choices which pupils made when they went into their last two years, many of them cut themselves off from further development in some skills areas. For example, by not taking a science, drama, technical studies or outdoor education, a pupil might have no opportunities to develop fine, or even gross, motor skills, or plan an activity as a member of a group or make guesses, examine evidence and draw conclusions, and so on.

Another interesting and useful activity was when employers and others examined the skill needs of young adults in the situations in which they saw them. Again and again, the conclusions of the *A–Z Study* have been supported, and teachers have realized how few opportunities there are during the school day whereby pupils are encouraged to be versatile, show initiative, work as members of a team, and so on.

To remedy some of the deficiencies which were perceived, some schools have introduced a compulsory course including opportunities for the development of social and life skills. Others are hoping that the increased awareness of skills which has come about through teachers analysing their own contribution will bear fruit in improved classroom practice.

A number of working groups have recognized the important contribution that work experience can make to the curriculum. One school sent out the whole of its fourth year on two weeks' work experience. The effect on the local community was electrifying, and the pupils gained tremendously in self-confidence and motivation in many cases. More than that — because they had been told to observe what skills they had to use and saw others using, they were able to report back in those terms to their teachers and be helped to see the relevance of at least some of their school work.

Yet another very exciting activity was undertaken at a school with some enthusiastic photographers on the staff. Slides were produced showing a variety of skills — practical, communication, literary, social — in use both in school and in other local places of work.

Some working groups interviewed recent school-leavers to find out what their perceptions are of the relation between what they did in school and what they now had to. Evidence from this source and from many contacts between teachers and other adults reveals that the whole business of skill acquisition and application is quite complex. For example, acquisition of a skill in the context of a classroom may be successfully achieved, but it does not necessarily follow that a pupil will be able to apply that skill, say addition of fractions, in conjunction with other skills of measurement, when, say, cutting or joining in a workshop. There is some evidence that letting pupils know what skills they are acquiring and practising, and talking to them about the idea of application and context, may help transferability and putting skills together to achieve a result.

Inevitably, participation in the project has led many teachers to think about what their pupils have to offer and can do, particularly in terms of recording their achievements in the form of a profile. That, however, is the subject of another article.

Conclusion

The project is thus to do with the *curriculum* which youngsters experience before leaving school looked at in terms of skills to be learned and used. That is the first essential feature of Skills.

The second essential feature is the emphasis within the project on *co-operation*. It is about co-operation between pupils and teachers, between teachers, between teachers and other adults. Co-operation between pupils and teachers is essential if skills are to be learned as well as taught. Co-operation between teachers is essential if pupils are to receive a coherent curriculum. Co-operation between teachers and other adults is essential *if*:

(a) the partnership between teachers and society is to mean something practical;

(b) skills needed by young people in a variety of situations are to be continuously reviewed;

(c) the experience of adults other than teachers of the contexts and applications of skills is to be of help in planning classroom activities.

References

The A–Z Study: Differences Between Improvers and Non-improvers among Young Unskilled Workers, the Industrial Training Research Unit Ltd, 1979.

Basic Skills Unit, 18 Brooklands Avenue, Cambridge CB2 2HN. Send for details of materials produced.

219

16

The Work Introduction Course at the Colchester Institute

AVRIL LOFTHOUSE

Imagine you are 16 and just leaving school. Learning, communication and relating to lots of different people have probably always given you problems. You've left school . . . now what? You can't get a job . . . well, you discovered at school that you're a bit of a failure . . . this just confirms it, doesn't it. What happens to those youngsters who leave school still experiencing difficulties? The present financial cut-backs, together with the effect technology has had on employment patterns, mean that fewer and fewer young people are entering employment straight from school. For the less-able young person with few, if any, recognized skills, the future must indeed seem very bleak. A long period of unemployment, of inactivity, will often result in regression of skills such as literacy, numeracy, and the social skills they had such difficulty acquiring; the late developer may just be maturing and so seeing the relevance of what he or she is being taught. It is in an attempt to use this period of enforced unemployment profitably that we offer the Work Introduction Course.

Background to the Course

The Work Introduction Course is part of the Manpower Services Commission Youth Opportunities Programme, a thirteen-week full-time course for unemployed 16–19 years olds who not only have been unable to find work but who would, most probably, have difficulty keeping any job they did find. Their problem may be connected with poor motivation and attitudes; lack of self-confidence; immaturity or a poor self-image. It may be associated with physical or sensory handicaps or with social and general disadvantages. It is on this wide target group that the WIC concentrates, aiming to improve employability and pave the path from school to an adult working life.

In the final selection for the 15 places on each course, there is close liaison between the WIC course tutor and all the supportive agencies — the Specialist Careers Officer for MSC courses, schools, medical services, School Psychological Services, etc. — and each intake is considered in terms of individual priorities and overall structure. In spite of a dislike of labelling, it is difficult to describe the youngsters who have been on the WIC without categorizing them, if only by the schools they went to. Students so far have come from both day and residential schools, from schools for the ESN(M); maladjusted; epileptic; partially hearing; partially sighted; physically handicapped; for delicate children; and, of course, from most of the local comprehensives.

So many of the youngsters on the Course have rejected school and/or failed there that a conscious effort is made to ensure that the WIC bears as little resemblance to school as possible. We have two tremendous advantages over schools: firstly, all our students are here voluntarily and may leave any time they wish; secondly, they are paid a training allowance — in 1981–1982 this was £23.50 per week — which has to be earned by effort, by regular attendance and by good timekeeping. As with employment, 'if you don't earn your money you don't get it, and you may be asked to leave'.

Course structure and content

The main elements of the WIC are always social and life skills, work experience, vocational exploration, counselling, skills training, together with literacy and numeracy if needed. A small amount of training for leisure is also included. There is great flexibility, because what is actually taught must reflect the needs of those particular students, thought of in terms of what is

(a) vital for coping with the complexities of adult life;
(b) helpful to enrich the quality of life;
(c) useful in the 'work situation',

together with 'back-up' for other lecturers and Work Experience employers.

There are few set rules and regulations, apart from the general one of adapting to whatever situation you may be placed in: the aim is to become self-disciplined. At first, many students find it very difficult to realize and cope with the fact that they are responsible for their own decisions — and the results of those decisions — albeit there is someone to offer help, advice and guidance if needed. Far better to make mistakes during the Work Introduction Course than afterwards in a job or on a full-time work experience placement with a firm. So many of youngsters' initial mistakes are the result of ignorance of accepted standards of behaviour and lack of experience in the work situation.

Each course starts with two weeks of assessment and exploration, when we get to know each other; the students learn their way around the large campus and find their way to the College Annexe which is over a mile from the main site. It is during this assessment time that an evaluation is made of the academic level of each student, and his or her interests, skills, hobbies, etc., are noted. We try to find if he or she has already decided on a particular type of job and whether it is likely to be realizable in the near future. It is only very occasionally that we come up against problems such as 'M', who wanted to work in a coal mine (which are non-existent in this area of Essex), yet was equally adamant that he had to live at home and didn't want to travel far to work! A visit to the pre-warned Job Centre proved to him the impossibility of his request, and he was willing to look at other possible areas of employment.

Even when they do not know what type of work they would like, most young people have definite opinions on what they do *not* want to do, which helps to narrow the options. If an ambition is unlikely to be realized in the immediate future because of a shortage of abilities and skills, it is suggested that students work towards acquiring these, but in the meantime think of some other type of employment. Who is to say they will *never* achieve their dreams even if currently it does seem unlikely?

During this initial assessment fortnight, individual programmes are planned with each student, taking into consideration his or her needs, interests, known abilities and the local employment scene. With only 13 weeks on the Course, the progress of each individual young person through the WIC needs to be managed and directed in such a way that he or she derives maximum benefit from the short stay.

In the first few weeks, everyone is expected to follow the basic timetable and attempt all the skill training offered. Later, individual interests can be followed, and if anyone really dislikes a subject, an alternative can usually be found. With only 15 students and a large college, it is often possible to 'in-fill' one of the WIC students into other existing courses. For example, 'F' decided he was interested in 'having a go' at bricklaying, and he was able to join a class of apprentice bricklayers on day-release in the College Construction Department. Although he joined in with the theory section, most of the day was of a practical nature. He was found to have a natural talent for bricklaying. Even though he probably will not succeed in becoming a qualified bricklayer, he has since acquired, and held, a semi-skilled job with a local builder.

At least one day each week is set aside for work experience, when the students go out of the college to different firms in the district. Shops, supermarkets, factories, warehouses, restaurants, laundries, builders, builders' merchants, garages, garden centres, and various small firms have all co-operated. Once the young person has expressed an interest in a particular type of work, a suitable placement is found for her or him. No payment is required from the firm and the youngster is covered by our insurance. The employer offers training and an insight into that particular job, and in return acquires an extra pair of hands which hopefully become increasingly of more use. We have had extraordinary co-operation from local employers, and they often provide their temporary 'employee' with free lunch, teas, and so on.

Very occasionally, a particularly difficult, withdrawn or unreliable student is kept in the college to start her or his work experience. 'P' worked with the Institute's maintenance staff for several weeks before he was thought reliable enough to work 'outside' with a firm of builders' merchants. However, whenever possible, all the students go out into 'real-life work situations'. On the one hand, the youngster gains experience, on the other, work experience acts as a trial period for the employer. A carefully matched placement sometimes leads to the offer of paid employment, even in the case of a young person not having the required formal qualifications. Many employers would sooner employ someone they know, someone who has proved he or she can do the job and is partially trained, who has the 'right attitudes' and who fits in with his other employees, than take on an unknown quantity.

Behaviour and attitudes

An important element of the WIC is concerned with attitudes. Whatever their ability level and whatever their type of employment, young people will have to have what are generally referred to as 'the right attitudes'. They will need to understand what is acceptable behaviour for an employee; how to cope with many new situations; how to relate to the many different people they are going to meet in their adult life; and to accept that he or she is the 'junior' and may often get the mundane tasks. It has been possible to find employment for a very slow-learning youngster who is clean and tidy, a good time-keeper, friendly and willing, and who works to the best of his ability. It has not been so easy for one who is of far higher ability but who is lazy and lacks good personal hygiene.

A great deal of thought is given to employers' needs, both in group discussions and in one-to-one counselling sessions. An unsatisfactory or unsuccessful time at school has so often resulted in a poor self-image and in both a denial of 'establishment values' and an opting out of the system. Yet to get a job — always supposing there are any available — the young person usually has to conform to expected standards to some degree: at an interview, how many of us would risk employing someone who appears aggressive, disgruntled, uninterested and none too clean?

After all the time spent considering employers' needs, we discovered the *A - Z Study* (1979). If only we had known about it earlier, how much time we could have saved! The *A - Z Study* looked at school-leavers of lower ability and their styles of behaviour during their first year of employment, ranging from the best (A types) to the worst (Z types). There was general agreement that in their jobs type A and type Z differed not so much in operative skills as in personal behaviour and attitudes. Behaviour factors mentioned by employers and their order of priority are given by Mike Cahill in the preceding chapter (figure 17).

Although these employers' requirements are all carefully considered, it is worth remembering that it is not necessarily the young person's fault that she or he has failed to get a job. They *may* have traits unacceptable to an employer, but all too often they are unemployed because of the recession and because the jobs suitable for youngsters of lower ability are disappearing. 'Why haven't I got a job? What's wrong with me?' is the poignant question that is the most difficult to answer.

So far, each Work Introduction Course has had a different timetable, but the example in figure 18 shows some of the skills offered.

For workshop sessions, there are always some of the students doing something different from the main group, partly because of individual interests and partly because 12 is the maximum workshop number for reasons of safety. Ideally, when working with the lower ability student there should be no more than about eight in practical sessions, although individual personalities have to be considered. How one personality can have an effect on the constitution of the whole group is illustrated by the following example. 'J' came to the WIC never having been on a bus, a train or shopping on her own, and she stood waiting for other people to do everything for her. One memorable time in a catering class she was given an opened tin of fruit and a strainer and told to strain off the thick juice. What the lecturer had failed to mention was that she would need a bowl under the strainer! The juice slowly dripped over the workbench and on to the floor, with 'J' watching it. That lecturer decided that the group would become totally unproductive with more than one 'J'. Final group sizes have to be flexible enough to cope with safety, personality, ability, and so on.

Other skill training on the timetable can be seen to include automobile engineering, which covers mechanical and body repairs; DIY — which is

	09.00	10.00	11.00	12.00	13.00	14.00	15.00	evening
M	Work experience day — each student with a local firm							
T	Social and life skills		Auto-engineering			Sheet-metal work (including wrought-iron work, brass, welding)		
W	Social and life skills		Working with plastics / Small-tool work / Typing			Visits or visiting speakers		
Th	Social and life skills					Catering — including survival cookery		
F	Sport		DIY			Printing / Woodwork / Grooming — in hairdressing salon		

Fig. 18 A basic timetable for the Work Introduction Course.

anything considered useful around the home. The sheet metal work is a great favourite with both boys and girls. We do not differentiate between 'masculine' and 'feminine' subjects and, in fact, several boys have opted for the hairdressing and catering. The session called 'grooming' has a dual purpose: it helps the youngsters learn to present themselves to their best advantage and to get their hair styled, washed and set — free; and it improves their standards of hygiene which may, indeed, have been a contributory factor to their unemployment. During the two-hour sport sesssions, as many different activities as possible are experienced; basketball, squash, trampolining, table tennis, darts, five-a-side football, canoeing, etc. We have found so many to be non-swimmers that swimming is to be included in future.

Methods

The social and life skills teaching concentrates on 'doing', using many different methods. This variety helps maintain interest and minimize any limitations in concentrations. One of the many books on methods is Priestley and McGuire's handbook (1978) which we have found to contain several practical suggestions. For role-play and for learning and practising interview techniques, we use the closed-circuit television in the college studios. After the initial shyness of appearing before cameras and the shock of seeing themselves on television, there is soon an increase in confidence. Students find the studios great fun and derive much benefit from them.

224

Literacy and numeracy are not taught from school-type books, nor as separate subjects, but as functional necessities of life. Form-filling, using post office facilities, completing time-sheets and application forms, understanding 24-hour timetables, etc. — the students are encouraged to collect any forms they come across and these provide the basic materials. With such a wide range of abilities within the group, the better readers tend voluntarily to help the less skilful, who accept this help with little embarrassment. Although assessment and evaluation continue throughout the 13 weeks, there is very little formal standardized testing. One exception is the *Holborn Reading Scale*, used to give a quick and approximate level of reading ability. Literacy levels of the first 45 students were as follows:

Holborn score in years	Number of students
< 7.0	8
7.0 – 9.0	12
9.0 – 12.0	13
> 13.0	12

For two hours each week there are opportunities for one-to-one tuition (in the style of Adult Basic Education classes) for any student who both needs and wants help. If he or she is 'anti-literacy', there is little point forcing him or her over and above the compulsory timetabled sessions.

Visits have included the Citizens' Advice Bureau, factories, supermarkets, magistrates' court, etc., but one of the most popular places has been the Crown court. The atmosphere, the jury, the judge in his robes and wig is something they have only seen on television before and it usually promotes fruitful discussion.

The Work Introduction Course is in its third year now and during that time there have been the inevitable teething troubles in introducing into a college of further and higher education what is usually referred to as 'the new FE student'. Some of the WIC students have settled into the college without any difficulty, but many have not done so. They fail to be accepted in social situations, and in college they are the group that squabble amongst themselves, gang up against somebody weaker and generally fail to meet the college's 'standard of conduct' code. Immaturity can so often result in behaviour that annoys other people; *they* are the students who play in the lifts and *they* are the students who are shatteringly honest. One lecturer came to complain that a WIC student had told him his lesson was dead boring; in all his years of teaching he had never been told he was boring! Perhaps other students have learned to be more tactful; all too often the WIC student says exactly what he or she thinks, and that opinion is not well received.

Summary

The less-able young person needs goodwill shown towards him or her, and work needs to be taught in basic, stimulating, well-prepared and clearly explained short packages. STRING — Short-Term Realizable Interesting Goals — is required when dealing with low ability and/or a limited span of concentration. Emphasis must, of necessity, be on methods, changing often from one method to the next. If at all possible, methods are used that most probably have not been widely used in schools, because so often the WIC youngsters are those who have failed at and rejected school. For example, because our television studios are a novelty, they make role-play and interviewing much more fun and are not associated with their previous failure.

A short thirteen-week course in isolation would be far from satisfactory, so throughout the course the MSC representative from our local careers office is a frequent visitor, and she works very closely with the WIC course tutor. For any student still unemployed at the end of their 13 weeks, much effort is put into matching him or her with a suitable WEEP (Work Experience on Employers' Premises) placement. This means that for a further six months, training can be given and follow-up provided, thus consolidating those skills just learned.

So often further education has the course and fills it with suitable students; with the Work Introduction Course, we tend to have the students first and must adjust the course to suit them. This opposing outlook presents problems for many existing lecturers who have been teaching the subject before the student and would prefer to continue in this manner. The concept 'it is the doing that is equally as important as the finished article being made' is sometimes difficult for the traditionalist to take. Yet, more and more of our colleagues are accepting the challenge of these new FE students. Without their interest and co-operation, it would be virtually impossible for the Work Introduction Course to succeed. As with any new venture, there have been set-backs, but changes initiated through experience and on-going assessment minimize these set-backs, and the course is constantly evolving to best benefit its students.

References

The A–Z Study: Differences between Improvers and Non-improvers among Young Unskilled Workers, the Industrial Training Research Unit Ltd, 1979.

Priestley, P., McGuire, J., et al., Social Skills and Personal Problem-solving — a Handbook of Methods, Tavistock Publications, 1978.

Conclusion and guidelines

——————MARTIN HUGHES——————

'It is apparent that all is not well with the curriculum, but the causes of the malady are complex and the remedy unclear. A long period of convalescence is impractical and it is recommended that all available skill, expertise and equipment be used to sustain the patient at the highest possible level of functioning until further investigation indicates a suitable course of treatment.' Such a diagnosis is rather gloomy and the prognosis not very promising but, allowing for a little poetic licence, this medical analogy illustrates the problems facing those endeavouring to plan effective strategies for pupils with learning difficulties. In the short term, the present curriculum must be made as efficient and as relevant as possible, but in the longer term, there would appear to be a strong case for serious rethinking of its context design and development.

Factors influencing curriculum change

Curriculum problems are obviously not restricted to the education of pupils with learning difficulties and, although the emphasis here is on one particular segment of the school population, any proposed solutions must be seen in the light of a much wider context. The complex nature of the task facing the planners is not limited to any one area of experience, but permeates the whole spectrum of learning.

A developmental approach has indicated that there are common features throughout the period from the pre-school years to late adolescence, and it is evident that the impact of a rapidly changing technological world will result in a reappraisal of the role of schools within our society. Teachers are having to face an ever-increasing diversity of challenges, as advances in technology not only have implications for strategies, methods, techniques and resources within schools but for the quality of life and the prospects of employment thereafter.

The factor of falling school rolls has received considerable attention in educational literature, but its cumulative effect, when combined with a failing economy, has yet to be fully appreciated. The decrease in real numbers influences day-to-day organization, pupil-teacher ratios, career prospects and resources available — all of which concern the staff — but the implications for those with learning difficulties are even more problematic. In an ideal world, a reduction in numbers would mean a decreased demand on existing resources, more accommodation, more time for small group and individual work, the opportunity for teachers to take advantage of in-service training and the chance to evaluate their work as individuals and members of larger groups. Although reality paints a much harsher picture, there still remains an urgent need for a concerted effort to make a realistic evaluation of the objectives, strategies, content and methods of the present curriculum and the role of the teacher within it.

Unlike the law, education does not have a series of virtually watertight definitions that would help to establish a clear framework for fruitful discussion. Nowhere is this more obvious than in the literature on the school curriculum, and this lack of agreed terminology compounds what is already a demanding study. There is, as yet, insufficient research into the problems of children with learning difficulties and into the strategies that could be devised to meet them. There is also, to date, no really adequate means of disseminating such knowledge in a form that is easily accessible to teachers.

Two strands within the curriculum

Looking at the more immediate problems, there are two discernible strands which are interdependent, overlapping and complementary but which, for the sake of convenience, will be discussed separately. The first strand is concerned with what might be described as the instrumental aspect of the curriculum. This is the more explicit side of teaching and learning, and is predominantly the realm of knowledge, judgements and procedures. It is the more tangible area, therefore easier to define, plan, implement and monitor. It lends itself to clearer guidelines and structures, and is more easily encompassed in policy documents, syllabuses and schemes of work. The format may include objectives, strategies, methods and techniques and have integral monitoring procedures. Alternatively, the format may be much more loosely structured, virtually unstructured or not exist in written form at all. In short there is a wide variety in the ways schools express their approach to teaching — thus it can vary from the prescriptive to the virtual laissez-faire.

In whatever form the plans are made, the actual implementation will be subject to a variety of factors outside the planners' control. The number, quality, experience, expertise and morale of the staff, for example, will act as a modifier of any proposals. Differences of philosophy on educational issues, particularly where plans are not based on consensus but are arbitrarily imposed, can severely restrict, if not negate, official policy. Inadequate resources in terms of time, money, space and equipment can at best put a severe brake on progress and at worst convince the disillusioned that change is either not worth the effort or practically impossible.

The second strand of the discussion places greater emphasis on the expressive aspects of the school's work and provides a link between the overlapping areas of the overt and the hidden curriculum. This is where attitudes, expectations, standards and relationships of both pupils and staff all contribute to the general ethos and provide the milieu in which the pupils learn to a greater or lesser degree. It can be argued that the hidden curriculum is a far more potent source of social learning than any planned classroom procedure, but this of course does not imply that pupils should be left to sort out what they can from a series of basically unstructured, though valuable experiences. Certainly, pupils with learning difficulties need guidance if they are to profit from the kaleidoscope of stimuli that occurs in any school.

Since this element of the pupils' learning is far less tangible and far more difficult to quantify than the more academic input, its influence as a complementary and reinforcing agent has often been underestimated in the past. In addition to the quality of the academic element, success depends to a great extent on pupils accepting the school's priorities and, consequently, if pupils do not feel able to identify with them, the efficiency of learning is reduced. The underlying assumption that pupils should postpone immediate gratification in order to increase the chances of ultimate success may well result in the keen, able, well-motivated and family-supported pupils completing their homework regularly and successfully. For those lacking these attributes and advantages, failure to achieve the set standards may not only diminish scholastic progress, but also strengthen the foundations of disillusion. Ambition, drive and success may be worthy traits, well rewarded in a competitive society but, should they appear to be the principal criteria for assessing personal worth in school, then it will be no surprise if certain pupils gradually find the school's standards both unattainable and less than relevant.

Long before they leave school, many pupils, despite their learning difficulties, are aware of their inadequacy in terms of the school's expectations. They can, in varying degrees, compare their own performance with that of classmates and others in their year group, and arrive at a rough approximation of their place on the academic ladder. Any reappraisal that does not take these factors into consideration will build up problems for the future and weaken the foundations of any new proposals.

Influences within a school

The values underlying any school's hidden curriculum do not lend themselves to simple analysis because, while schools have much in common as institutions, each also has a marked individuality due to a combination of variables peculiar to it. Since conditions and circumstances change, there is no clear pattern, and some less-favoured inner-city schools generate a more conducive atmosphere for learning than some environmentally-advantaged institutions.

It is, however, possible to categorize broadly pupils' reactions to the school's priorities in order to illustrate the range of attitudes in any one school. At one end of the continuum there are pupils who are totally committed to the school's priorities and who share the aspirations and standards of their teachers. A second category comprises those who may well have reservations about many facets of school life but who decide, at least outwardly, to conform in order to gain maximum benefit. A considerable number of others appear to drift along with the system, not out of any deep sense of commitment to the school's expectations, but more in a mood of passive acceptance. The next group, among whom are many with learning difficulties, are those who do not fully comprehend the intricacies of academic and social life that surround them. They are unlikely to initiate any collective disturbance, but can be influenced for better or worse by more dominant peers. The hard core, who constitute the remainder of the pupils, also contains many who have failed academically and who reject the school's value-system. This rejection may be passive and express itself in a sullen acceptance punctuated by periods of absence, or it may be more active, where clashes with authority are expected or even engineered.

It is this final group that can exercise an influence out of all proportion to its numbers in disrupting teaching and learning, syphoning off time and energy to deal with behaviour problems and regrettably infecting a larger group of the more passive and uninterested pupils. Should the employment prospects become any more bleak because of technological developments or a lasting recession, then the curriculum planners will have an even more daunting task in trying to ensure that pupils and teachers are working towards a common goal.

External influences

Just as there are many internal influences which ensure that more is learned than taught in school, there are also external influences on the pupils' capacity to learn. The whole of the pre-school period and most of the time between the ages of five and 16 is spent outside the formal academic environment, and it is these experiences that can have a profound effect on educational progress.

There is a growing body of sociological research on the effect of the home background, child-rearing practice and parental interest on pupils' attitudes and attainment at school. It is no longer realistic to assume that the education of children is the sole province of teachers, since parents, employers and a wide range of social agencies have valuable contributions to make. The value of the family as a force in education can be too easily underestimated, but the earlier the start, as well as the longer the period of systematic teaching, the more the chance of success there is in remedial programmes.

The importance of home involvement in these early years is amply illustrated in the case study on the Parental Involvement Project. The emphasis was on prevention at an early stage, so that children did not arrive at the age of formal schooling without efforts being made to reduce, if not eradicate, environmental deficits. Warnock supports this wider embrace of education and counsels against too narrow a view of the teachers' role. The restoration of self-confidence, the increase in self-awareness, the extension of acceptable communication skills and the fostering of independence and motivation must all be seen within the context of the whole family to produce maximum benefit and a better foundation on which the teacher can build.

It is not only in the early years, however, that partnership in education should be seen at work. In the case study of an inner-city secondary school, the fostering of social skills to increase pupils' life-chances was not left to teachers alone. Particular problems were broken down into component parts and appropriate programmes were devised to meet these needs. Self-awareness, self-confidence and self-esteem cannot be acquired in a vacuum, so that opportunities had to be found for realistic decision-making and the refining of social skills in appropriate settings. The co-operation of employers and other interested adults was necessary to complement the drive and initiative of the staff to give pupils practice in coping with everyday living. There is evidence also that society in general and employers in particular do not feel happy with the standards of many school-leavers. Apart from academic inadequacies, the work introduction courses confirm the importance of attitudes, behaviour and personal contact skills if adolescents are to make a successful transition from school to adult life.

Teaching strategies

Evidence from the primary school stresses the value of a well-thought-out language policy which takes into account emotional, physical and environmental variables, as well as the more obvious intellectual development. Early language deficit impedes the growth of logical thinking and proves to be a cumulative burden throughout the later stages unless early remedial action is taken.

At the secondary level, attitudes, concept levels, resources and materials must all be taken into consideration to achieve the development of effective strategies. The same picture emerges in pursuing mathematics and science throughout the compulsory years of schooling. Positive attitudes need to be fostered to replace the negative ones so common among those who experience learning failure. Feelings about a subject persist long after the particular content is forgotten, and early traumatic experiences tend to stifle future desires to experiment. Basic problems of language and comprehension inhibit the grasp of more technical skills, and the teachers' task of promoting flexibility in thinking is made all the more exacting.

Good geography teaching at the primary level is said to be based on carefully conceived plans which incorporate a coherent structure of learning appropriate to pupils at their particular level of conceptual development. This is extended by a sequence of learning experiences to ensure continuity into the middle and secondary years of schooling, where teachers are encouraged to evaluate, classify and specify their objectives, content and methods of teaching. The same difficulties are experienced with pupils here as in any remedial class in that a short concentration span, weak comprehension skills, limited writing ability and difficulty with abstract ideas are common features. Pupils are found to need good habits of study, better organization of approach, co-operation in the use of resources, intelligent reading of instructions and an increase in self-reliance. What geography teachers are said to lack is firm evidence from research of the precise kinds of difficulties pupils experience in learning geography, together with an explanation of these difficulties and guidance as to the methods of remedying the most common of them.

The same plea is echoed in history, where it is pointed out that not enough is known of the capabilities of the less able. The examples quoted illustrate some of the limitations of pupils' thinking but there is no simple classification of difficulties. History involves the comprehension and analysis of evidence about people, and it can be argued that poor verbal skills can mask the actual level of understanding. In common with others, pupils with learning difficulties need a variety of experiences to help them appreciate the world in which they live. They need to find their personal identity through a widening of their horizons from studies of other times and places. It is true that they will be constrained by the state of their cognitive development, their social situation and their affective experiences, but it is the teachers' task to mediate between historical evidence and their limited construct system. A weak grasp of the concept of time restricts many pupils in history, but the approaches suggested to ameliorate the situation are based on the same principles as the normal curriculum. The guiding rules are that, whilst modifications can be made, the nature of the subject should not be violated and the tasks should be conceptually realistic so that pupils are offered the opportunity to assess evidence at their own level.

The curriculum as a whole

It has been argued that too often the focus of attention has been on the teaching difficulties of teachers and how they can be resolved, rather than on the learning difficulties of pupils and how they can be reduced. This is perhaps too harsh an indictment of a profession which has had to cope with ever-increasing pressures in recent years, but it does suggest a shift of emphasis from a narrower area of professional specialism to a more comprehensive study of curriculum problems. This is not meant to imply that all teachers should become teachers of general subjects, but that existing expertise should be augmented by a wider knowledge of the factors that affect the education of pupils in school.

In the longer term, planning will have to be concerned with the curriculum as a whole rather than with valuable but piecemeal developments. A study of curriculum development since the introduction of compulsory education shows that many major modifications have taken place, but the acceleration of social change in recent years has placed undue pressure on the system. Those concerned with the education of the less able have long been aware of the growing inadequacy of the traditional framework, but the temptation to replace it with *ad hoc* arrangements must be resisted. Too often the proposals for remedial education have been based on an assumed list of characteristics and deficiencies of pupils, not always supported by firm evidence from research. This has stemmed from feelings of frustration where children are thought to be failing to benefit from the present régime. Advocates of change, however, should base their case on a detailed analysis of the curricular needs of such pupils to ensure appropriateness, balance, coherence and proper evaluation. Precipitate action to ensure an alternative curriculum for any section of the school population immediately leads to problems of what to include, what to leave out, what are the criteria for selection of pupils, when should such selection occur and how, if at all, should pupils regain the mainstream? Would energies be better devoted to a study of ways in which the main curriculum could be adapted so that all have education based on the same principles but differing in strategy, method and content according to particular needs? This presupposes informed analyses by remedial teachers in co-operation with colleagues from other areas to clarify specific teaching intentions and learning outcomes. Such discussions could produce more broadly based planning, not only of objectives relating to content but, equally important, objectives concerned with the learning process itself. This teamwork would reduce areas of conflict between colleagues, which have more often been the product of misunderstanding of each other's priorities rather than deep-seated professional antipathy. The argument in favour of adaptation rather than the attempt to create an alternative curriculum based on different principles is supported in the opening chapter by the listing of principles which provide a framework for considering modifications.

Discussion has ranged widely over the shortcomings of what is currently taught in schools and suggestions have been made that any future plans should take into consideration the eight areas of knowledge, outlined in recent DES documents, to which all children should have access. It is from these areas that appropriate objectives could be derived which in turn could specify the skills, knowledge, attitudes and work habits to be acquired, as well as the level expected.

Current provision has emphasized, perhaps over-emphasized, basic skills to the possible impoverishment of the rest of the curriculum. The extent to which this has occurred is not clearly documented, but both special schools and remedial departments have been taken to task for a lack of balance in intellectual development and social adjustment. Whatever the truth of the matter, future planning will have to take account of the fact that pupils who do not achieve academic success and have correspondingly more difficulty in finding employment often have the added burden of social and emotional immaturity. Even in a more favourable economic climate, these pupils are unlikely to find jobs on the basis of their intellectual attainment and are prone to dismissal on the grounds of poor relationships with peers and adults. It is essential, therefore, that both cognitive development and social adjustment are not merely pious aspirations, but are the product of a clearly defined policy based on relevant and realizable objectives and implemented by a well-thought-out strategy.

Planning will need to start from an assessment of the current situation so that the nature of the problem, the likely timescale, the professional implications and the necessary resources are among the variables considered. Such planning will need to take place at national level, and it is here that professional organizations concerned with children experiencing learning difficulties can supplement the evidence of HM Inspectorate, local advisers and other interested parties. At school level there is also a definite need for action, so that information and informed opinion can go up the channels of communication rather than passively waiting for official policy to filter down.

There is in existence a fund of information and professional expertise that needs co-ordinating, so that ideas can be cross-fertilized and more efficient strategies developed. This relatively untapped reservoir of expertise can be further expanded by teachers analysing their own roles in a systematic manner, so that the foundations can be laid for future progress. Unless the teacher is aware from informed observation over a period of time, as well as from a profile of test results, of the basal level of individuals, then the relevance of existing objectives will be hard to evaluate. If colleagues as a whole share markedly different philosophies on educational issues, the likelihood of a coherent policy, actively supported across the continuum of learning, is remote. Differences in interpretation will exist in any group of teachers but, if policy is not regularly discussed and reviewed, they can become ends in themselves and no amount of curriculum planning will avoid their effect on both the overt and the hidden curriculum. Unrealistic targets can be set which do not allow for limited staff experience and expertise in particular areas, and the implications of falling rolls on the redeployment of staff are likely to make this factor more rather than less common. At a time of cutbacks in resources, a possible increase in teaching loads and general professional insecurity, the idea of further time being devoted to refurbishing professional skills may not be of universal appeal. Unless, however, some strategy is devised to better equip teachers to meet new challenges, then the present arrangements will become progressively more out of tune with the changing educational scene.

Resources

A further measure of the appropriateness of the curriculum is the availability of the resources needed to implement and maintain it. Policy statements, syllabuses and schemes of work may well appear sound if examined in isolation, but if they are based on assumptions about resources that cannot be met, then their validity is called into question. Planning must be realistic and, however frustrating it may be, if there is insufficient finance, time, accommodation and staffing, then either further resources must be found, or objectives and strategies have to be modified accordingly. The principles on which planning is based must be sufficiently flexible to allow for contraction and possible expansion to accommodate the vagaries of future economic developments.

Striving for a balance

In addition to being appropriate to pupils' needs, any future curriculum must also be balanced. The breadth and depth of teaching cannot be formally fixed, but the need to allow pupils access to a wide spectrum of knowledge has already been argued. Obviously, children with learning difficulties must not be faced with too broad a span, or they will fail to see any pattern in their learning. However, conversely, narrow concentration on specific areas can prove both boring and unproductive. The dimensions of mastery/awareness and understanding/familiarity have been suggested as guidelines for planners in deciding where the emphasis should lie in particular circumstances, so that both content and process objectives could be realized. Concept development does not follow the dictates of any timetable, but it is more likely to occur where provision is made for a wide variety of experiences to enable the pupil to build up more than a series of unconnected skills. A common problem in the education of pupils with learning difficulties is the achievement of the right blend of pace and reinforcement, as too much of the former produces bewilderment; whereas over-subscription to the latter virtually guarantees a loss of interest. The optimum point of balance will vary according to changing circumstances, but only frequent monitoring will ensure that extremes are avoided.

Continuity and liaison

Official reports such as Bullock and Warnock have shown the limitations of planning that does not take into consideration the whole of the pupils' school career. A successful curriculum must have overall coherence, both vertically and horizontally. Schools are obviously restricted in the age-range they cover, but if this produces a series of end-on developments which do not take full cognizance of what has gone before and what is likely to follow, then the pupils will lurch from one development to another. Responsibility for overseeing the successive stages of schooling is more in the hands of the LEA than in those of individual institutions, but teachers, both individually and in professional organizations, can make use of the facilities of teachers' centres, for example, to collate ideas and disseminate findings.

Within the school, curriculum policy should encourage continuity throughout a particular age-span and ensure liaison across a particular year-group. Colleagues may well pass on information incidentally or at a personal level but, unless this aspect is adequately organized, some children will not receive the lasting support they deserve. The disruptive pupil is unlikely to let anyone overlook his or her needs, but the more withdrawn pupils, who do not pose overt behaviour problems, suffer because they are less likely to claim the immediate attention of a harassed teacher. This theme of continuity and liaison is obviously dependent upon an efficient and comprehensive recording system, particularly for those with learning difficulties. Without such a system there is either unnecessary duplication or considerable difficulty in capitalizing on the pupils' previous experiences, as well as not having the advantage of earlier diagnoses and evaluation. Since structure, support and a good self-image are essential ingredients of success, it is important that teachers have access to all the relevant information so that they can offer the maximum assistance.

Faced with these problems, many schools have resorted to models consisting of, for example, particular objectives, to provide the framework for future progress, but others have argued that the work of the school cannot be adequately portrayed in such a manner. It is regrettable that some proponents of particular models are prone to overstatement in suggesting a panacea for all ills, but it is equally unfortunate that the reaction can be so strong as to dismiss curriculum models out of hand.

Allowing for differences in terminology and conceding that objectives models are not without their weaknesses, there would appear to be sufficient evidence to state that schools need to examine their goals (both academic and non-academic) to see that they are relevant, reasonable and realizable within the resources and constraints of their particular situation. Over a period of time, changes in the composition of any school population can produce a conceptual mismatch between the demands of the syllabus and the ability of the pupils. The readability levels of school texts, for example, have not received the attention they deserve, and this has added to the number of pupils experiencing difficulty. Negative attitudes in mathematics can have their roots in language problems, yet readability levels of texts have not been widely investigated.

Teaching and learning styles vary with individuals, and obviously there is no one ideal method, but it is an area that would warrant further research. Organization can make or mar any school's efforts, but here also there is no clear evidence of the optimum conditions for those who are failing. Teachers need more information from research to indicate how best they can use limited resources and what range of options is open to them.

Future needs

The variety and individuality which typify the English and Welsh education system can be both a strength and a weakness for curriculum planners. National surveys, cross-sectional studies and, to a lesser extent, longitudinal investigations rely heavily on the written submissions of the intended curricula of a number of schools. What may well emerge will be at best helpful guidelines, but these will need to be supplemented by a wider analysis of the problems facing teachers in their own schools.

The traditional role of the teacher as expert, guide, facilitator and shepherd of a particular group of children must be reviewed. The ability to organize, stimulate, encourage, explain, guide and control will be necessary, but not sufficient, attributes to meet future demands. In-service training, however it is funded and organized, cannot be restricted to the refurbishing of classroom-based skills, for the focus of attention must be much wider. It is true that professional expertise, the management of resources, the ability to foster good classroom relationships and a sound knowledge of content and process have previously constituted the firm basis of a successful professional role. As curriculum change, however, gradually gathers momentum, it will require a rethinking of the remedial teachers' function, since the idea of 'first aid' for survival, administered to individuals or small groups by an expert in basic techniques, will no longer suffice.

Skills in relationships, assessment, diagnosis, programme planning and evaluation must be applied to a much broader canvas. Training, qualifications and experience must be geared to curriculum design and implementation on a much larger scale, so that remedial expertise is preventive by reducing the mismatch in the content and process of objectives, wherever possible. This would be a departure from current practice for many, as traditionally the remedial teacher has seen it as his or her task to accept rather than develop overall strategies and work within the confines of schemes initially geared to other needs. This practice has arisen, not primarily from the ignoring of problems of the less able by colleagues with other interests, but from the overloading of the present curriculum structure with demands it was never designed to withstand.

Changes in attitude

Major reforms start from small beginnings, and one of the first stages towards improving the lot of pupils with learning difficulties must come from the breaking down of the insularity of remedial work. This change is obviously a two-way process that requires willingness and changes of attitude on both sides.

Teachers have been known to assume that some of their problems could be 'solved' by the removal of pupils to the care and responsibility of remedial specialists. This transfer may have been viewed in a positive light as being in the child's best academic and social interests, or in a negative sense of deep-felt relief that there is a 'sin bin' to which the recalcitrant and the failing could be despatched. Such a move may relieve tension at teacher level, but is not necessarily a constructive procedure from the pupils' point of view, since it fosters the idea that learning problems are not the province of the ordinary teacher. Remedial specialists, for their part, have been known to foster a mystique about their activities and operate in small-group situations in relative isolation, thus widening the gap between themselves and their colleagues. Attitudes do not change overnight, and it will not be until action-research provides more information about coping with learning difficulties that much headway will be made in staffroom discussions. Yet the evidence offered throughout the contributions to this book indicates the generality of the learning problems faced by all teachers, and the wealth of experience that can be drawn from everyday activities.

Various research findings have presented different perspectives on the curriculum process, but all have shared the common concept that the teacher is the crucial factor in the development of the pupils' ability and potential, regardless of the area of study concerned. The importance of a flexible teaching style, openness to new forms of management and the willingness to take on varied roles should be the hallmark of all teachers.

In particular, the universality of general language skills as the basis of academic success across the whole spectrum of learning has shown how unreal it is to see the remedial teachers' role as divorced from that of their colleagues. The language environment of the classroom, for example, is an essential element in the teaching of geography, for the pupils must grasp the meaning of the technical terms which contribute to the structure of geographical concepts. The real danger is that, unless the teacher has access to the skills that will remedy this situation, the pupils will be excluded from tasks requiring literacy and numeracy. The fact that they may reconcile themselves to tracing, drawing and shading may reduce discipline problems, but does little to stimulate the imaginative thinking they so obviously lack. In science, it was made clear that the teacher, without becoming a language specialist, needed to develop pupils' confidence and skills in talking, reading and writing as a prerequisite to understanding more technical knowledge. Pupils need opportunities to practise and refine their powers of observation, ability to classify, predict, experiment and explain. The co-operation provided in practical work not only enables them to learn from their peers, but to build up social skills necessary in later life. Research into skills required for employment and adult life indicates the gaps in our knowledge about what should be taught, what is being taught and the degree of overlap and omission.

Remedial teachers, therefore, must be aware that, unless they become involved in decision-making at the highest level in school, they will have little influence on the demands made on their charges, nor on the size of the resources necessary to support them. This influence has been less pervasive than it should have been because of the narrow educational structure which seems to typify remedial education in most schools. Until relatively recently it was an aspect of education which had a limited career structure, few opportunities of specific professional qualifications and still does not enjoy a high status. If the value of remedial work is to be more widely recognized, the assessment, diagnostic, prescriptive and therapeutic aspects of the role must not overshadow the supportive and liaison elements.

Summary

In drawing together the strands of this discussion, it is important to remember that the Warnock Report should not be regarded as a total blueprint for the future, but as the basis for continuing research and development. Much is still unknown and much of what is known is not sufficiently disseminated.

If there is to be real progress, the attitudes of teachers, parents and pupils need to be favourable. Systematic study must further replace intuitive guesswork, and the extent of change will be influenced by the resources available, and governed by the degree of official priority it is given.

There needs to be more widespread acceptance that remedial work requires as much skill and professional expertise and is as rewarding in human terms as any other field of education. Such recognition will not come easily, and will have to be earned by the results of professional expertise and the development of a tradition of well-organized research. Future progress lies not in further isolating pupils, but in preparing them (in the vast majority of cases with their fellows) for the practicalities of adult life. Whether this is in the field of employment, increased leisure opportunities or what has been termed 'significant living without work' will never be certain, but the curriculum of the future will need sufficient in-built flexibility to cope with this range of possibilities. Society is constantly evolving, and the social reality of today is different from that of 15 years ago and indeed 15 years hence. The process of renewal will not leave education untouched, so that intellectual and social skills, positive self-concepts and capability of adjusting to change and attempting to understand it will be among the objectives of the future. There is little wonder, therefore, that curriculum planners have been hesitant to take decisions where there are no right answers and where no-one is sure of the consequences. Nevertheless, there is sufficient evidence from a wide cross-section of the curriculum to suggest that a co-ordinated plan of campaign for the future is both feasible and necessary for the education of pupils with learning difficulties.

Subject index

Author index